THE HUNLEY:
SUBMARINES, SACRIFICE, & SUCCESS IN THE CIVIL WAR

by
Mark K. Ragan

Narwhal Press Inc.
Miami/Charleston

THE HUNLEY

973.757
R141

Library of Congress Catalog Card Number: 99-074431
ISBN: hard cover 1-886391-42-4
ISBN: paperback 1-886391-43-2

Classifications suggested by the publisher: Alabama history; archeology; Civil War; diving; *H.L. Hunley*, submarine; naval history; salvage; shipwrecks; South Carolina history; submarines; underwater archeology; wrecks

Cover: Illustration, mural in the City of Mobile Museum showing the crew of the *Hunley* in the submerged submarine, used by permission and courtesy of the City of Mobile Museum.

Title Page: "Submarine Torpedo Boat *H.L. Hunley*" by Conrad Wise Chapman. Katherine Wetzel photo of the original painting in the collection of the Eleanor S. Brockenbrough Library, The Museum of the Confederacy, Richmond, Virginia.

Revised Edition

© Copyright 1995, 1999 by Mark K. Ragan and Narwhal Press Inc.

Published by Narwhal Press Inc., 1629 Meeting Street, Charleston, South Carolina, 29405.

This book is dedicated to my great-great-grandfather
John W. Ragan,
who went off to war with the Tennessee Militia and never returned.
His fate and final resting place remain a family mystery to this day.

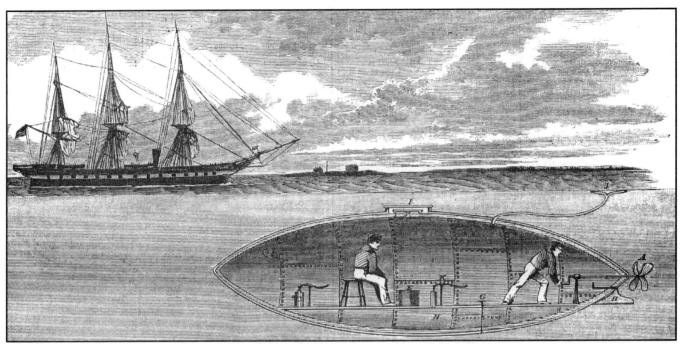

Artist's concept of the inner workings of a Confederate submarine. Engraving from *Harper's Weekly*, November 2, 1861.

John K. Scott squeezes through the narrow hatch of the privateer submarine "Pioneer" at a dock in New Orleans.
Drawing by Greg Cottrell.

TABLE OF CONTENTS

James R. McClintock was an engineer in New Orleans. By the fall of 1861 McClintock had become involved in the design and construction of a true submarine. His role in the development of first the "Pioneer," and finally the "Hunley," has properly earned him a place in the annals of submarine warfare. U.S. Navy Historical Center photograph of Daguerreotype circa early 1860's, courtesy Naval Historical Foundation (donation of McClintock's grandson, Henry C. Loughmiller).

CREDITS & ACKNOWLEDGMENTS

I would very much like to thank the following individuals and organizations, whose own work, help and/or encouragement has aided me in my research, explorations, and writings relating to the *Hunley*.

First and foremost, I would like to thank Caldwell Delaney, Museum Director Emeritus, Mobile City Museum, who alerted me to all kinds of documents used in this book. Incidentally, it was Delaney who, in 1991, officially received from the Sons of Confederate Veterans the Confederate Medal of Honor on behalf of the crew of the *C.S.S. Hunley*.

Second, I want to thank and congratulate all of the people who participated in NUMA's ultimately successful efforts to relocate and positively identify the *Hunley*. Those efforts were spearheaded and funded by best selling author and underwater explorer Clive Cussler, who in turn generously credits Ralph Wilbanks, Wes Hall, and Harry Pecorelli with the success. Among the many others who worked with NUMA was Mark Newell with the South Carolina Institute of Archaeology and Anthropology. Without the persistence of Cussler and his people, the *Hunley* may have been left to rust into oblivion. Their collective role has been of the utmost importance to the *Hunley's* story, and they should be proud of it for the rest of their lives.

The following historians all helped me and deserve individual recognition: John T. Hunley, Richard Sullivan, Sally Necessary, Chris Amer, Robert Neyland, Richard Wills, Barbara Volgaris, Sen. Glenn McConnell, William Still, Richard Pizer, Cynthia Middleton, John Brumgardt, Dan Dowdy, Brian Pohanka, Charles Stuart, Mike Zeigler, E. Lee Spence, Major Roy Houchin, John H. Friend, Richard Hovis, Ted Savas, Sidney H. Schell, Frank Furman, and William C. Schmidt Jr.; James Kloeppel, author of *Danger Beneath the Waves*; Barbara E. Taylor and Charles Torrey of the Mobile City Museum.

Steve Hoffius and Pat Hash of the South Carolina Historical Society; the staff of the Nimitz Library at the United States Naval Academy; John M. Coski and Cory Hudgins of the Museum of the Confederacy, Richmond, Virginia; Dr. Harold Langley, Head Curator Naval History Department, Smithsonian Institution; John E. White, Manuscripts Department, University of North Carolina; the staff of the Valentine Museum, Richmond, Virginia; the staff of the Mobile Historic Preservation Society; George Schroeter and George Ewert of the Mobile City Library; the staff of the Library of Congress; Caval Cante, Curator of the Naval Archives, Naval Historical Center, also helped me with my research and deserve credit and thanks.

Tom and Sally Robinson, proprietors of Charleston Scuba; chartered me their boat and gave me invaluable technical assistance during my 1993 expedition. Divers who donated their time and worked with me on my expeditions included: Beth Simmons, who is now my wife; Greg Cottrell, fellow submarine owner and naval artist, who is associated with me in my submarine business; and Stan Fulton, who is also Vice President of Narwhal Press. Stan also contributed financially to my expeditions. All of their contributions were important and appreciated.

Sincere thanks also go to the following archivists attached to the National Archives, William E. Lind, Becky Livingston, Mike Meier, Mike Pilgrim, and especially Dianne Blanton, whose tips and suggestions led me to several files and other sources of information I otherwise would have overlooked.

Sincere appreciation is also extended to Richard A. Dalla Mura, N. Patrick Mellen, E.D. "Ned" Sloan, Jr., E. Lee Spence, and Sarah M. Williams, who helped Narwhal Press edit this book.

Mark K. Ragan
April 5, 1999

CHARLESTON

MERCURY

EXTRA:

Passed unanimously at 1.15 o'clock, P. M., December 20th, 1860.

AN ORDINANCE

To dissolve the Union between the State of South Carolina and other States united with her under the compact entitled "The Constitution of the United States of America."

We, the People of the State of South Carolina, in Convention assembled, do declare and ordain, and it is hereby declared and ordained,

That the Ordinance adopted by us in Convention, on the twenty-third day of May, in the year of our Lord one thousand seven hundred and eighty-eight, whereby the Constitution of the United States of America was ratified, and also, all Acts and parts of Acts of the General Assembly of this State, ratifying amendments of the said Constitution, are hereby repealed; and that the union now subsisting between South Carolina and other States, under the name of "The United States of America," is hereby dissolved.

THE

UNION

IS

DISSOLVED!

With these words, Charlestonians were informed that South Carolina had officially seceded from the United States. Courtesy of U.S. National Archives.

FOREWORD

The maritime history of Mobile Bay spans more than five centuries. In that long period of time many colorful and exciting events have taken place: Clumsy galleons gave way to clippers, and steam sent even the most beautiful sailing ships into oblivion. The battle of Mobile Bay, one of the most crucial battles in the development of naval warfare, proved the navies of the world obsolete.

But among all these events none other grips the imagination as does the designing, building and launching in Mobile of the Confederate submarine *Hunley*.

From the time of DaVinci man has struggled to perfect a submersible warship which could attack and sink an armed surface foe, and here at last it was.

In this book Mark Ragan has traced the career at Mobile, and at Charleston when the shallow water of Mobile Bay proved unsuited to submerged operations. He has searched the primary sources more diligently than anyone preceding him, and he has unearthed a wealth of material never before used in writing the submarine's story.

With a real narrative flair he has woven this mass of information into a readable account which will probably take its place as the definitive history of the first submarine to sink a warship.

> Caldwell Delaney
> Museum Director Emeritus
> City of Mobile

On March 25, 1991, the Sons of Confederate Veterans, pursuant to an act of Congress CSA, awarded each of the men of the final crew of the "Hunley" the Medal of Honor of the Confederate States of America for "uncommon valor and bravery involving risk of life above and beyond the call of duty in defense of his homeland and its noble ideals." The medal was officially accepted on their behalf by Caldwell Delaney. Photo courtesy: Museums of the City of Mobile.

Horace Lawson Hunley, wealthy resident of New Orleans, gave his fortune, his name, and his life to the world's first militarily successful submarine. He was a lawyer, legislator, merchant, submarine promoter. He and his crew died when the Confederate States submarine "H.L. Hunley" was accidentally trapped on the bottom of Charleston Harbor, S.C., October 15, 1863. U.S. Naval Historical Center photograph (courtesy of the Louisiana State Museum, New Orleans, Louisiana).

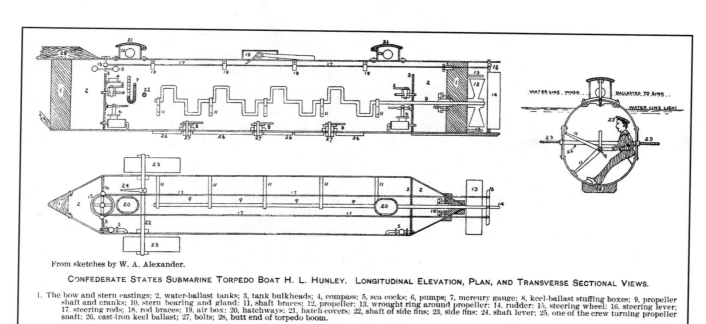

From sketches by W. A. Alexander.

CONFEDERATE STATES SUBMARINE TORPEDO BOAT H. L. HUNLEY. LONGITUDINAL ELEVATION, PLAN, AND TRANSVERSE SECTIONAL VIEWS.

1, The bow and stern castings; 2, water-ballast tanks; 3, tank bulkheads; 4, compass; 5, sea cocks; 6, pumps; 7, mercury gauge; 8, keel-ballast stuffing boxes; 9, propeller shaft and cranks; 10, stern bearing and gland; 11, shaft braces; 12, propeller; 13, wrought ring around propeller; 14, rudder; 15, steering lever; 16, steering wheel; 17, steering rods; 18, rod braces; 19, air box; 20, hatchways; 21, hatch covers; 22, shaft of side fins; 23, side fins; 24, shaft lever; 25, one of the crew turning propeller shaft; 26, cast-iron keel ballast; 27, bolts; 28, butt end of torpedo boom.

Diagram of the *H.L. Hunley* from the *Official Records of the Union and Confederate Navies in the War of the Rebellion.*

INTRODUCTION

During the fall and winter of 1863-64, a small iron submarine prowled the waters outside Charleston Harbor. Operating at night with only a single candle to illuminate it's crude depth gauge and compass, it was not uncommon for this hand cranked submarine to venture six or seven miles out to sea in search of an enemy warship. On several occasions the little submarine surfaced for air so close to blockading enemy ships that her crew could hear singing through the sub's open hatch.

On the night of February 17, 1864, the Confederate torpedo boat *H.L. Hunley* became the first submarine to sink an enemy ship. A torpedo was attached to the hull of the United States Steam-Sloop-of-War *Housatonic* and detonated. Although the agreed signal to light a shore beacon to guide the small submarine back to dock was observed and answered after the successful attack, the *Hunley* and her crew of nine were never heard from again.[1]

Numerous books about the War Between the States (commonly called the Civil War) have touched on the exploits of the *Hunley*, but their brief accounts are usually incomplete, distorted and/or loose with the facts. The monument located at White Point Gardens in Charleston, dedicated to the crews who lost their lives during diving operations, states that the exact number of accidental sinkings and men lost may never be known. The only thing that all accounts agree on is that the *Hunley* was the first submarine to sink an enemy ship during wartime. It was a feat that would not be repeated until World War I, over fifty years later.

The men who volunteered for duty in this small submarine were entering a realm which few in the nineteenth century knew much about. This took extraordinary courage as they knew that oxygen depletion within a confined area could cause suffocation within a very short period of time. Once the sub's hatches were closed and she was submerged more than a few feet, there would be no way to replenish the air supply. If the *Hunley* became trapped while submerged, the crew could do little but wait for the end. A lighted candle was used to illuminate their few instruments, as well as warn the crew when the air was going foul. The faint light given off by this tiny flame probably never reached beyond the first couple of crew members - causing the men in the rear of the craft to turn the propeller shaft in near-total darkness, all placing their fate in the hands of the man at the forward diving planes.

At least two crews were killed during training operations in Charleston Harbor. After each accident the submarine was raised by divers and a fresh group of volunteers stepped forward to take their late comrades' places at the propeller shaft. By one eye-witness account, volunteers had come forward to re-man the submarine before the bodies of the previous crew were removed.

Ever since I was a child I have been interested in the Civil War. My appetite was whetted over the years as I used metal detectors to acquire a shoe box full of mini-balls as I searched battlefields from North Carolina to Pennsylvania.

During the summer of 1977, I journeyed to Warren, Maine, to take a class on submersible piloting from retired World War II submarine Captain George Kittredge. Upon completing the course, I became a qualified mini-sub pilot, and now operate a two man K-250 dry sub of my own. My growing knowledge of small submersibles, combined with my life-long interest in the war, lead me on my search to learn the true story behind the tiny Confederate submarine *Hunley*.

My research has been exhaustive, having gone through thousands of Confederate and Union documents at the National Archives and other libraries around the country.

During the course of my search, I was very fortunate to correspond and meet Caldwell Delaney, Museum Director Emeritus, Mobile City Museum, which is located in the city where the *Hunley* was built. In 1991 Delaney was chosen by the Sons of Confederate Veterans to accept the Confederate Medal of Honor on behalf of the crew of the *Hunley*.

While discussing my research with Delaney, he encouraged me to include everything I discovered, and to tell the complete story of the *Hunley*. Several times while writing this book, I would come to a point in the story that I felt I could pass over rather quickly. It was during those moments of fatigue that Delaney's words echoed in my ears compelling me to tell the complete history of this Confederate diving machine. I would then put down my pen and break until I was refreshed enough to follow his advice.

This story is based solely on the facts I have uncovered. The details have been derived from letters, invoices, orders, diaries, telegrams, dispatches, eye witness accounts, period newspaper articles, diagrams, photographs, requisitions, supply lists, harbor reports, vessel papers, crew member war records, boards of inquiry, deserter's testimonies, ship logs, period maps, obituaries and post-war interviews.

This search has taken me flying over the area of operations in a chartered plane and to diving on the wreck site of the *Housatonic* with an underwater metal detector. My own submarine remained in Charleston for nearly a year while we planned and finally searched for the *Hunley's* final resting place with a towed magnetometer. The story I tell is a culmination of the efforts I have just described.

On May 11, 1995 (Just twelve days before the first edition of this book was planned to go to press), underwater explorer and author, Clive Cussler, announced that he and his dive team (in cooperation with SCIAA), had discovered the hull of the missing *Hunley* several miles outside Charleston Harbor.* I had been in contact with Cussler several times in the past, and in fact been provided with a chart by him, showing the location of the *U.S.S. Housatonic*, which helped greatly in my own moderately financed search.

Since I myself had unsuccessfully searched for the *Hunley* the previous summer, I had personally felt that the wreckage still existed, and had hoped, but not really expected, that it's fragile remains might be discovered in my lifetime. I was optimistic that this would indeed be the case, but the excited announcement of May 11, with it's national media coverage, came as a stunning surprise.

Within twenty four hours following the formal announcement I received a telephone call from Clive Cussler, and was informed of many details that had not been revealed to the media. We (Narwhal Press and myself) therefore delayed publication of the first edition for several months so as to include several particulars in the conclusion of the book regarding the search, discovery and condition of this unique Confederate diving machine that is unquestionably a national treasure.

I hope that the reader will enjoy the narrative style in which I have presented the many fascinating characters, and events that surround history's first successful military submarine.

Mark K. Ragan

* E. Lee Spence's claim to discovery of the *Hunley* prior to NUMA's discovery is discussed in Appendix on page 234.

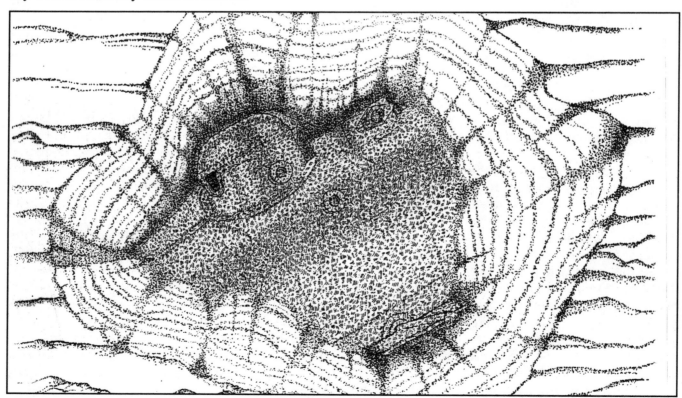

The wreck of the "Hunley" as partially excavated by NUMA. Sketched by NUMA diver Wes Hall May 3, 1995.

A "SMASH" FOR JEFF.

This political cartoon portrayed the frustration that must have been felt by Confederate president Jefferson Davis as he found the Confederate navy bottled up Southern ports. Engraving from Harper's Weekly, *November 2, 1861.*

Fort Morgan was one of the many fortifications hastily constructed by the Confederates in defense of Mobile and other Southern ports. Photo courtesy of the U.S. National Archives.

Confederate privateers were issued commissions, similar to the blank one shown above. The commission issued for the "Pioneer," described her as a "Submarine Propeller" with armaments consisting of a "Magazine of Explosives." Blank commission courtesy of the United States National Archives.

CHAPTER ONE
Experimental Submarines Built in Besieged City of Mobile

"From the Chesapeake to the mouth of the Rio Grande, our coast is better fitted for submarine warfare than any other in the world." – Rev. Franklin G. Smith (Confederate inventor)

Whether the War Between the States was fought over slavery or over State's rights will probably be argued by our descendants forever. The storm clouds that erupted into America's bloodiest conflict loomed on the horizon long before the first shot echoed across Charleston Harbor in the spring of 1861. From Alexandria, Virginia to Brownsville, Texas, the headstrong South, determined to be an independent country, prepared to back up it's secession from the Union with powder and shot.

The young Confederacy seized forts, arsenals, mints and shipyards that had belonged to the United States. A central government was hastily set up at Montgomery, Alabama, later moved to Richmond, Virginia, dedicated to the right of the Confederate States to decide their own affairs.

The South had originally hoped to leave the Union in peace, and to sever it's ties with Washington without the bloody struggle their ancestors had faced with London over eighty years before. Some in the North were content to let their Southern cousins leave, one, however, was not. The newly elected President of the United States, Abraham Lincoln, was determined to preserve the Union that had been proclaimed in 1776, and was willing to use force if necessary. Three days after the guns fell silent at Fort Sumter, President Lincoln called for 75,000 volunteers to put down what was claimed to be an unlawful rebellion. The War Between the States had begun.

One of Lincoln's first and most critical problems was how to cut the recently seceded South off from badly needed European munitions and supplies. Europe had always been leery of such a large country in the Western Hemisphere; it was in their best interest that the United States should fragment.

Both the Secretary of the Navy and the Attorney General advised Lincoln in vain not to use the word blockade in his April 19th proclamation.[2] They believed that by using this word, which endowed both sides with specific legal rights and obligations, the Confederacy would be entitled under international law to recognition by foreign governments. Although a country could effectively close its own ports through the passage and enforcement of tax laws, a blockade was a defined

act of war that was only recognized as legal when used against the harbors of an enemy nation. The formal declaration of a blockade was therefore tantamount to admitting that the fight was not a civil war or rebellion but a war between two nations.

While eager volunteers flocked to recruiting stations North and South, their governments purchased any vessels that could float. At first the South considered the proposed blockade to be ridiculous. How, they thought, could the thirty-five hundred mile coastline of the Confederacy be effectively patrolled? In a few months, astonished citizens of coastal cities began to see the masts of unfriendly warships anchored outside their heavily defended harbors.

By late spring of 1861 the Confederate Congress had passed a bill authorizing the government to issue commissions to private citizens who wished to act as privateers.[3] Southern

General Lovell, Confederate States military commander of New Orleans.
Photo Courtesy of the U.S. National Archives.

A New Orleans street as it appeared in the Fall of 1861. Perhaps the "Pioneer" was rolled down this same street on her way to the New Basin Canal.
Photo courtesy of U.S. Army Military History Institute.

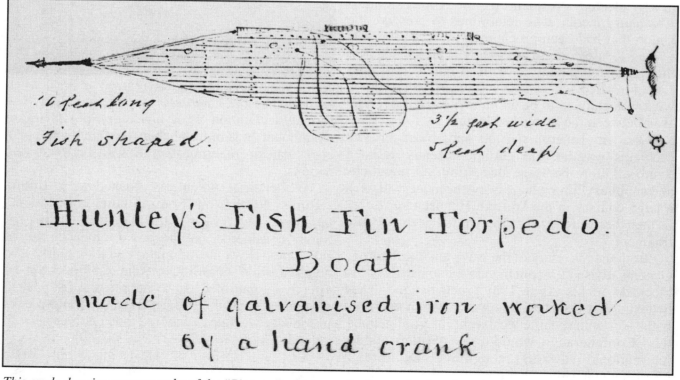

This crude drawing appears to be of the "Pioneer," which was the first and only submarine in history that was actually commissioned as a privateer. The "Pioneer's" official documents listed her dimensions as 34' in length and 4' in depth.
Diagram from the Willis Collection in the U.S. Library of Congress.

Admiral David G. Farragut commanded the Naval attacks on both New Orleans and Mobile. During the Battle of Mobile Bay he ordered his fleet forward with the words: "Damn the torpedoes, full steam ahead."
U.S. National Archives photo.

leaders realized that the only hope of ultimate victory rested in breaking the blockade that was beginning to cut them off from badly needed European supplies and munitions. By mid 19th century, most governments had outlawed the practice of privateering on the high seas. However, desperate times called for bold measures; all over the South, commissions were granted to groups and individuals who had fabricated everything from iron rams to floating gun batteries.

During this period of flag waving and mobilization an interesting article was being written in the South compelling it's citizens to build submarines in which to defend their shores. The article in question appeared as a letter in the *Columbia (Tennessee) Herold* and was re-printed in many newspapers throughout the Confederacy. The letter was written by Reverend Franklin Smith, a highly respected chemist and inventor who owned one of the finest laboratories in the South. [4]

Excerpts from his letter advocating submarine construction appeared all over the Confederate States as follows.

"June, 10, 1861, SUBMARINE WARFARE, Excepting our privateers the Confederate States have not a single ship at sea. Throughout our southern seaports, men of a mechanical turn and of the right spirit must go to work, maturing the best plans for the destruction or the capture of every blockading ship.

From the Chesapeake to the mouth of the Rio Grande, our coast is better fitted for submarine warfare than any other in the world. I would have every hostile keel chased from our coast by submarine propellers. The new vessel must be cigar shaped for speed - made of plate iron, joined without external rivet heads; about thirty feet long, with a central section about 4 X 3 feet - driven by a spiral propeller. The new Aneroid barometer made for increased pressure, will enable the adventurer easily to decide his exact distance below the surface." In closing Rev. Smith stated the following:

"I am preparing a detailed memoir on Submarine Warfare, discussing matters not proper to be spoken of here, illustrated with engravings. Copies of the pamphlet will be sent to the mayors and municipal authorities of southern maritime cities. Applications from individuals must be made through the local authorities."[5]

Later that summer, a copy of that article may very well have been read in the small New Orleans

shop of James McClintock and Baxter Watson. At the outbreak of the War the two men were in the steam gauge manufacturing business, fabricating and supplying parts for steam engines throughout Louisiana.[6] Within weeks after hostilities had erupted, the two partners had designed, built, and sold two bullet making machines to the Confederate government for which they were paid one thousand dollars.[7]

It is not known from where the two men came up with their scheme to construct a vessel capable of traveling beneath the water, No documents have survived from the early days of their venture, so much can only be guessed at. All that is known for sure is that by late fall of 1861 their three-man submarine boat was well under construction at the Leeds foundry not far from their shop. The unique craft was fabricated from sheets of 1/4 inch plate bolted to an iron frame; the bolt heads being hammered into counter sink holes to provide as smooth a hull surface as possible. A small spiral propeller at the stern, turned by hand, provided mobility, while diving planes on either side enabled the vessel to sink and rise as desired.[8]

At some point during the early phases of construction another Louisiana gentleman eagerly joined McClintock and Watson in their unique underwater adventure.

Horace L. Hunley was Deputy Collector of Customs at New Orleans as well as a wealthy lawyer and planter. In the early months of the war he had realized the importance of keeping the supply lines with Europe open in a way which few in the new Confederacy understood. He had led an expedition to Cuba in June of 1861 to obtain arms and secure a safe route to and from Louisiana. In a letter to the Confederate Secretary of War, his supervisor, F.H. Hatch stated, "The report of H.L. Hunley, who had charge of the expedition, will be valuable in transferring arms and munitions to the Confederate States."[9]

It's obvious that Horace Hunley was a capable person to have been put in charge of such an important expedition, although whether he was a submarine enthusiast from the start of the War, or merely a patriot dedicated to breaking the blockade by any means available may never be known. All that is known is that from the time Captain Hunley joined McClintock and Watson until his death in 1863, he remained intimately involved with the nuts and bolts of this unique undersea adventure.

By early February, 1862, the small submarine

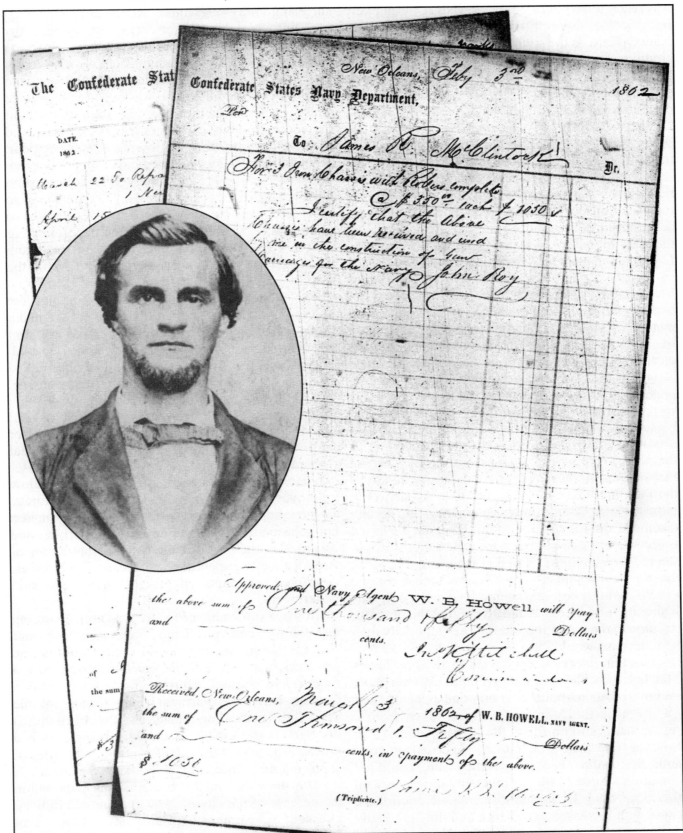

Prior to the Civil War, James R. McClintock was the youngest licensed riverboat captain on the Mississippi. The above invoices are evidence of how closely he worked with the Confederate Navy who monitored his submarine tests with great interest. Invoices courtesy of the U.S. National Archives. Photo courtesy of the U.S. Naval Historical Center and McClintock's grandson, Henry C. Loughmiller).

was ready to be put through her trials. One can only imagine the looks on the faces of the citizens of New Orleans as the strange craft was hauled behind straining horses on the way to its launching at the New Basin Dock. Nothing like this strange contraption had ever been seen before, and the commotion it caused must have been thrilling. For security reasons, only the builders, owners, and select members of the military, were permitted to actually view the first trials.

Pioneer, as she was later christened, proved to be quite seaworthy, requiring only minor modifications to stop the leaks that trickled into the dark interior of her hull. With all the leaks plugged, the tiny submarine was towed down the canal to Lake Pontchartrain to continue testing.

From a post war letter written by James McClintock to one-time Confederate underwater explosives designer Matthew Maury, we get a good picture of what these early underwater tests were like: "In the years 1861, 62, and 63, I in connection with others was engaged in inventing and constructing a submarine boat or boat for running under the water at any required depth from the surface. At New Orleans in 1862 we built the first boat, she was made of iron 1/4 inch thick. the boat was of a cigar shape 30 feet long and 4 feet in diameter. (Same dimensions prescribed in the Smith letter of 1861.) This boat demonstrated to us the fact that we could construct a boat that would move at will in any direction desired, and at any distance from the surface. As we were unable to see objects after passing under the water, the boat was steered by a compass, which at times acted so slow, that the boat would at times alter her course for one or two minutes before it would be discovered, thus losing the direct course and so compel the operator to come to the top of the water more frequently than he otherwise would."[10]

From an interview conducted in 1872 by James McClintock with representative of the British Navy (Who wished to build a submarine boat of their own) comes the following extracts taken from a report that is still on file at the British Admiralty in London. "He (Mr. McClintock) supposed on good authority, that the boat he was then using could not contain a supply of air for himself and an assistant for more than 15 minutes; increased confidence came with increased experience and they gradually prolonged the time during which they remained submerged until they found they were able to remain below for a period of two hours without suffering any serious inconvenience." Of McClintock's depth monitoring instrument the following was written. "The depth (of the submarine) was constantly indicated on an ordinary mercurial system gauge fixed immediately opposite the pilot - one end of which was open to the outside water. Each 1/2 inch of Mercury represents about one foot of immersion." As to monitoring the speed of the vessel the following lines appear. "McClintock states that when under weigh beneath the surface, it is quite impossible to ascertain whether the vessel is progressing as there are no passing objects by which to recognize the fact of motion; on several occasions when experimenting with his boat they continued working the crank when all the time the boat was hard and fast in the mud."[11]

In spite of these apparent short comings the owners and backers applied for and were granted a Letter of Marque (privateering commission) from the Confederate government on March 31, 1862. Their invention was officially described as a "Submarine Propeller" with her armament (i.e. torpedo) consisting of a "magazine of powder." She measured thirty-four feet from bow to stern, and was four feet in diameter with conical ends. Her narrow hull was painted jet black to help conceal the craft while running beneath the surface. Her skipper was a man named John K. Scott, a fellow employee at the Customs House with Horace Hunley. Scott and his crew of two were granted a commission to cruise the high seas, bays, rivers and estuaries in the name of the Confederate States of America and were entitled to a share of all vessels destroyed or captured in the name of said government.

It's not known how *Pioneer* was utilized during her short career. From the time of her commissioning as the world's first sub-marine privateer, until the fall of New Orleans, hardly a month had passed. During that period, Union Captain David G. Farragut (Flag Officer of the West Gulf Blockading Squadron), had concentrated his fleet at the mouth of the Mississippi, pushed northward past Forts Jackson and St. Philip, capturing the "Crescent City" in late April of 1862.

If or how the small submarine was deployed in the defense of the city of New Orleans can only be guessed at. Some historians have stated that *Pioneer* may have prepared to engage the fleet with other privateering vessels known to have taken part in the battle. Unfortunately all we have to go on is

of the chances in the next c...
his chances in the next c...

☞ The torpedo boat, of which we made mention, this morning, was sold at public auction to day, at noon, for forty-three dollars. It cost, originally, twenty-six hundred.

☞ There was a very h... this morning, so we are infor... sons who in their earnest ... the mythical worm which ... posed to be crawling around ... boor, never fail to rise with ... A heavy white frost is ... to indicate rain, and so, n... present beautiful weather ... change on the morrow.

BALLS TO NIGHT.—Th... regalia and mask ball of ... No. 9, Order of Seven ... place to night at the G... corner of Bienville ... Alley. A soirée dansa... the Concordia Club at ... ...night. Refre...

AUCTION SALES.

☞ A torpedo boat, which was built in this city or hereabouts during the war, and which is now lying on the banks of the New Canal, near Claiborne street, is to be sold at public auction to-day, by the United States authorities, at 12 o'clock, at the Canal street entrance of the Custom-House. The boat in question, which is built of iron and weighs about two tons, was sunk in the Canal about the time of the occupation of the city by the Federal forces, in 1862. It was built as an experiment, and was never fully perfected, and is only valuable now for the machinery and iron which is in and about it.

As Farragut's fleet approached, Hunley, Watson and McClintock scuttled their first submarine in New Orlean's New Basin Canal, and fled to Mobile to carry on their experiments. From the New Orleans *Picayune*, February 15, 1868.

Farragut's fleet passing the forts below New Orleans. Photo courtesy of Massachusetts Commandery Military Order of the Loyal Legion and the U.S. Army Military History Institute.

Union naval officers demand the surrender of New Orleans. Frank Leslie's Illustrated News 1862.

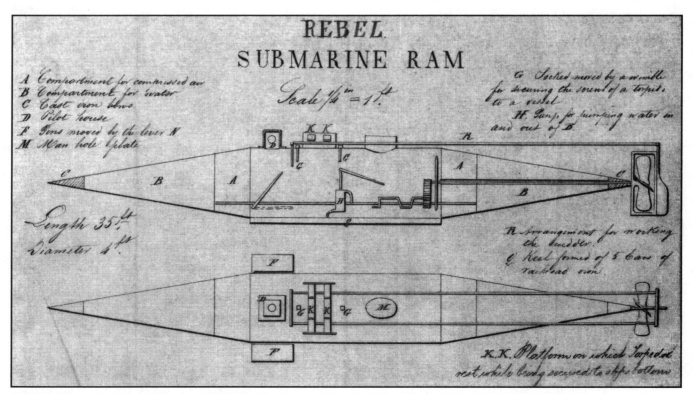

"C.S.S. Pioneer" as drawn by fleet Engineer Shock soon after the fall of New Orleans. National Archives.

a passing sentence from the post war McClintock letter to Maury stating "The evacuation of New Orleans lost the boat before our experiments were completed."

With the collapse of the city, retreating Confederates burned and destroyed anything that could be used by the victorious Union forces. One Union naval officer who witnessed the carnage later wrote, "The river and shore were one blaze, and the sounds of explosions were terrific." While smoke from thousands of burning cotton bales filled the sky, it would appear that Hunley, Watson and McClintock followed the example set by their retreating army, and hastily scuttled their invention in the New Basin Canal. With the city in panic, our trio returned to their shop on Front Street, gathered up what diagrams and notes they could and joined the mob of refugees now clogging the roads leading from New Orleans. With little more than the shirts on their backs the disappointed inventors made their way to Mobile, Alabama with hopes of building a second, more formidable submarine boat.

The sudden collapse of New Orleans sent shock waves through the Confederacy. With the loss of the city, access to the Mississippi was now denied, and a valuable seaport lost. Shortly after the Stars and Stripes had once again been unfurled over City Hall, the hastily scuttled submarine was found by Union sailors and dragged to shore. With the discovery of the derelict submarine causing some concern among the sailors in the fleet, officers from the Engineering Department were immediately summoned to examine the machinery aboard this strange contraption.

G.W. Baird, a young engineer's assistant, accompanied his superiors on an inspection of the craft. The following text is from an article Commander Baird wrote for the U.S. Naval Institute early this century: "When a third assistant aboard the *Pensacola* during the Civil War, I had the pleasure of assisting Second Assistant Engineer Alfred Colin in the measurements and drawings of a submarine torpedo boat which had been fished out of the canal near the 'New Basin' between New Orleans and the Lake Pontchartrain. Mr. Colin's drawing was sent by the Fleet Engineer (Mr. Shock) to the Navy Department.

The boat was built of iron cut from old boilers, and was designed and built by Mr. McClintock, in his machine shop in the city of New Orleans. She was thirty feet in length; the middle body was cylindrical, ten feet long, and the ends were conical. She had a little conning tower with a manhole in the top, and small, circular, glass windows in its sides. She was propelled by a screw, which was operated by one man. She had vanes, the functions of which were those of the pectoral fins of a fish. The torpedo was of a clockwork type, and was intended to be screwed into the bottom of the enemy's ship. It was carried on top of the boat, and the screws employed were gimlet-pointed and tempered steel.

Mr. McClintock (whom I met after the Civil War had ended) informed me that he had made several descents in his boat, in the lake, and succeeded in destroying a small schooner and several rafts. He stated that the U.S. Steamers *New London* and *Calhoun* had been a menace on the lake, and this gave rise to the torpedo boat; but before an attack was made the fleet of Farragut had captured New Orleans, and his boat was sunk to prevent her from falling into the hands of the enemy."[13]

While searching through a file entitled *Letters Received by the Secretary of the Navy from Officers Below the Rank of Commander* (National Archives), a fantastic stroke of good luck yielded the mysterious diagrams that had been "sent by the Fleet Engineer (Mr. Shock) to the Navy Department." From the letter that accompanied this detailed drawing of Mr. McClintock's *Rebel Submarine Ram* we read the following.

"Flag Ship *Pensacola*. Western Gulf Blockading Squadron, off New Orleans. G.W. Fox (Assistant Secretary of the Navy) My Dear Sir: Some few weeks since I had some duty calling me to a place known as the 'New Basin' where I discovered a Submarine Machine. I embraced the first favorable opportunity and examined it, got its history and had a drawing made of it, a tracing of which I send you as a curiosity.

The history of the machine is simply this. In the early part of Admiral Farragut's operations here the gun boat *New London* was a perfect terror to the Rebels on the lake, so it occurred to them if they could get a machine that would move underwater, they could succeed in securing a torpedo to the bottom of the ship, move off, touch the wires, and thus terminate her existence. They finally got the thing done, made a good job of it, got it overboard and put two men in it, they were smothered to death. The thing was a failure and a monument to badly expended talents. J.H. Shock, Fleet Engineer,

General Dabney H. Maury, nephew of underwater explosives expert Matthew Maury, and Confederate military commander of Mobile. Photo reproduced from the U.S. Library of Congress.

Western Gulf Blockading Squadron."[14] (If Mr. Shock's history of the *Pioneer* is true, it would appear that Mr. McClintock failed to mention the fact that two men had died of asphyxiation while testing the vessel in either his post war interview with Commander Baird or letter to Matthew Maury.)

The extraordinarily detailed diagram of the submarine that accompanied the above communication is indeed a treasure, for nothing more other than a brief description of the *Pioneer* existed prior to it's discovery. From the look of the plans it could be presumed that the finished vessel was a menacing looking engine of war and quite striking in appearance.

From the small forward (box shaped) observation tower the pilot could maneuver the vessel beneath a ship and screw in the torpedo that rode in the rack bolted to the top of the black iron hull. With a large differential gear placed at the base of the propeller shaft, two men could have easily provided the necessary power to propel the vessel both above or below the surface. From the low placement of the forward diving planes it could be assumed that the vessel may have experienced stability problems while diving, for on later projects these fins were moved higher and placed on the horizontal axis.

Unfortunately for history the *Pioneer* was auctioned off as scrap soon after the war, for a short announcement found in the February 15, 1868 issue of the *New Orleans Picayune* states the following.

"AUCTION SALES: A torpedo boat, which was built in the city or hereabouts during the war, and which is now lying on the banks of the New Canal, near Claiborne Street, is to be sold at public auction to-day, by the United States authorities, at 12 o'clock, at the Canal Street entrance of the Custom House. The boat in question, which is built of iron and weighs about two tons, was sunk in the canal about the time of the occupation of the city by the Federal forces, in 1862. It was built as an experiment, and was never fully perfected, and is only valuable now for the machinery and iron which is in and about it."

Later that day the following brief statement appeared in the afternoon edition. "The torpedo boat, of which we made mention this morning, was sold at public auction to-day at noon, for forty-three dollars. It cost, originally, twenty-six hundred."

In the course of my research into the history of this Confederate submarine, I found the skipper of the *Pioneer*, John K. Scott, conspicuously missing from the post New Orleans phase of our story. Upon further investigation I discovered that shortly after the fall of the city, he enlisted in a Louisiana Infantry Regiment, went to war, and was never heard from again.[15] As for the other players in our drama, McClintock, Watson, and Horace Hunley, they arrived in Mobile and immediately sought an audience with the proper Confederate authorities, presented their privateering commission and their submarine diagrams, and were eagerly granted the full cooperation of the military defenders of the city.

As luck would have it, Mobile's commanding general was receptive to most ideas regarding underwater obstructions for use in the defense of his harbor. Major General Dabney H. Maury, nephew of Matthew Maury, the underwater explosives expert to whom McClintock would later write, was fascinated with the groups invention. Nicknamed "Old Puss in Boots," stemming from his short stature and perpetual wearing of thigh high cavalry boots, this open-minded commander made sure that every assistance possible was granted the newly arrived inventors.

Throughout this chaotic period, the besieged city of Mobile was alive with activity. From the numerous battle-worn regiments that arrived to help strengthen the harbor defenses, mechanics, engineers and machinists were withdrawn and placed on detached duty in the numerous shops and foundries involved in the city's war production.

Among the many soldiers placed on detached duty was Lieutenant William Alexander, a young, sandy-bearded, mechanical engineer. An English immigrant who had arrived in Mobile barely two years before the War began.[16] At the start of hostilities, he enlisted in Company "A" 21st Regiment Alabama Infantry, a unit that had recently sustained heavy casualties at the Battle of Shiloh. He, along with other members of the recently arrived 21st, was placed on temporary duty at the Park & Lyons machine shop near the harbor on Water Street.

It was here that Baxter Watson, Horace Hunley, and James McClintock appeared one day with diagrams and drawings of their strange invention. For several weeks Alexander and his men had been boring out the barrels of hundreds of old Mississippi rifles to make them compatible with military ammunition.[17] Alexander's superiors ordered him to place the conversions on hold and

This old building at the corner of Water and State Streets in Mobile, was the Park and Lyons machine shop where both the "American Diver" (a.k.a. "Pioneer II") and the "Hunley" were built. It was still serving as a machine shop when this photo was taken in 1960. Unfortunately, this building has since been destroyed. Courtesy U.S. Naval Historical Center.

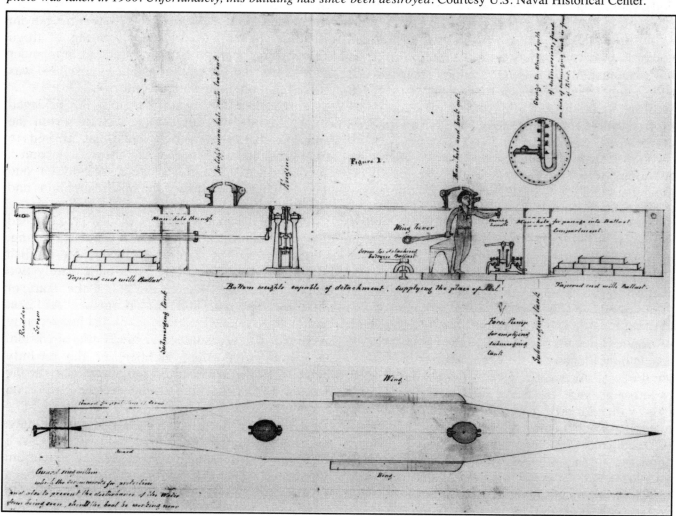

Top and side views of what appears to be the "American Diver"/"Pioneer II" submarine with her (electric?) motor in place, drawn by James McClintock it included the notation: "We built the second boat, also of iron 1/4 inch thick. She was built with square sides, with ends tapered like a wedge." British Admiralty.

give his full attention to the diagrams submitted by the three strangers. All in the shop must have been flabbergasted by the proposed project. The reader must remember that this was 1862, eight years before Jules Verne would captivate the world with his undersea adventure 20,000 Leagues Under the Sea, and few in the Victorian Age dared dream that such inventions were possible. With the full backing of the military, our three newly arrived inventors unrolled their numerous diagrams and set the shop's bewildered company to work on the daring project.

The outstanding facilities at the Park & Lyons machine shop made it the obvious choice for the construction of their second submarine boat. The facility boasted two large cranes, a foundry located in the back, as well as the finest machine shop in the city.[18] While going through Park & Lyon receipts at the National Archives, I was disappointed to find no documents associated with submarine construction. However, I realized that although the partners were given the full cooperation of the military authorities, they were not provided with any government funding for their submarine experiments. It's known from a letter written later in the war that Horace Hunley provided all the funding for the second vessel's construction. It would have been to him that all the receipts were addressed, not the government. This would account for the absence of related documents among the archive's Confederate collection.

The main reason I was searching through the wartime documents of Park & Lyons had to do with the fact that no Civil War period diagrams, drawings, or requisitions have so far come to light pertaining to this second submarine. I had hoped that a sketch of the craft could be among the collection's faded papers. There is also some confusion over this second vessels name as evidenced, in part, by the late war testimony of a Confederate deserter who worked in the Mobile shop. He called her the *American Diver*.[19] By other accounts she was known as *Pioneer II*. Having not been able to sort out the true name of this mysterious craft, I shall refer to her from this point on as *American Diver/Pioneer II*.

From the scanty records connected with this second submarine, evidence would suggest that our group of Louisiana inventors attempted to build a craft far too advanced for her technological times. From the previously quoted, post-war letter of James McClintock, we read this passage:

"We built a second boat at Mobile, and to obtain room for machinery and persons, she was made 36 feet long, Three feet wide and four feet high. Twelve feet of each end was built tapering or molded, to make her easy to pass through the water." McClintock then went on to write the following unbelievable passage. "There was much time and money lost in efforts to build an electro-magnetic engine for propelling the boat." This one sentence alone can be viewed as striking evidence as to how far ahead of their times these underwater visionaries actually were. The idea of powering their little submarine with an electric motor could be viewed as ingenious considering the era in which they were working. From evidence to be presented later, it would seem that electric motors capable of propelling such a vessel did in fact exist during the Victorian Age, for a late-war letter sent by Baxter Watson to the Confederate War Department states that an engine of "electro-magnetism" capable of powering such a craft could be purchased in New York City at a cost of $5000 dollars.

Returning once again to McClintock's post war letter to Matthew Maury we learn that the electric motor built for the submarine "was unable to get sufficient power to be useful". Unfortunately for history, McClintock remained silent as to how the group had tested their electric motor and it may never be known just how close these New Orleans inventors had come to fabricating history's first electrically powered submarine boat.

Although the electric motor built for the *American Diver/Pioneer II* was an apparent failure, evidence found within the Confederate Patent Office record books show that a patent on such a device may in fact have been issued, for an entry dated December 8, 1862 (the same time period in which testing of the electric motor would have taken place), in the aforementioned book states that a patent was granted to a Mr. J.G. Wire of New Orleans, Louisiana for a *Machine for Operating Submarine Batteries*. Unfortunately most of the diagrams submitted to the Richmond Patent office were destroyed at the end of the war, and its therefore probable that the blueprints for Mr. Wire's unique motor for operating a submarine battery will remain a mystery.[20]

From the archives of the British Admiralty in London comes highly detailed drawings of a submarine boat drawn by Mr. McClintock that appears to match his description of the *American*

Matthew F. Maury

Much of what we know about the "Hunley" and the two submarines that came before her, comes from a post-war letter written by James R. McClintock to Matthew F. Maury. Maury was an internationally acclaimed scientist and a former Confederate underwater explosives designer. Letter courtesy of the Library of Congress. Photo courtesy U.S. Naval Historical Center.

Diver/Pioneer II when the electric motor was still in place. If the comical character and the free-hand drawn bench behind him were removed from the drawing, we would be left with a highly detailed engineering diagram that could easily serve as a construction guide (see diagram page 26).

Surviving records indicate that several months were spent designing and redesigning the power source by which the submarine was to have been propelled. With the failure of the electric motor our determined inventors turned to a more conventional means of propulsion, a small custom built steam engine.[21] Some historians have pointed out what they saw as the folly of incorporating such a system. They believed a steam engine would have quickly used all available oxygen. It is my opinion that this compact steam engine was designed to build up great pressure within its boiler while running on the surface, extinguish the fire before submerging; and run on the remaining pressure. Remember McClintock and Watson were steam gauge manufacturers. They, more than anyone, would have known the limitations of such a system. Obviously they must have considered it feasible to have attempted its use. This same concept was later utilized in an experimental European submarine with great success.[22]

Unfortunately, as with the electric motor, the steam engine also proved to be a failure, perhaps due to the scarcity of materials in wartime Mobile. The engine was removed and a propeller shaft, designed to be turned by four men, was installed. By mid-January, 1863, the *American Diver/Pioneer II* was ready for sea.[23]

Throughout this period of experimentation, southern ports were slowly succumbing to the pressures of the federal blockade. By early 1863 the only Confederate harbors that remained open were Mobile, Alabama, Charleston, South Carolina, Wilmington, North Carolina, and Galveston, Texas. More and more, the blockade runners ceased to bring in European luxury items, opting instead to fill their low silhouetted hulls with arms and ammunition. It was this ever eroding situation that helped bring the Mobile project to the attention of the Confederate Navy Department in Richmond.

Admiral Franklin Buchanan, one time commander of the Confederate ironclad *Virginia* (ex-*U.S.S. Merrimack*), had been sent to Mobile in late 1862 to take charge of the city's naval defense. From his letter book, now in the collection of the University of North Carolina, we find that he was in constant communication with Secretary of the Navy, C.S.A., Stephen R. Mallory, in Richmond. Much can be learned regarding the *American Diver/Pioneer II* and her effectiveness from the following letter dated February 14, 1863: "Sir: I have the honor to acknowledge the receipt of your letter of the 27th relating to Mr. McClintock's submarine boat. Mr. McClintock has received from this state, from General Slaughter commanding her, and myself all the assistance and facilities he requested to complete his boat, and within the last week or ten days we succeeded in getting a man from New Orleans who was to have made the 'magnetic engine' by which it was to have been propelled. I have witnessed the operations of the boat in the water when propelled by hand, the steam engine being a failure and had to be removed.

On that occasion it's speed was not more than two miles per hour. Since then other trials have been made all proving failures. The last trial was made about a week since when the boat was lost off this harbor and was sunk, the men came very near being lost. I never entertained but one opinion as to the result of this boat, that it should prove a failure, and such has been the case. The original intention of going under a vessel and attaching a torpedo to her was abandoned, the torpedo or explosive machine was to have been towed by a rope from the boat and when under the vessel was to have been exploded. I considered the whole affair as impracticable from the commencement."[24]

From the above letter, it becomes quite clear that the *American Diver/Pioneer II* did not come up to expectations. McClintock himself later wrote in his letter to Maury, "I afterwards fitted cranks to turn the propeller by hand, working four men at a time, but the air being so closed, and the work so hard, that we were unable to get a speed sufficient to make the boat of service against vessels blockading this port."

In spite of the little submarine's apparent drawbacks, a document does in fact exist suggesting that an attack on the federal fleet was attempted sometime during the first weeks of February. Evidence of this alleged attack can be found within several faded pages of testimony given by a Confederate deserter named James Carr, a nineteen year old New York native who claimed to have been conscripted into the Confederate Navy while working on a Mississippi river boat docked near New Orleans.

Admiral Franklin Buchanan was in charge of the Confederate naval defenses at Mobile. Although, as a gentleman, submarine warfare offended his sense of fair play, he realized that it could be effective militarily.
U.S. Naval Historical Center photograph, courtesy F.B. Owen, Cleveland, Ohio.

This battle scarred lighthouse stood near the entrance to Mobile Bay during the Civil War.
Photo courtesy of the U.S. National Archives.

Modern view of Mobile Bay. Photo by Mark K. Ragan.

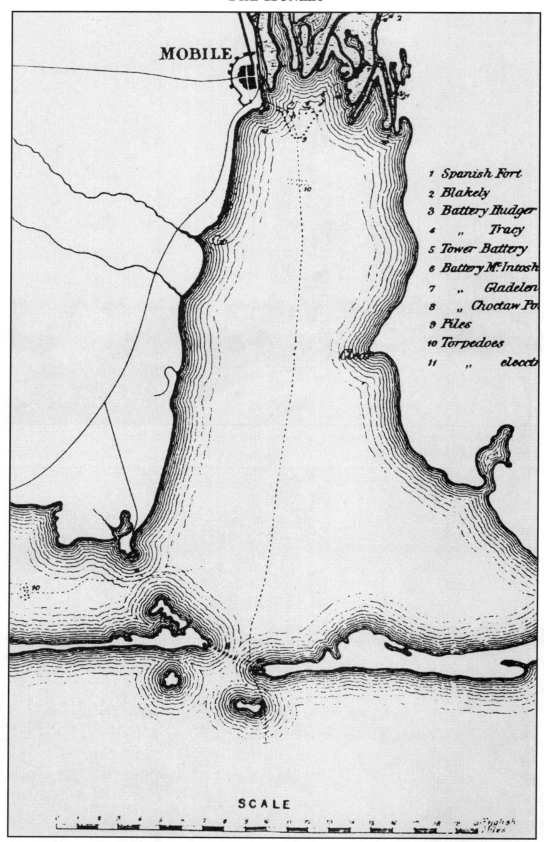

1 Spanish Fort
2 Blakely
3 Battery Hudger
4   „   Tracy
5 Tower Battery
6 Battery McIntosh
7   „   Gladeler
8   „   Choctaw Po
9 Piles
10 Torpedoes
11   „   electr

SCALE

Somewhere along the line running down the center of this chart, rests the second submarine built by Horace Hunley and James McClintock. The "American Diver"/"Pioneer II" went down in a storm while being towed to Fort Morgan. She has never been found.
Adapted from chart in *A Treatise on Coastal Defense*, Von Scheliha, 1868.

On February 23rd, after being sent ashore to hunt for oysters, James Carr and two sailors attached to the gunboat C.S.S. Selma deserted their vessel and surrendered to the crew of the U.S.S. Clifton anchored near Horn Island.

After being questioned about Mobile's defenses and the armaments of the C.S.S. Selma, Carr told the following story that remains something of a mystery to this day. From his sworn testimony we read the following lines:

"On or about the 14th (February), an infernal machine, consisting of a submarine boat, propelled by a screw which is propelled by hand, capable of holding five persons, and having a torpedo which was to be attached to the bottom of a vessel and exploded by means of clockwork, left Fort Morgan at 8 p.m. in charge of the Frenchman who invented it. The intention was to come up at Sand Island, get the bearing and distance of the nearest vessel, dive under again and operate upon her; but on emerging they found themselves so far outside of the island and so strong a current (setting out) that they were forced to cut the torpedo adrift and make the best of their way back. The attempt will be renewed as early as possible."[25]

From the contents of James Carr's testimony it would appear that he was quite convinced that an attack on the blockading fleet had indeed been attempted by a five man submarine matching the description of the American Diver/Pioneer II, and that the vessel in question towed her torpedo (for he claimed it had to be cut adrift) in the same manner described in the Buchanan letter of February fourteenth.

Both chief designer James McClintock and engineering officer Lieutenant Alexander's post war writings fail to mention any attempt made on the federal fleet. In fact the post war writings of James McClintock fail even to mention what became of the vessel. All we really know about the vessel, other than what can be discerned from the Buchanan letter, comes from a post war news article written for the New Orleans Picayune by Lieutenant William Alexander. From an excerpt taken from that article we read the following. "It (the submarine) was towed off Fort Morgan, intended to man it there and attack the blockading fleet outside, but the weather was rough, and with a heavy sea the boat became unmanageable and finally sank, but no lives were lost."[26]

Although no contemporary documents have come to light regarding the alleged submarine attack described by Confederate deserter James Carr, it could be quite possible that some form of attempt did in fact take place; for it's recorded in the files of the Mobile Bar Pilots Association that a Mobile Captain Named George Cook was to have taken the vessel out - and it may have been while under his command that the attempt described by James Carr took place.[27] Unfortunately little has survived from wartime Mobile that could shed more light on this question.

Shortly after the loss of the little vessel, Admiral Buchanan received a short inquiry concerning the submarine from the Confederate Navy Department. It appears that Baxter Watson had written to Naval Secretary Mallory informing him of the loss and requested some form of government assistance in the salvage of the vessel. Malloy's inquiry to Buchanan seemed to ask the question of whether such an operation was justified. In response to The secretary's question, Buchanan sent the following communication.

" Hon: S.R. Mallory, Secretary of the Navy, Richmond Va. Sir: I have the honor to acknowledge the receipt of your letter of the 23rd with enclosed communication from Baxter Watson relating to his submarine boat. On the 14th I addressed you on that subject. Mr. McClintock spoken of by me was one of the partners associated with Mr. Watson. The boat can not be of any possible use in Mobile Bay in consequence of its shallow water. I don't think it could be made effective against the enemy off the harbor as the blockading vessels are anchored in water too shallow to permit the boat to pass under."[28]

With all hope of salvage abandoned, the small submarine's exact location was soon forgotten. She rests to this day exactly where she sank on that February morning so long ago; perhaps one day her rusting hull will be rediscovered and she'll take her rightful place as a national maritime treasure of these now reunited states.

Throughout the construction of this second submarine, it's sole financier,[29] Horace Hunley, had been intermittently called away on government business. Since the early days of the war he had remained closely involved in several operations related to breaking the federal blockade by any means available.[30] Hunley's submarine activities appear to have been only part of his overall efforts towards achieving this goal. It's not known how much Captain Hunley invested in this second ill-fated venture; no records have come to light

Receipt for $3,000 payment for 20 Singer torpedoes. National Archives

Diagram of a Singer underwater contact mine.
From "Texan gave world first successful submarine." 1916

The Honorable Stephen Mallory, Secretary of the Navy, Confederate States of America, would have had a keen interest in the submarine experiments being conducted in Mobile, but apparently questioned the feasibility of submarine warfare. National Archives.

In contrast to to Mallory, Captain Peter Murphy of the C.S.S. Selma saw great potential in submarines and, in a post war letter, wrote that he considered the "Hunley's" harbor trials "a perfect success." Naval Historical Center

indicating the total cost of the unlucky craft. With the loss of this second vessel, our discouraged inventors must have felt that submarine warfare would become a reality only in the distant future. Without government assistance, construction of yet another craft was doubtful.

It was at about this time that an organization of patriotic engineers was being formed at Mobile, Alabama of which Horace Hunley, James McClintock and Baxter Watson would soon become members. Under guidelines set fourth by the Confederate government this group would be entitled to 50% of the value of all vessels of war and other Federal property destroyed by means of their inventions. "With the necessary ammunition and materials for manufacturing their devices, as well as free transportation for both men and machines."[31]

The group's founder was a 37 year old burly Texan named Edgar C. Singer, a self-styled mechanical engineer from Port Lavaca, who, along with a small group of ex-Texas Artillery Men, were then manufacturing the most widely used underwater contact mine in the Confederacy. In the early weeks of April, 1863 this group consisting of J.D. Braman, R.W. Dunn, B.A. (Gus) Whitney, D. Bradbury, James Jones, and several others, had entered into a contract with the military defenders of Mobile, Alabama to mine Mobile Bay with Singer's Torpedoes. Within weeks after the signing of this contract Horace Hunley, James McClintock and Baxter Watson were asked to join the unique organization.[32]

With encouragements from the three new members from New Orleans who had already built two underwater vehicle's, the "Singer Submarine Corp" (as they would later call themselves), decided to invest in an underwater torpedo boat submitted for consideration by the eager McClintock, Hunley and Watson.

From the ranks of this unique organization, four men stepped forward to buy shares in the proposed venture. Mr. E.C. Singer, the group's founder, and chief explosives designer, purchased 1/3 of the vessel at a cost of $5,000 dollars; Horace Hunley retained another third and sold the remaining shares to R.W. Dunn, B.A. Whitney, and J.D. Braman, bringing the total cost of the submarine boat to $15,000 dollars, quite a considerable sum in 1863.[33]

With financial backing secured, construction of the third and final craft was begun at the Park &

Lyons machine shop under the direction of Lieutenant Alexander and James McClintock. From a post-war article written by William Alexander, we get an invaluable first hand description of this innovative diving machine:

"We decided to build another boat, and for this purpose took a cylinder boiler which we had on hand, 48 inches in diameter and twenty-five feet long (all dimensions are from memory). We cut this boiler in two, longitudinally, and inserted two 12-inch boiler iron strips in her sides; lengthened her by one tapering course fore and aft, to which were attached bow and stern castings, making the boat about 30 feet long, 4 feet wide and 5 feet deep. A longitudinal strip 12 inches wide was riveted the full length on top. At each end a bulkhead was riveted across to form water-ballast tanks (unfortunately these were left open on top); they were used in raising and sinking the boat. In addition to these water tanks the boat was ballasted by flat castings, made to fit the outside bottom of the shell and fastened thereto by 'Tee' headed bolts passing through stuffing boxes inside the boat, the inside end of the bolt squared to fit a wrench, that the bolts might be turned and the ballast dropped, should the necessity arise.

In connection with each of the water tanks, there was a sea-cock open to the sea to supply the tank for sinking; also a force pump to eject the water from the tanks into the sea for raising the boat to the surface. There was also a bilge connection to the pump. A mercury gauge, open to the sea, was attached to the shell near the forward tank, to indicate the depth of the boat below the surface. A one and a quarter inch shaft passed through stuffing boxes on each side of the boat, just forward of the end of the propeller shaft. On each side of this shaft, outside of the boat, castings, or lateral fins, five feet long and eight inches wide, were secured. This shaft was operated by a lever amidships, and by raising or lowering the ends of these fins, operated as the fins of a fish, changing the depth of the boat below the surface at will, without disturbing the water level in the ballast tanks.

The rudder was operated by a wheel, and levers connected to rods passing through stuffing-boxes in the stern castings, and operated by the captain or pilot forward. An adjusted compass was placed in front of the forward tank. The boat was operated by manual power, with an ordinary propeller. On the propelling shaft there were formed eight cranks at different angles; the shaft was supported by

AN ACT

To amend an act entitled "An Act recognizing the existence of war between the United States and the Confederate States, and concerning Letters of Marque, Prizes and Prize Goods, approved May 6th, one thousand eight hundred and sixty-one."

SECTION 1. *The Congress of the Confederate States do enact*, That the tenth section of the above entitled act be so amended that in addition to the bounty therein mentioned, the Government of the Confederate States will pay to the cruiser or cruisers of any private armed vessel commissioned under said act, twenty per centum on the value of each and every vessel of war belonging to the enemy, that may be sunk or destroyed by such private armed vessel or vessels, the value of the armament to be included in the estimate. The valuation to be made by a board of naval officers appointed, and their award to be approved by the President, and the amount found to be due to be payable in eight per cent. bonds of the Confederate States.

SEC. 2. That if any person who may have invented or may hereafter invent any new kind of armed vessel, or floating battery, or defence, shall deposit a plan of the same, accompanied by suitable explanations or specifications, in the navy department, together with an affidavit setting forth that he is the inventor thereof, such deposit and affidavit (unless the facts set forth therein shall be disproved) shall entitle such inventor or his assigns to the sole and exclusive enjoyment of the rights and privileges conferred by this act, reserving, however, to the Government, in all cases, the right of using such invention.

APPROVED May 21, 1861.

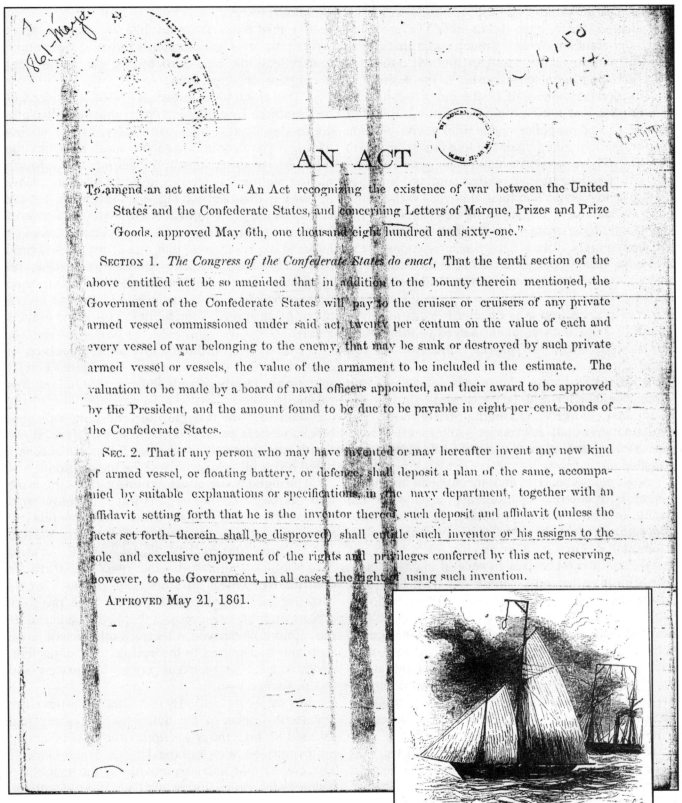

Confederate Congressional document that outlined the monetary rewards that would be granted to southern privateers.
National Archives

Insert shows the special rigging suggested by northern political cartoonists for vessels employed in the chase of southern privateers.

brackets on the starboard side, the men sitting on the port side turning on the cranks. The propeller shaft and cranks took up so much room that it was very difficult to pass fore and aft, and when the men were in their places this was next to impossible.

In operation, one half of the crew had to pass through the fore hatch; the other through the after hatchway. The propeller revolved in a wrought iron ring or band, to guard against a line being thrown in to foul it. There were two hatchways - one fore and one aft - 16 inches by 12, with a combing 8 inches high. These hatches had hinged covers with rubber gaskets, and were bolted from the inside. In the sides and ends of these combings glasses were inserted to sight from. There was an opening made in the top of the boat for an air box, a casting with a close top 12 by 18 by 4 inches, made to carry a hollow shaft. This shaft passed through stuffing boxes. On each end was an elbow with a 4 foot length of 1-1/2 inch pipe, and keyed to the hollow shaft; on the inside was a lever with a stop-cock to admit air."[34]

Sometime during the construction of this submarine which was to be christened H.L. Hunley, Lieutenant George E. Dixon, an officer in the 21st Alabama (William Alexander's regiment), enters our story and remains until its mysterious conclusion.

A Kentucky native and mechanical engineer, Dixon had entered Confederate service in the spring of 1861, leaving his post as an engineer aboard a river boat to enlist as a private in the 21st Alabama Regiment. During his two years of service, he had taken part in several engagements, rising through the ranks along the way. Due to a severe leg wound he received at the Battle of Shiloh, he may have walked with a limp, which may have been responsible for relieving him of active field duty. It's very possible he also may have been on detached duty with Alexander at the Park & Lyons shop (several sources seem to indicate this). Unfortunately, his war record at the National Archives has no details as to his duties while convalescing in Mobile.

By now the strain of two long years of war was showing in the blockaded Confederacy. Prices of the most common pre-war commodities had shot up and continued to rise. On the home front the war was taking a terrible toll; by now the South had invested all it could in materials and manpower. In battle after battle, men on both sides continued to be killed by the thousands with no end to the

slaughter in sight.

At this point I would like to share a letter written by my grandmother's great grandmother, that reflects the hardships felt on the home front during this unhappy time.

"The Honorable Jefferson Davis, President of the Southern Confederacy, Sir: I must beg leave to address you a few lines petitionary. I am a widow having two daughters and no adult male on the farm. I have three sons in the service and a fourth having died on his way from Fort Delaware where he was a prisoner having been captured by the enemy in the great fight at Richmond (the Battle of Malvern Hill). Under existing circumstances it looks to me reasonable that one of my sons should be released from service to attend to my farm and his brothers in the neighborhood. Will you sir be so good as to allow me the privilege as to have one of my sons at home? Your humble petitioner Francis Pearce."[35]

Although grandmother Pearce received a cordial reply from one of President Davis' secretaries, family records indicate that no one was released.

With the war dragging on, the once ridiculed blockade were proving to be very effective. If the South was going to realize her independence, this hated blockade would have to be broken soon.

Throughout the construction of the submarine that carried his name, Horace Hunley was continually being called away from Mobile on services related to the war effort. By early May of 1863, these duties had taken him to central Mississippi on military business.[36] While there, he continually wrote to his old friend James McClintock, begging for details and progress reports on their latest project that had to succeed. If the submarine proved effective, others would be built and transported to the various port cities then under siege; the blockade could be broken and independence won.

In mid-July of 1863, shortly after the devastating news of the defeat at Gettysburg had reached Mobile, the *H.L. Hunley* slid down wooden ramps into the harbor at the Theater Street Dock.[37] The crowd that had assembled for the launching watched the proceedings with great expectations. Could this be the invention that would put an end to the terrible blockade?

The submarine launched that day was no *Pioneer*. Experience with their previous projects had taught our determined inventors what worked

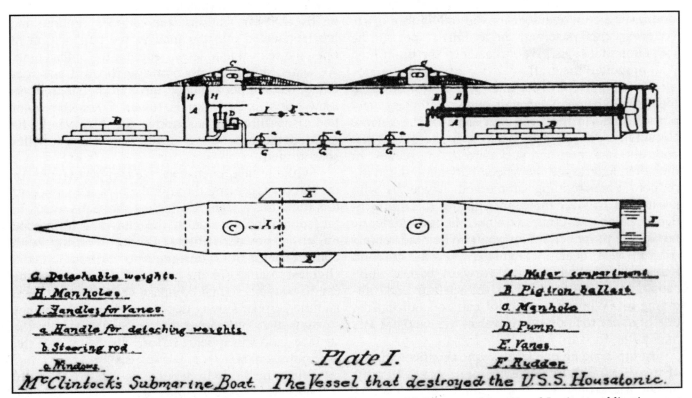

In a letter written in 1902, William Alexander stated that this diagram, which appeared in a Naval Institute publication, was not the "Hunley," and went on to write "After the capture of New Orleans McClintock went to Mobile where he built the submarine in Plate I. I don't know where McClintock is living, but hope he will assist in correcting this error." Since the sketch had been made in McClintock's presence it may mean that this is a fairly accurate drawing of the "American Diver" (a.k.a. "Pioneer II") even though it is incorrectly labeled as "The Vessel that destroyed the U.S.S. Housatonic."
Courtesy of the U.S. Naval Institute.

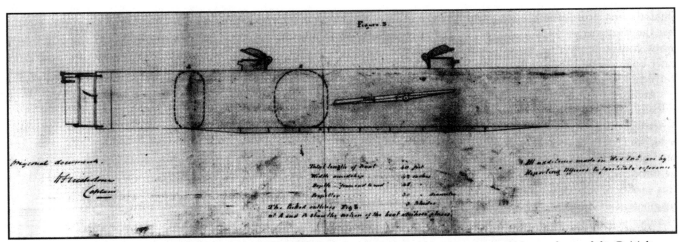

The "Hunley" as drawn by designer James R. McClintock while attending a secret meeting with members of the British Admiralty during the fall of 1872. Accompanying this diagram was a document stating "She was built of iron 3/5 inch thick, 40 feet long, 42 inches wide in the middle and 48 inches high, fitted with cranks geared to her propeller and turned by 8 persons inside of her. She was a beautifully modeled boat, and worked to perfection." British Admiralty

and what didn't. From past trials, it was learned that the submarine would tilt while submerged whenever a crew member moved only a foot or so. To arrest this problem, an assigned spot at the propeller shaft was given to each of the eight men who propelled the craft.

The skipper or ninth man in the crew stood in the forward hatch, peering through small glass view ports located at the front and sides of the narrow conning tower. In one hand was the lever that controlled the port and starboard diving planes. In the other, he grasped the wheel that manipulated the rudder. When running submerged, it was he who knelt next to the candle, monitoring the dimly lit depth gauge and compass while the anxious crew turned the propeller's crankshaft. When the cabin's oxygen was nearly exhausted, it was he who manually pumped out the forward ballast tank, causing the craft to rise to the surface and life-giving air. Without a doubt, it can be said that the fate of every man on board was in the hands of this man at the forward hatch.

At this time no one knows who this first skipper of the *Hunley* was. However logic would suggest that he was probably one of the engineers or owners of the craft. In my own opinion, it was either Dixon or McClintock; both men later commanded the small submarine, so it seems safe to say that one of them was at the diving planes during her harbor trials. Regardless of who piloted the novel craft that day, all who witnessed the underwater tests agreed that this third submarine boat was a success.

Satisfied with their small submarine's performance, James McClintock and his old partner, Baxter Watson, arranged a demonstration of the *Hunley's* attack capabilities for Mobile's Naval commander, Franklin Buchanan. Buchanan, being from the old school of naval tactics, viewed such inventions as underwater mines and submarine boats to be infernal machines, inhuman in their method of attack, by giving the enemy no chance to defend themselves. This chivalrous view was shared by many during the Victorian Age. However the South was starting to lose the war, and any invention that would help defeat the oncoming enemy was now eagerly welcome.

On the morning of July 31, 1863, an old, coal-hauling flat boat was towed to the middle of the Mobile River and anchored. On shore, several high ranking military officers had assembled to witness the destructive capabilities of a unique underwater diving machine.[38] Several hundred yards up river,

the *Hunley's* volunteer crew took turns squeezing through the submarine's narrow hatches. With all hands at their stations, the skipper ordered the hatches sealed and the man at the rear station to open the sea valve to let water enter the ballast tank. As water splashed into both the forward and rear tanks, the skipper watched through the small glass view ports in the conning tower. When the water had risen three inches above the black hull, he ordered the sea valves closed and the propeller shaft turned.

With the boat underway, the skipper steered for the flat boat, peering through the forward view port that remained a scant few inches above the water. In the submarine's wake, at the end of a long rope trailed a powder filled cylinder bristling with contact detonators designed to explode at the slightest touch. As they neared their target, the candle was lit, a final compass heading was taken, and the skipper slowly depressed the diving planes causing the submarine to descend beneath the surface and disappear before the eyes of the assembled crowd.

When the dimly lit depth gauge aboard the fully submerged vessel displayed twenty feet, the skipper leveled her off. As the crew continued to turn the crankshaft, the helmsman watched the compass needle swing slightly from side to side. Two or three minutes passed without a sound, except for the iron crankshaft turning in the hands of the anxious crew. Suddenly a huge concussion enveloped the tiny craft, causing the *Hunley* to shudder and list to one side.

Once the shock wave had passed and the small craft was once again stable, the skipper ordered the fore and aft ballast tanks pumped out. As the small vessel reappeared on the surface the heavy iron hatch covers were pushed open to the sounds of a cheering crowd. The *Hunley* had undoubtedly proven herself potentially lethal to any ship afloat.

By a fantastic stroke of good luck several eye witness accounts regarding these underwater experiments exist to this day. From a post war letter written by a Confederate general on duty in Mobile comes the following. "In company with Admiral Buchanan and many officers of the C.S. Navy and Army, I witnessed her (the *Hunley*) operations in the river and harbor of Mobile. I saw her pass under a large raft of lumber towing a torpedo behind her which destroyed the raft. She appeared three or four hundred yards beyond the raft and so far as I could judge she behaved as well under water as above it.

I will add that I witnessed her experiments more than a dozen times with equal satisfaction."[39]

Of the underwater tests conducted by the *Hunley*, Captain P.M. Murphey of the *C.S.S. Selma* (The ship from which James Carr had deserted in late February and testified as to the alleged submarine attack on the blockading fleet off Fort Morgan) would write. "Whilst lying at Mobile in company with my officers and others of the C.S. Navy, I witnessed the experiments of the Submarine Boat which appeared to be a perfect success." [40]

With the destructive potential of the small submarine no longer questioned, military commanders in Mobile unanimously decided to put the *Hunley* into action as soon as possible.

Due to Mobile's shallow water and relatively strong harbor defenses, it was decided that Charleston should be the *Hunley's* base of operations.[41] For over a month the city's fortifications had been subjected to a daily bombardment from the federal fleet. If Charleston fell only one other Atlantic port would be open to the dwindling blockade runners.

Within hours after the submarine had proven itself a worthy adversary for the enemy fleet, General Slaughter, (military commander of Alabama) penned the following letter of introduction to General Beauregard in far away South Carolina.

"Mobile, Alabama. July 31, 1863. My Dear General: This will be handed you by Messrs B. Watson and B.A. Whitney, the inventors of a Submarine boat which they desire to submit to you for examination, and if it meets your approval to test its usefulness in Charleston Harbor. So far as I am able to judge I can see no reason why it should not answer all our sanguine expectations. Nothing appears to me wanting but cool and determined men to manage it, but you will see and judge for yourself. Your Old Friend, John E. Slaughter."[42]

On the following day Admiral Buchanan sent a similar communication to Charleston's naval commander, John Tucker. Although Buchanan had been unimpressed with the *Hunley's* predecessor (the *American Diver/Pioneer II*), it would appear from the following lines that he was quite satisfied with this newest submarine.

"Naval Commandant's Office Mobile, Ala. August 1st, 1863. Sir: I yesterday witnessed the destruction of a lighter or coal flat in the Mobile River by a torpedo which was placed under it by a

Flag officer John Tucker was in command of Charleston's naval defenses. From the collection of Dr. Charles Perry

submarine iron boat, the invention of Messrs. Whitney and McClintock; Messrs. Watson and Whitney visit Charleston for the purpose of consulting General Beauregard and yourself to ascertain whether you will try it, they will explain all its advantages, and if it can operate in smooth water where the current is not strong as was the case yesterday. I can recommend it to your favorable consideration, it can be propelled about four knots per hour, to judge from the experiment of yesterday. I am fully satisfied it can be used successfully in blowing-up one or more of the enemy's ironclads in your harbor. Do me the favor to show this to General Beauregard with my regards. Very Respectfully Franklin Buchanan Admiral CSN."[43]

Shortly after Flag Officer Tucker received the above letter, Baxter Watson and Gus Whitney, our two submarine advocates, arrived at the busy Charleston Railroad station. With diagrams and drawings tucked under their arms, our weary travelers presented their credentials to the proper authorities and were immediately granted an audience with Charleston's military commander, Pierre Gustave Tousant Beauregard.

It was General Beauregard who had given the orders to fire on Fort Sumter on April 12, 1861. He had commanded the Confederate army at the First Battle of Manassas, and from the middle of 1863 had been assigned the task of improving Charleston's harbor defenses. A famous General, known both north and south as a commander with a flair for the unconventional, Beauregard examined the strange diagrams and listened to the wild scheme presented by the enthusiastic visitors from Mobile. With the situation at Charleston deteriorating daily, Beauregard wasted no time in approving shipment of the duo's amazing diving machine to his besieged city. On August 7, we find him sending the following message by dots and dashes over the busy telegraph wire to railroad agents on the line from Mobile to Charleston:

"PLEASE EXPEDITE TRANSPORTATION OF WHITNEY'S SUB-MARINE BOAT FROM MOBILE HERE, IT IS MUCH NEEDED."[44]

In Mobile, the Singer Submarine Corps received General Beauregard's telegram with great enthusiasm; at last their invention would be used against the enemy's fleet. Without delay, our small band of Confederate engineers addressed the problems associated with transporting their heavy submarine to faraway Charleston. The forty-foot craft was removed from the harbor, transferred to the railroad station and hoisted aboard two flatcars.[45] (The logistics involved in removing my own twelve-foot submarine from the water makes me appreciate all the more the problems faced by these Confederate submariners.)

From excerpts taken from a letter written by Lieutenant George Washington Gift (the naval officer assigned the task of transferring the *Hunley* to the Mobile railroad station), comes a rare first hand description of the *Hunley* as well as optimistic predictions regarding her future triumphs off South Carolina.

"*C.S.S. Gaines*, Mobile, August 8, 1863. My Dear Ellen: I have been employed during the past day or two in hoisting out of the water and sending away toward Charleston a very curious machine for destroying vessels, and which I certainly regard as the most important invention to us that could have been made. It is a submarine boat which is propelled with ease and rapidity underwater. But inasmuch as it will become in a very short time one

of the great celebrities in the art of defense and attack on floating objects I will run the risk of inflicting a short description.

In the first place imagine a high pressure steam boiler, not quite round, say 4 feet in diameter in one way and 3 1/2 feet the other - draw each end of the boiler down to a sharp wedge shaped point. On the bottom of the boat is riveted an iron keel weighing 4000 pounds. On top and opposite the keel is placed two man hole plates or hatches with heavy tops. They are just large enough for a man to go in and out. At one end is fitted a very neat little propeller 3 1/2 feet in diameter worked by men sitting in the boat and turning the shaft by hand cranks. She also has a rudder and steering apparatus.

Embarked and under ordinary circumstances with men and ballast she floats about half way out of the water and resembles a whale. But when it is necessary to go underwater there are compartments into which the water is allowed to flow, which causes the boat to sink to any required depth, the same being accurately indicated by a column of mercury.

Behind the boat at a distance of 100 to 150 feet is towed a plank and under that plank is attached a torpedo with say 100 pounds of powder. I saw them explode a vessel as an experiment. They approached to within about fifty yards from her keeping the man holes just above water. At that distance the submarine sank down and in a few minutes made her appearance on the other side of the vessel.

I consider it a perfect success! and in the hands of a bold man would be equal to the task of destroying every ironclad the enemy has off Morris Island (an island at the mouth of Charleston harbor) in a single night. It is perfectly safe and perfectly sure. She will be ready for service in Charleston by the 18th or 20th of this month."[46]

With the *Hunley* firmly secured to the flatcars, and probably covered for secrecy, our small band of underwater adventurers said farewell to Mobile as they set out with their unique cargo for the besieged city of Charleston.

Unloading cotton from blockade-runners at Nassau, New Providence. The Illustrated London News.

Blockade runner. Reproduced from the collections of the Library of Congress.

The little submarine was covered with tarpaulins and secretly transported from Mobile to Charleston.
Photo reproduced from the collection of the U.S. Library of Congress.

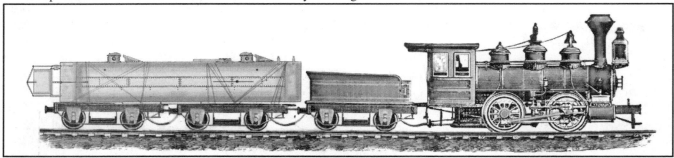

Too long to fit on a standard 20' flat car, the "Hunley" was cradled and tied down on two flatcars for her trip from Mobile.
Drawing adapted from sketch of *Hunley* by Caldwell C. Whistler and stock art of engine, coal car, and flatcars.

As the "Hunley" made its way to Charleston, she would have passed through the Atlanta rail station. Atlanta was the main transfer depot for the Confederate war effort. Civil War photo of the Atlanta switching yard and train barn, courtesy of the U.S. National Archives.

CHAPTER TWO
Charleston Harbor Becomes Submarine Proving Grounds

"If you wish to see war every day and night, this is the place to see it." – Lt. George E. Dixon (final commander of the *C.S.S. Hunley*)

On the morning of August 12, 1863, the locomotive hauling the small submarine and her weary crew slowly lumbered into the busy Charleston railroad station.[47] For over two days the submarine had made her way across the Deep South turning the heads of curious citizens as it made its way to the city that had witnessed the first shots fired in this bloody war. With the situation deteriorating daily, military leaders in the desperate city had waited eagerly for the arrival of the little diving machine that all hoped would put an end to the terrible blockade.

From the contents of the following telegram sent the day before the *Hunley's* arrival, we can get a good idea as to how anxious Charleston headquarters had been while waiting for their cargo from Alabama: "AUGUST 11, 1863, GENERAL MAURY HAS THE SUBMARINE BOAT BEEN SENT FROM MOBILE (STOP) IF SO WHEN DID IT LEAVE FOR CHARLESTON (STOP) SIGNED G.T. BEAUREGARD GENERAL COMMANDING."[48]

As the weary group of underwater raiders stepped down from the railroad car, their eyes were met with a scene far worse than that they had left in Mobile, for Charleston was under heavy siege. Wagons of military supplies rumbled through the streets. Convalescing soldiers, missing arms and legs, were a frequent sight. Women and children feared that their husbands, sons, and fathers might soon be needed to man the numerous earth works that encircled the harbor, and repel, with musket and bayonet, an expected all-out federal attack.

Charleston's primary harbor defenses consisted of Fort Sumter, located in the mouth of the harbor and garrisoned by about 350 men with 79 cannons of sundry caliber; and Fort Moultrie at the southern end of Sullivan's Island with 38 guns and about 300 men. Fort Moultrie defended the northern channel.[49] Between Sumter and Moultrie a string of underwater contact mines had been anchored to keep the enemy ironclads at bay. Guarding the southern entrance, at the tip of Morris Island, was Battery Wagner, currently under direct land attack from the Union infantry regiments that had recently captured the southern end of the island.

It was here at Battery Wagner, only a few short weeks before, that the 54th Massachusetts Colored Infantry Regiment spearheaded an attack that has come to be known as the African-American Bunker Hill and was featured in the movie Glory. Although the brave charge failed to dislodge the entrenched Confederates, the black soldiers who stormed the breastworks paved the way for other colored regiments to be formed by the United States Army. In all, about 6,000 Confederate soldiers manned the now battered defenses of the city known both north and south as the cradle of secession.[50]

From the city docks piled high with cotton, our newly arrived crew of sub-mariners could see Fort Sumter being reduced to rubble by the enemy batteries on Morris Island and ironclads at the harbor's entrance. It was plain to all who witnessed the siege of this once proud citadel of southern defiance that the tide of war was now turning against the ill-equipped Confederacy.

With the submarine now in the city, General Beauregard ordered the Engineering Department to unload the bulky craft and transfer it to a slip in the nearby harbor as soon as possible. While the small submarine was being unloaded from the two flatcars, word of the new secret weapon spread like wildfire throughout the war-weary city. Soon a curious group of onlookers had assembled around the mysterious boat and watched with eager anticipation as men and ropes strained to lift the bulky craft from its makeshift cradle. When the vessel was swung free from the two flat cars and rolled through the streets of the city, the delighted citizens of Charleston waved Confederate flags and cheered as this new threat to the hated Union fleet slowly lumbered past.

With the mere presence of the unique diving machine raising moral within the besieged city, General Beauregard, anxious to get the submarine into action as soon as possible, issued the following orders: "August 12th 1863. Major Hutson Chief Quarter Master, Department of S.C., Ga., & Fla. You will furnish Mr. B.A. Whitney on his requisition with such articles as he may need for placing his submarine vessel in condition for

Confederate commander of Charleston defenses, General P.G.T. Beauregard requested the "Hunley" be sent to Charleston to attack the enemy ironclads, but later feared that it was even more dangerous to her own crew. However, his concerns did not prevent him from ordering her into battle. Photo courtesy of U.S. National Archives.

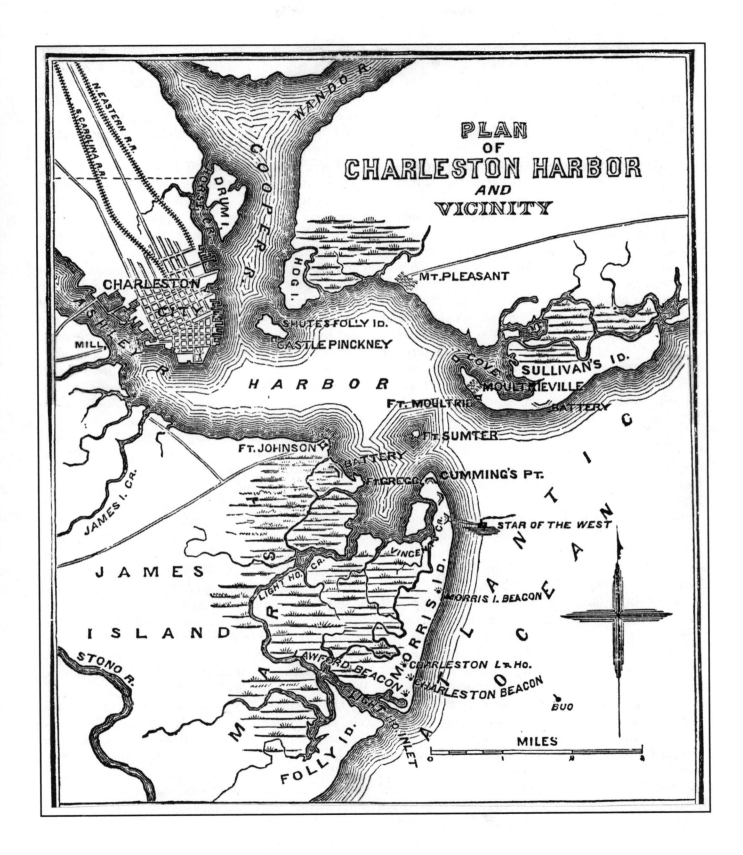

service. His requisitions will be approved subsequently at this office."[51]

Judging from the fact that the above order refers to the *Hunley* as "his (B.A. Whitney's) submarine vessel", it would appear that this recently transplanted Texas artillery man, was in all likelihood chief spokesman for the Singer Submarine Corps. Since the early part of the war Gus Whitney (along with E.C. Singer and most of the other members of Singer's group of torpedo engineers) had been enlisted men attached to Shea's Battalion of Texas Light Artillery stationed near Port Lavaca, Texas. In early 1863 he along with Singer and several other members of the Company, had been transferred to the Confederate Engineering Department following Singer's successful torpedo experiments. It would seem that Whitney and Captain Singer may very well have known one another before the war, and may have developed the widely deployed Singer contact mine together.[52]

As luck would have it, while searching through the thousands of Confederate documents at the National Archives, I was fortunate enough to locate a hastily written Charleston requisition signed by Gus Whitney on the very day the above order was issued. Although a bit confusing, it would appear that a quantity of lead and packing yarn was ordered.[53] At first glance this requisition seemed a bit strange. However, on further reflection I came to the conclusion that the lead was probably used as internal ballast or to seal joints, while the packing yarn was intended to pack the stuffing boxes that kept the water from entering the vessel through the various shaftways (for her propeller shaft and diving planes) that pierced her hull.

No records have been located indicating just where the *Hunley* was launched after her arrival in Charleston. Judging from the location of the railroad station, it's a good bet that her first point of entry was the dock at the end of Calhoun Street on the Cooper River. Once the small submarine was in the water, it would have been an easy task to tow the craft or manually propel it to any location around the harbor.

From a news article that appeared in the *San Antonio Express* in 1916, we learn that investor E.C. Singer arrived in the city a couple of days later to build the explosive devices that would be used against the blockading enemy fleet.[54] At about the same time that Singer arrived in Charleston, James McClintock received the following letter from a

very anxious Horace Hunley who was detained on military business in Mississippi: "I have been extremely anxious about your experiments at Charleston. It is not at all on the question of whether you will succeed in blowing up a vessel of the enemy, for I think that more than probable and of itself only a small matter. It is whether your success will be made available in effecting a real solid benefit to the Confederacy and conferring glory on it's originators.

I am anxious first and above all for a dead silence on your part that the enemy may be lost in uncertainty and mystery, which is more dreadful than any understood evil even of the greatest magnitude. Secondly, while in a panic if you succeed the enemy if properly pressed before he can make preparations to resist the consequences of your success might be possibly driven entirely from Morris Island, his works destroyed and guns spiked even if it be not possible to take and permanently hold the island and prevent it from being retaken. Therefore, as I cannot join you I would be glad to have you in conversation with General Beauregard if this reaches you before your experiment to ask him (by way of suggestion) if you should be so fortunate as to succeed, and if that success should create a panic and consequent retreat, if a rapid descent by vessels and men could not drive the enemy from the island.

If he should think that a panic and retreat of the enemies could effect such a result, then make every effort first to get him to prepare silently for such an event, and then by at least one spare torpedo for a second attempt make a heroic attempt to produce this panic. Remind your crew of Manassas and Shiloh and the consequences of faltering in the hour of success and make one grand effort and you may have cause to rejoice over the fruits of your labor and that like men in more exalted positions you did not stop to rejoice over your small gains let slip a vast success and immortal honor. Read this to Whitney. H.L. Hunley."[55]

During these first chaotic days in Charleston, our small band of sub-mariners were eagerly preparing their unique underwater weapon for action, as well as locate a suitable mooring from which to strike out at the ever-growing enemy fleet. On the same day that McClintock received the letter from Horace Hunley, General Jordan, Beauregard's Chief of Staff, relayed the following message to our newly arrived Mobile crew: "I am authorized to say that John Fraser & Co. will pay

Gus Whitney and Baxter Watson probably stayed in the Charleston Hotel during their short stay in the city.
Library of Congress photo.

over to any parties who shall destroy the US Steam ironclad *Ironside* the sum of $100,000, a similar sum for the destruction of the wooden frigate *Wabash*, and the sum of $50,000 for every monitor sunk. I have reason to believe that other men of wealth will unite and give with equal munificence toward the same end. At the same time steps are being taken to secure a large sum to be settled for the support of the families of parties, who, making any attempt against the fleet now attacking our outer works, shall fail in the enterprise, and fall or be captured in the attempt."[56]

One can better understand the size of this reward if you figure that $100,000 in 1863 gold was today's equivalent of about $2,000,000.

With this tantalizing offer, and with explosive expert E.C. Singer and staff now in the city, the following orders were issued to the arsenal commander: "Charleston, S.C. August 16th 1863. Major: The commanding General desires that you will render every assistance of material and labor to Messrs. Whitney and Watson, in the construction of torpedoes to be used with their submarine vessel which he regards as the most formidable engine of war for the defense of Charleston now at his disposition."[57]

At present I have been able to identify only one crew member, who accompanied the *Hunley* on her journey from Alabama. His name was Jeremiah Donivan, an eighteen year old native of Mobile who worked alongside Alexander at the Park & Lyons machine shop.[58] It's interesting to note that decades after the war had ended, Donivan, at the age of eighty-three still considered his short tour of duty aboard the submarine to have been the greatest adventure of his life. Although I have not been able to identify the other members of this first Hunley crew, it is reasonable to assume that they were from the Park & Lyons machine shop and/or Singer's group of engineers.

From names that appear on known requisitions, we can say with some certainty that Gus Whitney, James McClintock and Baxter Watson were in the city from the start. E.C. Singer, his assistant and fellow project investor, J.D. Braman arrived a couple of days later. And Horace Hunley, as we shall see shortly, arrived in the besieged city by August 20th, to help with the operations of his name sake. Although it's not known when fellow investor R.W. Dunn arrived in Charleston, an order from the Confederate Engineering Department in Richmond (dated August 10, 1863) clearly states

that he was then under orders to report at Charleston military headquarters as soon as possible. [59]

Although information is sketchy, existing evidence suggests that the *Hunley's* chief designer, James McClintock, was in command of the submarine with part owner, Gus Whitney, as his first officer manning the ballast tank pumps at the rear of the vessel.[60] Our two 21st Alabama engineers, George E. Dixon and William Alexander, appear to have been left behind in Mobile to continue their detached duty at the Park & Lyons shop. At this point in the operation, it can be said that this was a civilian effort under the jurisdiction of the military defenders of Charleston. However, with deteriorating conditions and the ever-growing threat of an all out enemy assault, this arrangement was destined to change soon.

From known dispatches and layout of Charleston harbor, it appears that an area known as The Cove, located behind Fort Moultrie at the end of Sullivan's Island, was the *Hunley's* first base of operations. By hugging the shore at the tip of the island, it would have been quite easy to avoid the numerous contact mines in the channel and gain access to the outer harbor and open sea.

At this point, I would like to remind the reader that for the most part we are dealing with Confederate military records, many of which were lost or destroyed at the end of the war. To say the least, the situation at Charleston during this period was desperate.

Ferocious duels between the heavily armored federal ironclads and Forts Sumter and Moultrie were almost a daily event. Across the channel, only a few hundred yards away, Battery Wagner, now cut off and alone, faced thousands of federal infantrymen and scores of large caliber cannon.

By night, swift, low-silhouetted blockade runners, loaded with medicine and arms, would frequently slip through the lines of enemy ships, and thread their way through the shoals and sandbars. If spotted by federal pickets, they would be greeted with a hail of shot and shell. In such cases they were known to have purposely run themselves aground under the protective guns of the batteries scattered along Sullivan's Island, on the premise that at least their cargo could be saved.

The exploits of this small band of sub-mariners could be considered a mere subplot in the greater drama that was taking place in this bastion of southern resistance. For the past couple of years,

The bark rigged, ironclad, screw steamer "New Ironsides," pictured above, was the "Hunley's" prime target during her first few weeks in Charleston. U.S. Naval Historical Center Photograph, courtesy of the U.S. Marine Corps Historical Center, Personal Papers Section, Collection of Henry Clay Cochran.

Confederate blockade runner "A.D. Vance" at Nassau, New Providence, Bahamas. The first information Washington received concerning the "Hunley" came from two engineers who were engaged in running the blockade from Nassau. U.S. Naval Historical Center photo of gift of Charles V. Peery. Extensively retouched for this book.

our newly arrived inventors had only seen the war from afar or read about the numerous battles in the Mobile papers. Now they were participating in, and witnessing one of the greatest naval sieges ever to have taken place.

With the small submarine now in a position to strike out at the federal fleet, our band of underwater raiders wasted no time in putting their ambitious plan into motion. From a soon to be quoted letter, we find that during the third week of August 1863, the *Hunley* made at least three nocturnal excursions against the enemy's fleet anchored at the harbor's mouth.[61] Keeping several feet below the surface, these southern inventors were awkwardly ushering in a new form of warfare that would come to change naval tactics forever. Rising to the surface every twenty minutes or so to replenish their dwindling air supply, McClintock could see the ironclads of the enemy's fleet silhouetted against the dark horizon through the subs tiny view ports. After several anxious moments, the ex-riverboat captain would once more depress the forward diving planes, causing the *Hunley* to again disappear beneath the dark surface. From within their cramped, dimly lit craft, our band of underwater warriors now turned their crankshaft within attack range of the very keels of the enemy's iron fleet. If luck and the currents were with them, perhaps tonight would be the night a death blow could be dealt to one of the unwelcome northern invaders.

From a food stuffs requisition filed by B.A.(Gus) Whitney, it would appear that the crew of the *Hunley* may have been associated or temporarily attached to the Charleston ironclad *C.S.S. Chicora.* - for the requisition in question was directed toward the Chicora's executive officer and the *"articles of subsistence"* requested, were taken from the ironclad's food stores. From this intriguing communication we read the following.

"*C.S.S. Chicora*, Charleston, S.C. August 22, 1863. To: John S. Banks, Sir: There is required for the use of the 'Torpedo expedition' (9) nine lbs. Bacon, (8) eight lbs. Bread, 1/4 lb. Tea, 1 2/16 lbs. sugar. Signed B.A. Whitney."

Since the above communication specially states that the food stuffs requested were "required for the use of the torpedo expedition", it could be assumed that the above mentions articles of subsistence were to be taken on board the submarine during one of her nocturnal expeditions. Since the submarine was most likely to remain at sea until the following

The Confederate ironclad Chicora is seen in this 1863 photograph. Collection of Dr. Charles V. Peery.

dawn, food and tea (tea being a stimulant) would have been invaluable in helping the men get through the long night.[62]

During my research, I was very fortunate to read a diary kept by Emma Holmes, a young South Carolina woman who lived in Charleston during this period. It is filled with the every day sort of events, so important to a true understanding of what was happening.

While reading entries penned between August 17 and August 27, 1863, I was surprised to discover that she had actually mentioned the *Hunley*, and gave a rather a good description of the craft. At this point I would like to share a few of Miss Holmes' entries with the reader regarding her observations around the city, as well as her description of the submarine boat she refers to as the *Porpoise*.

"August 19th, 1863. Went round to Uncle James to see the bombardment, which had been furious all morning. But the weather was very stormy yesterday, a strong east wind blowing, and all the vessels had drawn off, unable to stand the rough seas. Yesterday there were no casualties at Fort Sumter, strange to say, notwithstanding the furious cannonading.

August 21st, 1863. Mr. Earle came according to promise, for us to walk on the battery, to see the bombardment. it was a soft, but not brilliant moonlight night, and though we did not see but one shell burst, I enjoyed it very much. We returned about eleven and found several gentlemen in the drawing room with Mr. Bull playing and singing.

I was quite glad to meet Captain Tracey, he is a tall good looking, elegant gentleman, very intelligent and agreeable, and I enjoyed talking to him. He told us of the *Porpoise* - the cigar shaped

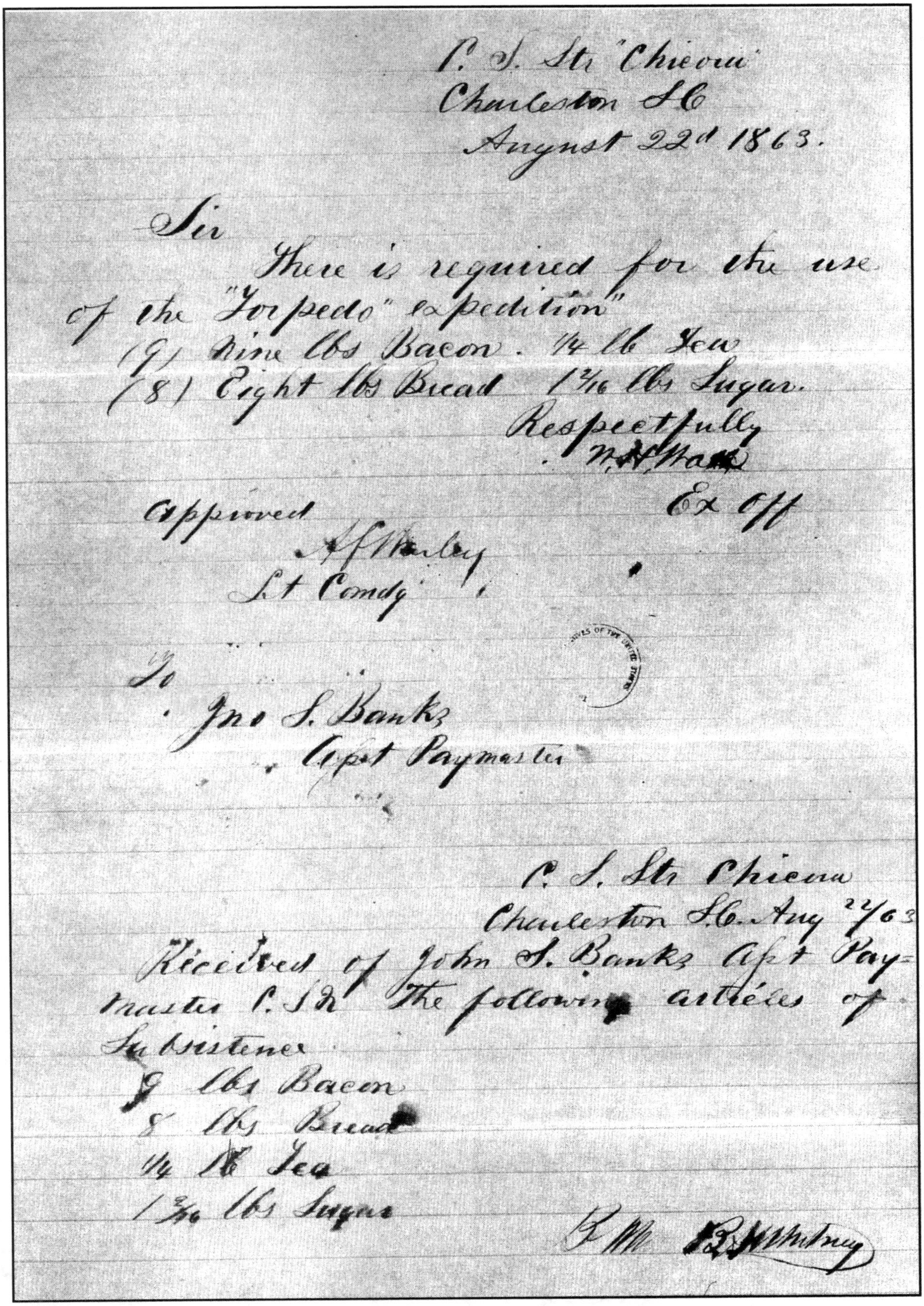

C. S. Str "Chicora"
Charleston SC
August 22d 1863.

Sir
        There is required for the use
of the "Torpedo" expedition"
(9) Nine lbs Bacon. ¼ lb Tea
(8) Eight lbs Bread 1 3⁄16 lbs Sugar.
                    Respectfully
                        W. H. Ward
                            Ex Off

Approved
    A F Warley
        Lt Comdg

To
    Jno S. Banks
        Asst Paymaster

                        C. S. Str Chicora
                    Charleston S.C. Aug 22/63
Received of John S. Banks Asst Pay-
master C. S. N. the following articles of
Subsistence
    9 lbs Bacon
    8 lbs Bread
    ¼ lb Tea
    1 3⁄16 lbs Sugar
                        F M B Whitney

Gus Whitney's requisition for supplies from the C.S.S. Chicora's food stores. National Archives.

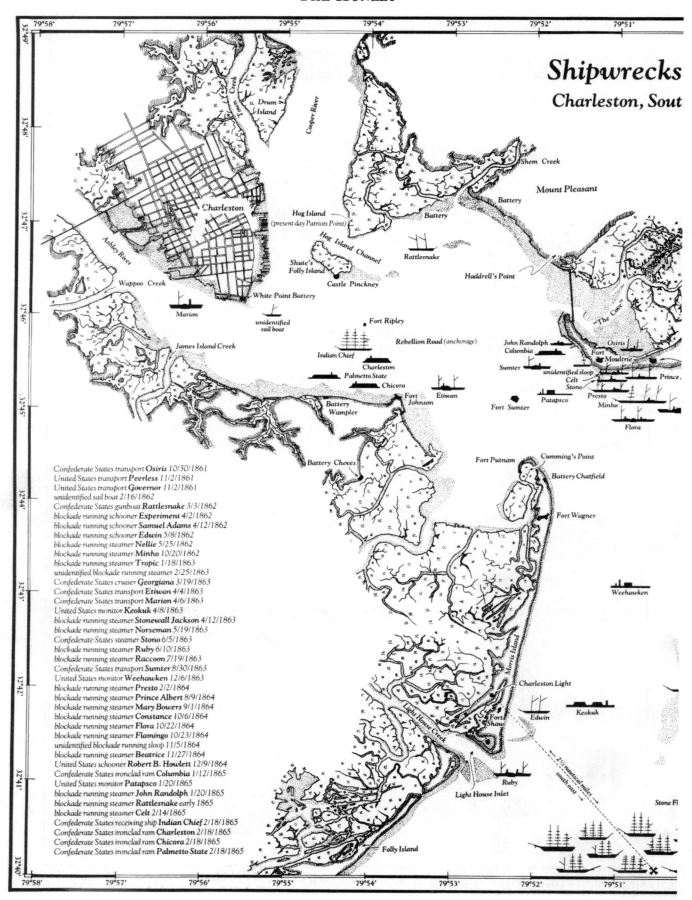

Shipwrecks
Charleston, Sout

Confederate States transport **Osiris** 10/30/1861
United States transport **Peerless** 11/2/1861
United States transport **Governor** 11/2/1861
unidentified sail boat 2/16/1862
Confederate States gunboat **Rattlesnake** 3/3/1862
blockade running schooner **Experiment** 4/2/1862
blockade running schooner **Samuel Adams** 4/12/1862
blockade running schooner **Edwin** 5/8/1862
blockade running steamer **Nellie** 5/25/1862
blockade running steamer **Minho** 10/20/1862
blockade running steamer **Tropic** 1/18/1863
unidentified blockade running steamer 2/25/1863
Confederate States cruiser **Georgiana** 3/19/1863
Confederate States transport **Etiwan** 4/4/1863
Confederate States transport **Marion** 4/6/1863
United States monitor **Keokuk** 4/8/1863
blockade running steamer **Stonewall Jackson** 4/12/1863
blockade running steamer **Norseman** 5/19/1863
Confederate States steamer **Stono** 6/5/1863
blockade running steamer **Ruby** 6/10/1863
blockade running steamer **Raccoon** 7/19/1863
Confederate States transport **Sumter** 8/30/1863
United States monitor **Weehawken** 12/6/1863
blockade running steamer **Presto** 2/2/1864
blockade running steamer **Prince Albert** 8/9/1864
blockade running steamer **Mary Bowers** 9/1/1864
blockade running steamer **Constance** 10/6/1864
blockade running steamer **Flora** 10/22/1864
blockade running steamer **Flamingo** 10/23/1864
unidentified blockade running sloop 11/5/1864
blockade running steamer **Beatrice** 11/27/1864
United States schooner **Robert B. Howlett** 12/9/1864
Confederate States ironclad ram **Columbia** 1/12/1865
United States monitor **Patapsco** 1/20/1865
blockade running steamer **John Randolph** 1/20/1865
blockade running steamer **Rattlesnake** early 1865
blockade running steamer **Celt** 2/14/1865
Confederate States receiving ship **Indian Chief** 2/18/1865
Confederate States ironclad ram **Charleston** 2/18/1865
Confederate States ironclad ram **Chicora** 2/18/1865
Confederate States ironclad ram **Palmetto State** 2/18/1865

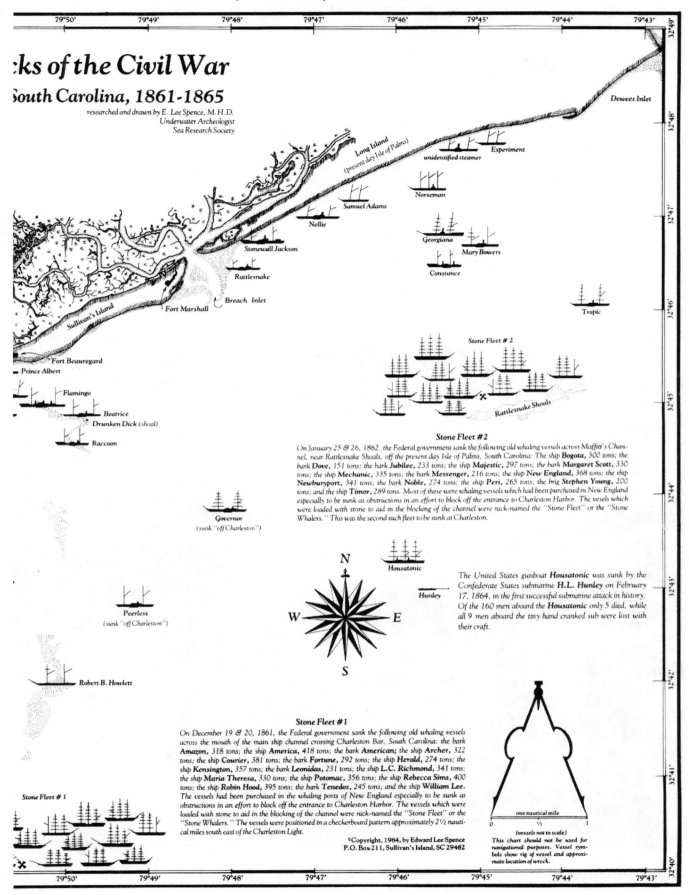

:ks of the Civil War

South Carolina, 1861-1865

researched and drawn by E. Lee Spence, M.H.D.
Underwater Archeologist
Sea Research Society

Stone Fleet # 2

On January 25 & 26, 1862, the Federal government sank the following old whaling vessels across Maffitt's Channel, near Rattlesnake Shoals, off the present day Isle of Palms, South Carolina: The ship **Bogota**, 300 tons; the bark **Dove**, 151 tons; the bark **Jubilee**, 233 tons; the ship **Majestic**, 297 tons; the bark **Margaret Scott**, 330 tons; the ship **Mechanic**, 335 tons; the bark **Messenger**, 216 tons; the ship **New England**, 368 tons; the ship **Newburyport**, 341 tons; the bark **Noble**, 274 tons; the ship **Peri**, 265 tons; the brig **Stephen Young**, 200 tons; and the ship **Timor**, 289 tons. Most of these were whaling vessels which had been purchased in New England especially to be sunk as obstructions in an effort to block off the entrance to Charleston Harbor. The vessels which were loaded with stone to aid in the blocking of the channel were nick-named the "Stone Fleet" or the "Stone Whalers." This was the second such fleet to be sunk at Charleston.

The United States gunboat **Housatonic** was sunk by the Confederate States submarine **H.L. Hunley** on February 17, 1864, in the first successful submarine attack in history. Of the 160 men aboard the **Housatonic** only 5 died, while all 9 men aboard the tiny hand cranked sub were lost with their craft.

Stone Fleet #1

On December 19 & 20, 1861, the Federal government sank the following old whaling vessels across the mouth of the main ship channel crossing Charleston Bar, South Carolina: the bark **Amazon**, 318 tons; the ship **America**, 418 tons; the bark **American**; the ship **Archer**, 322 tons; the ship **Courier**, 381 tons; the bark **Fortune**, 292 tons; the ship **Herald**, 274 tons; the ship **Kensington**, 357 tons; the bark **Leonidas**, 231 tons; the ship **L.C. Richmond**, 341 tons; the ship **Maria Theresa**, 330 tons; the ship **Potomac**, 356 tons; the ship **Rebecca Sims**, 400 tons; the ship **Robin Hood**, 395 tons; the bark **Tenedos**, 245 tons; and the ship **William Lee.** The vessels had been purchased in the whaling ports of New England especially to be sunk as obstructions in an effort to block off the entrance to Charleston Harbor. The vessels which were loaded with stone to aid in the blocking of the channel were nick-named the "Stone Fleet" or the "Stone Whalers." The vessels were positioned in a checkerboard pattern approximately 2½ nautical miles south east of the Charleston Light.

one nautical mile

0   ½   1

(vessels not to scale)

This chart should not be used for navigational purposes. Vessel symbols show rig of vessel and approximate location of wreck.

Confederate cannon in Fort Moultrie defended the entrance to Charleston Harbor.
Reproduced from the collections of the U.S. Library of Congress.

General T.L. Clingman, C.S.A., commanded Sullivan's Island located at the mouth of Charleston Harbor. When Clingman reported "I do not think it will render any service under its present management," the "Hunley" was immediately seized and placed under direct military command. Reproduced from the collections of the U.S. Library of Congress.

boat lately arrived from Mobile. It is forty feet long and can contain eight or nine men; it is worked by machinery and has fins like a fish, which enable it to dive. It can go twenty feet under water, then come up to within four feet of the surface and remain one or two hours while it sets off the torpedoes attached to it. It certainly is a wonderful thing, and we hope for it's success. It was to go out Saturday night to try and blow up the *Ironsides*, but I have heard nothing since of it."[63] Sometime during those first chaotic weeks in Charleston, the small submarine was closely observed, and studied by two steam engineers engaged in running the blockade from Nassau. From a letter received by Union Secretary of the Navy Gideon Welles, based on the engineers' description of the craft, we get a good idea of just how accessible the *Hunley* was to the inquisitive citizens of the isolated city.

"Nassau, August 24th, 1863. Sir: I am informed by two engineers engaged in running the blockade to Charleston, that there is a party of engineers in Charleston who have completed a submarine boat made of boiler-iron in the shape of a Spanish cigar and some forty feet in length, and by means of an air pump capable of remaining under water one hour with this machine. They plan to attach and blow up with torpedoes the ironclads, and men on the blockading squadron that come within reach. My informants inform me that they have examined the machine in all it's parts, and have no doubt of it's capability of accomplishing all the purpose. This infernal machine is all ready, and my only fear is that this mail will not reach you in time to put the squadron on their guard. Your Humble Servant S.G. Haynes."[64]

Upon receipt of this letter a copy was made and sent to Admiral Dahlgren (Commanding the South Atlantic Blockading Squadron off Charleston), who by then had heard rumors of the alleged submarine's existence from a small group of Confederate deserters. For reasons to be presented shortly it will be revealed why the Admiral dismissed this new underwater threat, and decided that a warning to the fleet was unnecessary.

On August 21st, perhaps fearing his men might be captured, the newly arrived Captain Hunley filed a requisition for nine uniforms to be worn by the McClintock & Whitney crew during their nocturnal patrols. "August 21,1863. SPECIAL REQUISITION: For nine grey jackets, three to be trimmed in gold braid. CIRCUMSTANCES: That the men for whom they are ordered are on special

secret service and that it is necessary that they be clothed in the Confederate Army uniform. H.L. Hunley."[65]

As further explanation, many in the Victorian Age considered such inventions as submarines and underwater mines to be "infernal machines," inhuman in their method of attack. If the small submarine were captured, the mere fact that her crew was wearing Confederate uniforms could make the difference between becoming prisoners of war, and being hung for involvement with a machine not recognized as a weapon for use in civilized warfare. In fact, most documents dealing with underwater mines and submarine boats were intentionally burned at Richmond to keep the names of those involved with such inventions secret from vengeful parties in the North.[66]

Less than twenty-four hours after this small band of submarine adventurers had received their new gray jackets, the war-weary citizens of Charleston awoke to the sound of a terrific explosion. From Morris Island over four miles away, the Union army had mounted a huge siege cannon aimed not at Forts Sumter or Moultrie, but at the very heart of the sleeping city. At 1:30 in the morning, August 22, 1863, the first shot was fired into Charleston. From then on as many as 100 exploding shells a day were indiscriminately hurled into the defiant city by this huge cannon, soon to be nicknamed "The Swamp Angel."[67]

On the day following this night of terror, the *Charleston Daily Courier* wrote a blistering editorial under the heading "The Bombardment." The first paragraph stated: "The startling events that have occurred since our last issue have opened up a new chapter in the history of the war. Our ferocious foe, maddened to desperation at the heroic obstinacy and resistance of his powerful combination of land and naval forces to reduce Fort Sumter and our batteries on Morris Island, tries the horrible and brutal resort, without the usual notice, of firing, at midnight upon the city, full of sleeping women and children, to intimidate our commanding general into a surrender of those fortifications. Our people are nerved for the crisis and with calm determination have resolved on making it a struggle for life or death."

The next day the citizens of Charleston were issued the following recommendation by the city's fire chief: "Incendiary Shells, the attention of house keepers and citizens generally is directed to the notice of M.H. Nathan, Chief of the Fire

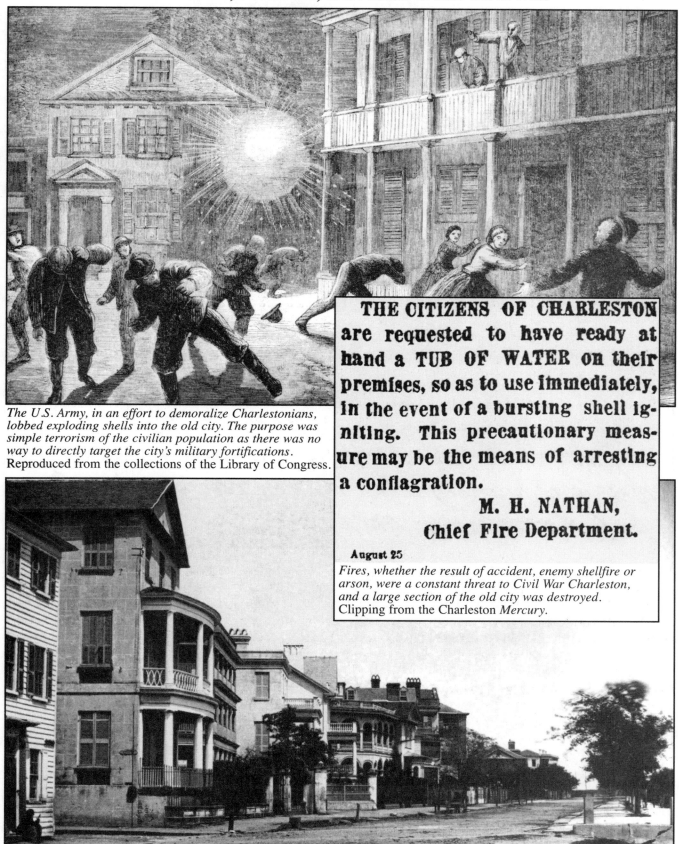

The U.S. Army, in an effort to demoralize Charlestonians, lobbed exploding shells into the old city. The purpose was simple terrorism of the civilian population as there was no way to directly target the city's military fortifications.
Reproduced from the collections of the Library of Congress.

THE CITIZENS OF CHARLESTON are requested to have ready at hand a TUB OF WATER on their premises, so as to use immediately, in the event of a bursting shell igniting. This precautionary measure may be the means of arresting a conflagration.

M. H. NATHAN,
Chief Fire Department.

August 25

Fires, whether the result of accident, enemy shellfire or arson, were a constant threat to Civil War Charleston, and a large section of the old city was destroyed.
Clipping from the Charleston *Mercury.*

Wartime photograph of homes on South Battery in Charleston. Several of these homes took direct hits from enemy guns.
Photo courtesy of the U.S. National Archives.

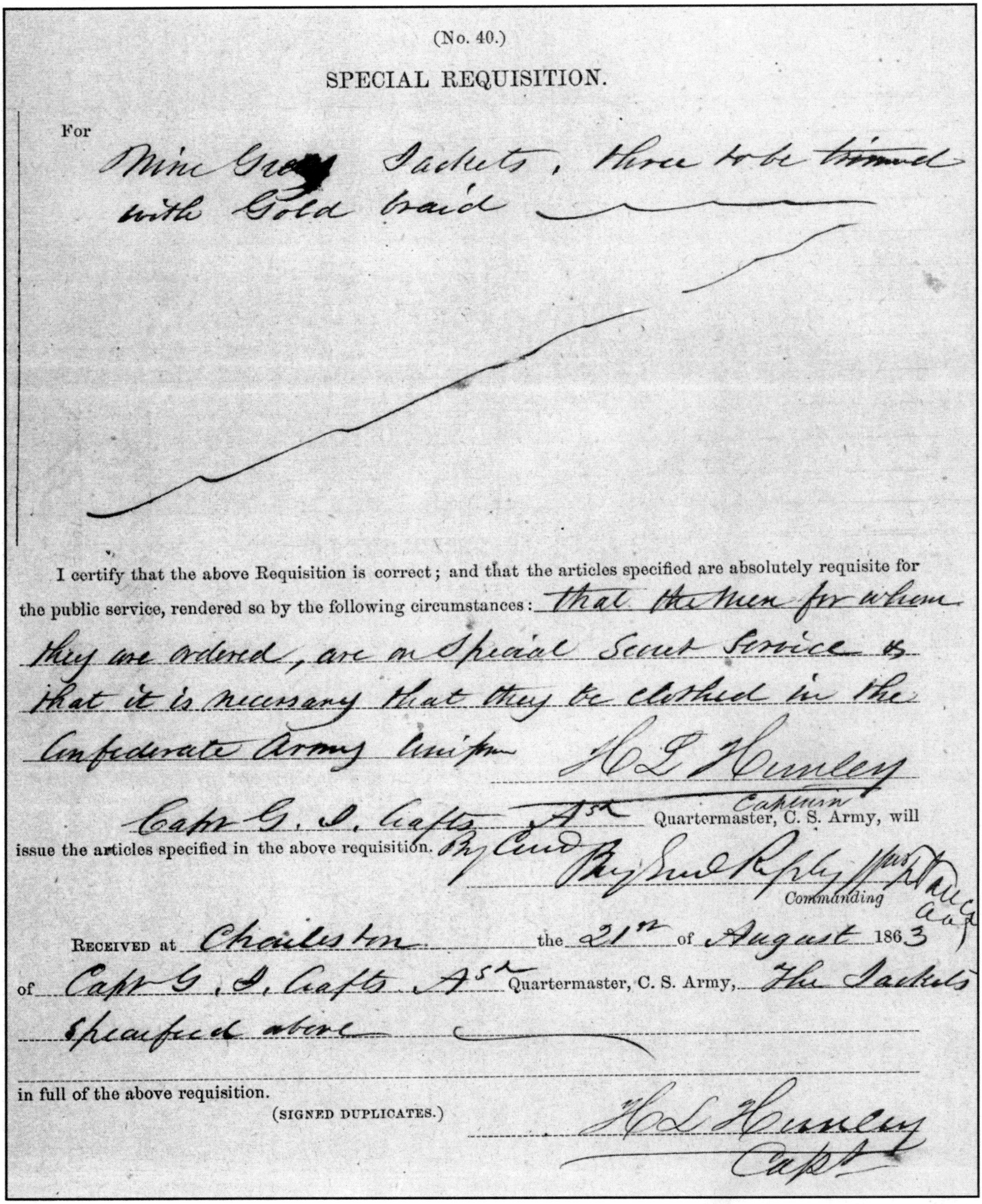

(No. 40.)

SPECIAL REQUISITION.

For

Nine Grey Jackets, three to be trimmed with Gold braid

I certify that the above Requisition is correct; and that the articles specified are absolutely requisite for the public service, rendered so by the following circumstances: *that the men for whom they are ordered, are on Special Scout Service & that it is necessary that they be clothed in the Confederate Army Uniform H L Hunley*

Capt G. I. Crafts A Qr ———— Quartermaster, C. S. Army, will issue the articles specified in the above requisition. *By Cmd* *Brig Genl Ripley* *Commanding*

RECEIVED at *Charleston* the *21st* of *August* 186*3* of *Capt G. I. Crafts A Qr* Quartermaster, C. S. Army, *The Jackets Specified above*

in full of the above requisition.
(SIGNED DUPLICATES.)

H L Hunley
Capt

"SPECIAL REQUISITION FOR: *Nine gray jackets, three to be trimmed with gold braid.* CIRCUMSTANCES: *That the men for whom they are ordered, are on Special Secret Service and that is necessary that they be clothed in the Confederate Army uniform. H.L. Hunley, Captain.*" Reproduced from the collections of the U.S. National Archives.

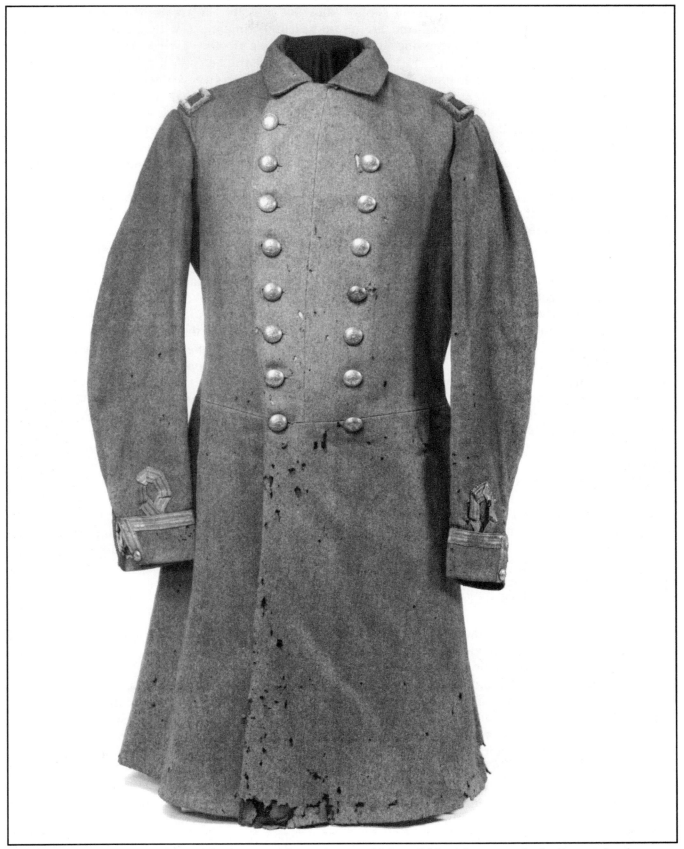

Confederate, double-breasted, naval frock coat similar to the one which would have been worn by Lt. Payne when he commanded the "Hunley." Reproduced by permission of the Museum of the Confederacy, Richmond, Virginia.

Department, recommending that a constant supply of water be kept on hand to extinguish the fire of the enemy's incendiary shells exploding in the city."

Turning once again to the diary of Emma Holmes, we read the following entry describing that first frightful night under the enemy's guns: "He (General Gillmore, commanding the Union forces on Morris Island), has turned his guns against a city filled with old men, women, children, and hospitals. I think I must have woke about three o'clock. Mr. Bull called out soon after to Rosa to listen to the shelling. It was a most peculiar fearful sound - the sharp scream or whiz through the air, and they sounded exactly as if coming over the house.

I was startled and much excited, but not frightened, but it produced a very solemn feeling, I lay with the windows partly open every moment expecting a shell might burst and kill me. I must have lain thus at least three quarters of an hour, when Rosa and Becca came down to my room so thoroughly scared they did not know what to do. I had never seen or heard of Rosa's being scared before, but this time she acknowledged she was so scared that her strength had utterly failed her, every limb ached, and she thought if she remained she would have fever.

She declared she could not move while the shelling was going on, for she was afraid to go upstairs. Her feelings had been similar to mine. She said she did not feel fit to die, yet every moment expected death."

On the following morning, Emma Holmes and her two sisters hastily gathered what possessions they could and fled to the state capitol at Columbia to stay with relatives.

With the city now under the very guns of the Union Army, military defenders of Charleston needed a bold combative action from the *Hunley* more than ever before. At about this time the Navy Department, anxious to learn why the small submarine had not yet made an attack, requested of the McClintock crew that a naval officer be allowed to accompany them on their next excursion. On considering this request, McClintock and the others came to the conclusion that a naval officer not familiar with the workings of their novel invention would simply get in the way; the request was denied.[68]

As the situation grew increasingly more desperate, and Battery Wagner likely to collapse any day, military leaders in the besieged city grew increasingly impatient with their cautious guests from Mobile. If this civilian crew could not, or would not attempt an attack on the blockading fleet, perhaps a military crew under the command of a bold and determined naval officer could.

In the early morning hours of August 23rd, a situation developed that may have contributed to the military's decision to seize the small submarine from her cautious civilian owners. At about three o'clock that morning a group of Union ironclads came to the harbor's entrance and commenced shelling Fort Sumter. Both Fort Sumter and Fort Moultrie returned fire as a thick fog rolled in, rendering the targets to both attacker and defender invisible. Upon the fogs lifting, it was seen that one of the enemy's ironclads had run aground and was dead in the water about 1,000 yards in front of Moultrie's guns. As the cannons from the fort started to sight in on the helpless monster, fog once again rolled in, causing the target to disappear from sight. In his report on the event, an irritated and disgusted General Clingman (commanding Sullivan's Island), stated that the enemy vessel would have been destroyed if only it had been in view for another thirty minutes.

With the opportunity of destroying one of the enemy's most powerful ships foiled, General Clingman was in no mood to hear excuses from the hesitant and thus ineffective *Hunley* crew. Shortly after writing his report on the botched attempt to destroy the grounded ironclad, Clingman sent the following note to his aide, Captain Nance: "The torpedo boat started at sunset but returned as they state because of an accident, Whitney says that though McClintock is timid, yet it shall go tonight unless the weather is bad."[69] Later that evening Nance received yet another unflattering message concerning the conduct of the *Hunley's* crew: "The torpedo boat has not gone out, I do not think it will render any service under it's present management."[70] With the sending of this last communication the fate of the small submarine's crew was sealed. Within twenty-four hours, the *Hunley* was seized by military authorities and turned over to the Confederate Navy; our small band of inventors from Mobile were out of a job.

With the *Hunley* now under the control of the Confederate government, a board of advisors was established to determine the value of the novel craft. From a document to be cited shortly, we learn that this group of naval experts calculated the value

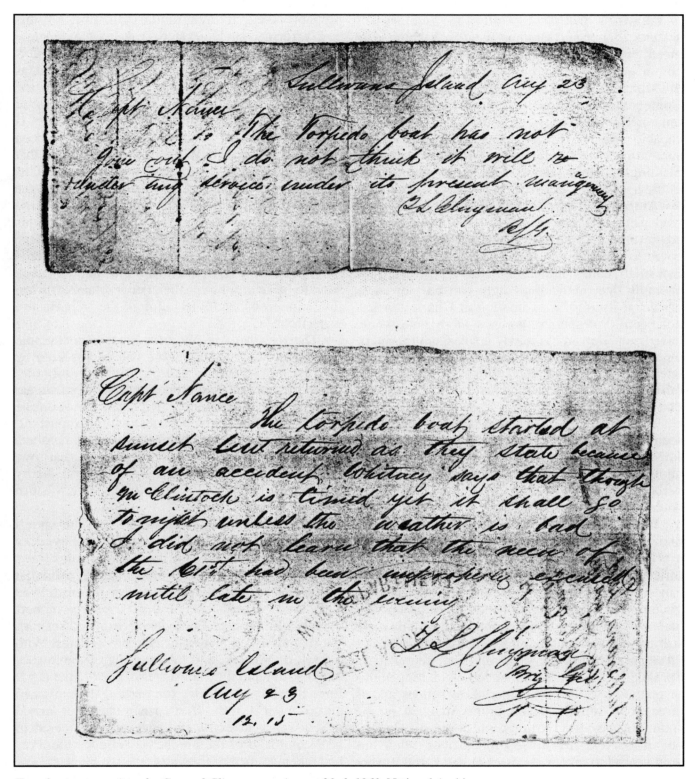

Two short notes written by General Clingman on August 23rd, 1863. National Archives.

of the unique diving machine at $27,500.[71] which was almost double the actual cost of the vessel's construction. However, there is no evidence that this sum was ever paid to the Singer group. All that is known is that shortly after the submarine's seizure, Singer and Braman went to Richmond to meet with the Navy Department concerning the continued deployment of underwater contact mines in Mobile harbor and other waterways in the Confederacy.[72] Whitney and Hunley appear to have remained in Charleston in some form of advisory capacity, while McClintock and the rest of the submarine's crew returned to Mobile to continue planting and maintaining underwater obstructions in the harbor.

At this point I would like to make it clear to the reader that McClintock and his crew of underwater adventurers were by no means cowards. The courage to venture several feet beneath the surface in a small, damp submarine to the very heart of the enemy's fleet night after night can be viewed as heroic in itself. If the situation at Charleston had not been so desperate, perhaps more time would have been allowed our newly arrived sub-mariners. One must remember that this was a civilian crew operating in the middle of one of the greatest military sieges in American history. The mere fact that McClintock put to sea in this unfamiliar besieged port against iron ships that had never been seen before in naval combat is commendable. If James McClintock and the Singer group had been allowed to retain command of the small submarine, perhaps the tragic events soon to be written of could have been avoided.

By August 26, the *Hunley* was undoubtedly under the full control of the Confederate Navy, with a volunteer crew at the propeller shaft and naval officer at the helm. From the following order we can see that although the submarine was now in government hands, some of the Singer group who had accompanied the submarine from Mobile were still present, continuing on in an advisory capacity: "August 26th, 1863, General: The bearer C.L. Sprague has come recommended as one ingenious in matters relating to submarine torpedoes and is directed to report to you to be attached to the submarine vessel of Whitney and company. He may be of service to the naval officer who has volunteered to take that vessel in hand, and it were well to place them in communication as also with Mr. Whitney."[73]

With the assigning of C.L. Sprague to the small submarine as its torpedo expert, it would appear that part owner, and under water explosives expert E.C. Singer had already left for meetings in Richmond. I have concluded that Sprague was probably the only non-military member of this newly formed and untested crew of Confederate sailors. As the reader may have noticed, Gus Whitney is still mentioned in the above order as having some authority or involvement with the *Hunley*; whether James McClintock and the rest of the crew had left Charleston by this date is unknown. This is the latest document I have been able to locate bearing Whitney's name. I found that shortly after the above order was issued, Gus Whitney, part owner and chief spokesman for the unusual invention, weakened, and died of pneumonia (possibly contracted as a result of his nocturnal activities aboard the damp submarine).[74] Thus the unfortunate Whitney might be considered the first casualty associated with this unique vessel, soon to be referred to as the "Peripatetic Coffin" in the numerous saloons along the Charleston waterfront.[75]

The fact that Mr. Whitney died of pneumonia only days after the submarine had been seized by the Charleston military is truly ironic, for an order found within the letter book of the Confederate Engineering Department (in Richmond, now on file in the National Archives) states that on August 22, 1863, Mr. B.A. Whitney and several other members of Singer's group of engineer's, were at that time under orders to be transferred to General Kerby Smith's Engineering Department in western Louisiana.[76]

The new volunteer skipper of the small submarine was Lieutenant John A. Payne, a distinguished veteran of the Confederate Navy assigned to the Charleston based ironclad *Chicora*.[77] A little more than a year before, Payne had served aboard one of the *Virginia's* support vessels during that Confederate ironclad's short, but distinguished, career at Hampton Roads. With the fall of Norfolk, and the scuttling of the history making ironclad, Payne was reassigned to the naval force operating in Charleston harbor. He had taken a keen interest in the *Hunley* ever since her arrival in the war-weary city, and eagerly volunteered to take command of the unique vessel once the navy had taken control of the craft.

From a 1914 article written for the magazine, *Confederate Veteran*, by Payne's fellow *Chicora* officer, Lieutenant C.L. Stanton, we learn that

This extremely rare action shot taken by Civil War photographer George Cook shows the destructive force of the cannon balls hurled into Fort Sumter by the Federal fleet. Copied from Miller's Photographic History of the Civil War.

This picture of an attack on Fort Moultrie is one of the only photos taken of Federal ironclads during combat. Photo by George Cook, copied from Miller's Photographic History of the Civil War.

Civil War engraving portraying the bombardment of Fort Sumter by ships from the South Atlantic Blockading Squadron. Harper's Weekly engraving.

Drawing showing the attack on Fort Sumter. Reproduced from the collections of the U.S. Library of Congress.

Appearance of Fort Sumter on Sunday afternoon, August 23, 1863.
Sketched from the "Beacon House" on Morris Island. Courtesy of the U.S. National Archives.

During the summer of 1863 the Union forces mounted a siege gun in the marsh between Morris Island and James Island to fire into Charleston. Note the soldiers playing cards in the lower left hand corner.
Photo courtesy of the U.S. National Archives.

Unfortunate Accident.—On Saturday last, while Lieutenants PAYNE and HASKER, of the Confederate Navy, were about experimenting with a boat in this harbor, she parted from her moorings and became suddenly submerged, carrying down with her five seamen, who were drowned. The boat and bodies had not been recovered up to a late hour on Sunday. Four of the men belonged to the gunboat *Chicora*, and were named FRANK DOYLE, JOHN KELLY, MICHAEL CANE and NICHOLAS DAVIS. The fifth man, whose name we did not learn, was attached to the *Palmetto State*.

The hatch closed on Charles Hasker's thigh, temporarily trapping him and seriously injuring him, as he escaped from the sub that drowned five of his comrades. The "Hunley" had been on the surface with her hatches open when she was swamped by a passing vessel. Adapted from a sketch by Greg Cottrell.

Payne was soon able to pilot the small submarine, and could be seen diving the novel invention under the numerous ships at anchor around the harbor shortly after taking command. A daring officer with little regard for caution, he wasted no time in preparing his raw crew of Confederate sailors for action against the ever growing enemy fleet.[78]

While James McClintock had practiced his men both day and night, evidence would suggest that Payne drilled his inexperienced crew only during daylight hours. Since the floating torpedo, or contact mine, towed by the small submarine could be seen in daylight, a night attack had always been seen as the only course of action. From the now well-quoted, post-war letter from James McClintock to Commodore Maury, we read the following passage regarding the casual way in which some viewed the *Hunley's* diving controls: "The boat and machinery was so very simple, that many persons at first inspection believed that they could work the boat without practice, or experience, and although I endeavored to prevent inexperienced persons from going underwater in the boat, I was not always successful in preventing them." McClintock is undoubtedly referring to the eager Payne and his crew of Confederate seamen.

Turning again to Stanton's 1914 article, we learn that he had volunteered for duty aboard the novel craft, but was instead assigned to watch duty aboard the ironclad *Chicora*. His replacement was Charles Hasker, an English immigrant who had served as a boatswain aboard the *Virginia* during her fierce duel with the *Monitor* at Hampton Roads. Recently promoted to lieutenant, Hasker was good friends with both Stanton and Payne, and shared their interest in the newly arrived submarine torpedo boat from Mobile.

It was shortly after Hasker joined Payne's newly formed crew of underwater raiders that disaster struck. After diving and surfacing the submarine several times around the harbor during the afternoon of the 29th, Payne ordered his crew to make for the docks at Fort Johnson to ready the vessel for an attack that would take place later that night. While the submarine was approaching the busy dock, or shortly after she had tied up, an accident occurred that caused the small craft to suddenly submerge with the hatches still open. In his own words we get a vivid description of what Hasker remembered of the event, and catch a glimpse of the terror felt by the trapped sailors as cold sea water spilled over the hatches causing the *Hunley* to rapidly plunge to the muddy bottom:

"I was anxious to see how the boat worked and volunteered as one of the crew. We were lying astern of the steamer *Etowah*, near Fort Johnson, in Charleston Harbor. Lieutenant Payne, who had charge got fowled (sic) in the manhole by the hawser and in trying to clear himself got his foot on the lever which controlled the fins. He had just previously given the order to go ahead. The boat made a dive while the manholes were open and filled rapidly. Payne got out of the forward hole and two others out of the aft hole. Six of us went down with the boat. I had to get over the bar which connected the fins and through the manhole. This I did by forcing myself through the column of water which was rapidly filling the boat. The manhole plate came down on my back; but I worked my way out until my left leg was caught by the plate, pressing the calf of my leg in two. Held in this manner, I was carried to the bottom in 42 feet of water. When the boat touched bottom I felt the pressure relax. Stooping down I took hold of the manhole plate, drew out my wounded limb, and swam to the surface. Five men were drowned on this occasion. I was the only man that went to the bottom with the 'Fish Boat' and came up to tell the tale." In reference to this event, McClintock later wrote. "Although she proved fatal to a number of persons, it was from no fault of the boat, or machinery, but want of sufficient knowledge of those in charge of the boat."[79]

Despite the fact that Hasker almost lost his life aboard the submarine, he appears never to have lost his interest in diving machines. From the 1918 book *The Submarine in War and Peace* written by Simon Lake (considered by many to be the father of the modern submarine), we find that shortly before his death in 1898 an aged Charles Hasker journeyed from his home in Richmond, Virginia, to meet with Lake. During his visit with the underwater inventor, Hasker is said to have related several stories about his adventures aboard the unlucky Hunley, as well as examine the "Argonaut submarine," recently completed by the New Jersey inventor. Lake stated in his book that he learned several tips from the ex-Confederate Naval officer, and considered him one of the few people of the day familiar with the problems associated with submarine boats.

Returning once again to that tragic day in late August 1863, we find the *Hunley* resting deep in the mud under 40 feet of water, with over half her crew now dead at the motionless propeller shaft.

THE HUNLEY

All who witnessed the terrible accident were stunned to see just how swiftly the small submarine had filled with sea water and vanished beneath the dark surface, silencing the muffled shouts of the helpless men still trapped inside.

When the gasping Hasker was spotted breaking the surface moments after the *Hunley* had disappeared it is reported that a young Midshipman named Daniel Lee threw off his tunic and dove in after the disabled lieutenant, who by his own description was "*more dead than alive.*" As Midshipman Lee pulled Hasker's near lifeless body towards the *Chicora* all waited anxiously for the faces of the other crew members to appear amidst the foam created by the sinking *Hunley*; but all that accompanied Lieutenant Hasker to the surface was black silt from the harbors cold muddy bottom. (as a small footnote to history it should be pointed out that Hasker's young rescuer, Midshipman Daniel M. Lee was from a somewhat illustrious southern family, for his uncle was none other than General Robert E. Lee, Commander in Chief of the Army of Northern Virginia.)[80]

From a letter sent to Beckie Honour from her husband stationed at Fort Johnson, comes a rare first-hand glimpse into the events leading up to that unfortunate day so long ago:

"Sunday morning August 30th 1863, My Dear Beckie: You doubtless remember, and perhaps you saw while in the city the iron torpedo boat which certain parties brought from Mobile to blow up the *Ironside*. They have been out three times without accomplishing anything, and the government suspecting something wrong, proposed to them to allow a naval officer to go with them on their next trial, which they refused. The boat was therefore seized and yesterday some men from one of the gun boats was placed in her to learn how to work her, and go out and see what they could do. Just as they were leaving the wharf at Fort Johnson, where I was myself a few minutes before, an accident happened which caused the boat to go under the water before they were prepared for such a thing, and five out of the nine went down in her and were drowned. The other four made their escape. They had not up to last night recovered either the boat or the bodies. Poor fellows they were five in one coffin."[81]

In his August 30 morning report, Fort Johnson's commander, Colonel Charles H. Olmstead, informs us that the accident which caused the small submarine to sink with five sailors happened as a result of the craft being entangled in some way with ropes and drawn on her side: "An unfortunate accident occurred at the wharf yesterday by which five seamen of the *Chicora* were drowned. The submarine torpedo became entangled in some way with ropes, was drawn on it's side and went down. The bodies have not yet been recovered."[82]

From the evidence presented, I feel that the above description may be in error, and am more inclined to believe the narration presented by Hasker who survived the fatal sinking and undoubtedly discussed the events leading up to the tragedy with his fellow survivors and friend Payne. If the submarine had been pulled over on her side, this fact would have been well-known to the men struggling to escape the submerging craft. An interesting passage from the previously cited Honour letter reads, "Just as they were leaving the wharf an accident happened which caused the boat to go under the water before they were prepared for such a thing." This account agrees with Hasker's description of the tragedy and is also compatible with McClintock's post-war statement, "Although she proved fatal to a number of persons, it was from no fault of the boat, or machinery, but want of sufficient knowledge of those in charge of the boat."

Regardless of exact circumstances which lead to the deaths of five seamen that day, the *Charleston Daily Courier* reported the unhappy story to the citizens of the city on the front page of the next morning's edition. "Unfortunate Accident - On Saturday last while Lieutenants Payne and Hasker, of the Confederate Navy, were about experimenting with a boat in the harbor, she parted from her moorings and became suddenly submerged, carrying down with her five seamen who were drowned. The boat and bodies had not been recovered up to a late hour on Sunday. Four of the men belonged to the gunboat *Chicora*, and were named Frank Doyle, John Kelly, Michael Cane and Nicholas Davis. The fifth man, whose name we did not learn, was attached to the *Palmetto State*."

From the book of pay receipts issued to the crew of the *C.S.S. Palmetto State* for the months of July and August, 1863, (found in the Eustace Williams Collection in the Mobile city library), we find the following entry penned next to the name of Absolum Williams: "Drowned in submarine battery on 29th August, 1863." With the name of this fifth unfortunate crew man at last having come to light, perhaps one day Williams' name can be inscribed

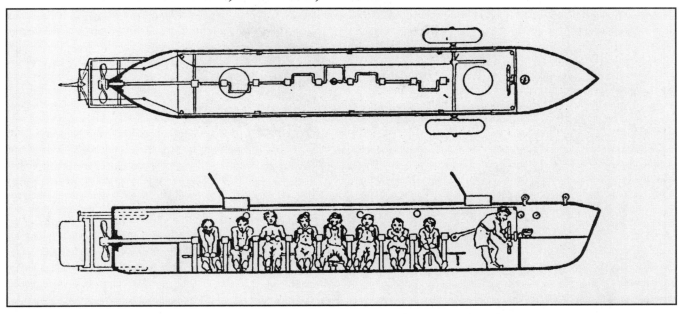

Diagram of the "Hunley" drawn by Charles Hasker during the summer of 1897 while visiting New Jersey submarine designer Simon Lake. McLure's Magazine, 1899.

Charles Hasker was pulled from the water by Daniel Lee following the "Hunley's" sinking near Fort Johnson. Navy Historical Center.

Daniel Lee (nephew of General Robert E. Lee) was a midshipman aboard C.S.S. "Chicora." From the collection of Dr. Charles Peery.

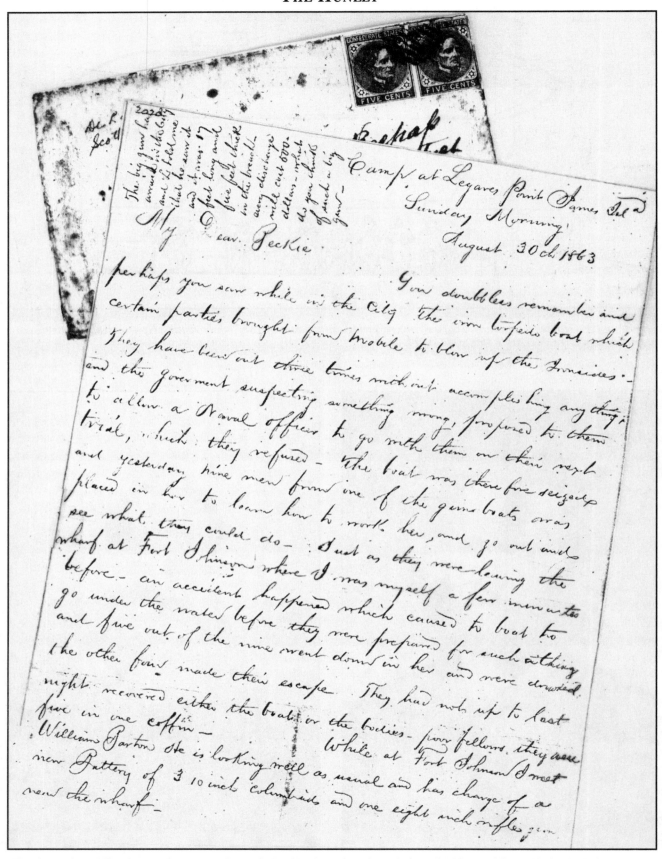

This letter from Theodore A. Honour to his wife Beckie describes the accidental sinking of the "Hunley" on the previous day. "Poor fellows, they were five in one coffin." Letter courtesy of the South Carolina Library.

next to those of his comrades on the *Hunley* monument at the foot of Meeting Street in Charleston.

From a newspaper article written some years later by an apparent crew member attached to one of the Charleston based ironclads comes the following lines:

"The *Palmetto State* was posted just west of Fort Johnson Wharf, and was made headquarters for the diving boat while awaiting a chance to slip out in the night and get amongst the Federal fleet. It (*Hunley*) was quickly manned by a crew of New Orleans longshoremen who had previously enlisted in the Confederate Navy at that place, and volunteered from on board the ironclads *Palmetto State* and *Chicora*, being part of their crew at that time.

Two of them I remember - Kelly, a New Orleans Irishman, a perfect and graceful physical athlete, and William Robinson (Apparently the other crewman who escaped through the rear hatch with torpedo expert Charles Sprague.), also from New Orleans, Australian by birth, and a giant in size and strength. In the frantic struggle for life Robinson's great strength took him out of the grasp of the terrible rush of water in the man hole. He followed the cause to the final shot. I saw him at Drewry's Bluff (The Confederate naval base on the James River, Virginia) three days before Richmond fell."[83]

From the above recollection it would appear that the *Palmetto State*, not the *Chicora*, was the *Hunley's* floating headquarters following her seizure by the Confederate Government. Although other sources seem to point to the *Chicora* as the submarine's support vessel, little can be said against the above narration, in light of the fact that it was obviously written by someone (the author of the article is unknown) who was apparently on board one of the ironclads, and had personally known some of the men involved.

At the South Carolina Historical Society, I happened on a collection of letters written during the war by Augustine (Gus) Smythe, a long time resident of Charleston and sailor, attached to the ironclad *C.S.S. Palmetto State*. His letters are filled with keen observations regarding life in a city under siege, and since I will be sharing several letters written by Smythe, I would like to introduce him to the reader with this note to his aunt.

"*C.S.S. Palmetto State*, August 30, 1863. Dear Auntie: We are always lying with steam up, and our anchor buoyed and ready to slip at a moments notice. We have had several alarms and are now quite practiced in getting up in a hurry. I and several of the officers sleep in hammocks swung on the gun deck. We never 'turn in' for a night without expecting and preparing to be called up at any moment.

We had quite a sad accident yesterday. A 'machine' we had here and which carried eight or ten men, by some mismanagement filled with water and sank, drowning five men, one belonging to our vessel, and the others to the *Chicora*. They were all volunteers for the expedition and fine men too, the best we had. It has cast quite a gloom over us. Strange, isn't it, that while we hear with indifference of men being killed all around us, the drowning of one should effect us so. Augustine."

With the loss of the *Hunley* and most of her crew, the exhilaration once felt in knowing that the South had a secret weapon that when unleashed would strike a death blow at the enemy's fleet was now dashed; there was no one to come to the city's rescue. If the submarine remained abandoned at the bottom of the harbor, little could be done but pray that the government in Richmond could negotiate a peace with the advancing Union forces. With no other offensive weapon at their disposal, General Beauregard and Flag Officer Tucker decided that the only course of action was to salvage the vessel, find another crew, and put the *Hunley* back into action.

Within 72 hours after the *Hunley* had disappeared off the end of the Fort Johnson wharf, the following telegram was dispatched to the commander of the first military District on the far side of Charleston Harbor. "General Ripley: Fish Torpedo still at bottom of bay, no one working on it. Adopt immediate measures to have it raised at once. Put proper person in charge of the work. Inform Lieutenant Payne of my orders. Sgn. General Beauregard."[84]

The monumental task of salvaging the submarine was given to civilian divers, Angus Smith and David Broadfoot.[85] These two Scottish immigrants held a virtual diving monopoly around Charleston harbor, and had been employed by the government several times before. The duo's specialty was performing the hazardous task of anchoring underwater contact mines by night at the mouth of the harbor, under the very noses of the enemy fleet. To be a deep sea diver in 1863 is in itself worthy of a book. Unfortunately most of the

No. 15.—

I
We, the Subscriber, do hereby acknowledge to have received of *Capt S Rich s Twelt*

being in full of our pay for the peri

Date.	No.	NAME.	OCCUPATION.	PERIOD OF SERVICE.			
				FROM	TO	MOS.	DAYS
Sept 8	1	C. L. Sprague	Torpedo Boatman	19 Aug	31 Aug.		12

water line when ballested to sink

water line light

Sketch drawn by crew member William Alexander.

74

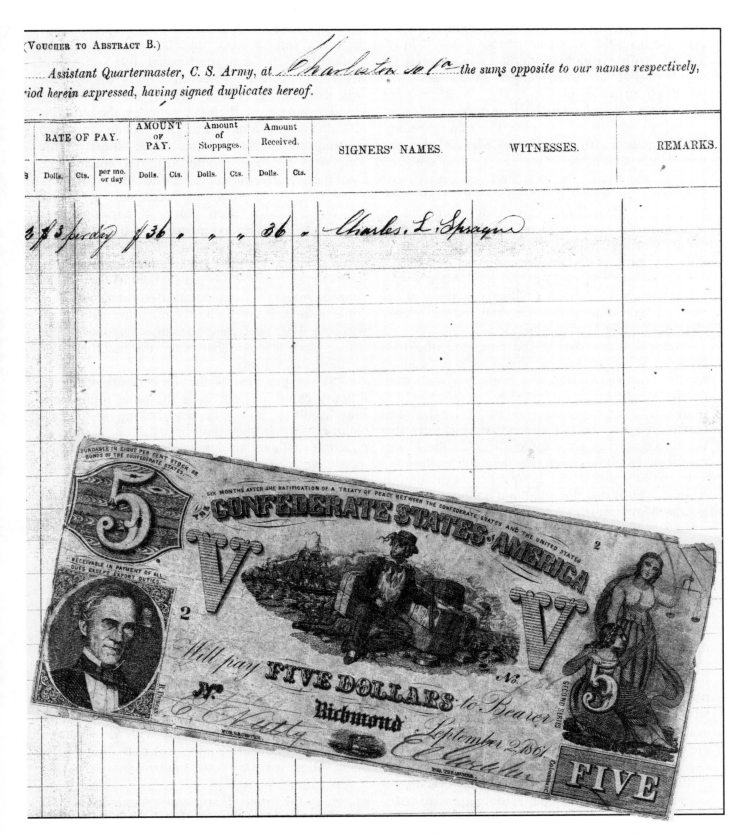

(VOUCHER TO ABSTRACT B.)

...... Assistant Quartermaster, C. S. Army, at *Charleston So Ca* the sums opposite to our names respectively, ...riod herein expressed, having signed duplicates hereof.

RATE OF PAY.			AMOUNT OF PAY.		Amount of Stoppages.		Amount Received.		SIGNERS' NAMES.	WITNESSES.	REMARKS.
Dolls.	Cts.	per mo. or day	Dolls.	Cts.	Dolls.	Cts.	Dolls.	Cts.			
3 per day			$36				36		*Charles L Sprague*		

Charles Sprague was assigned to the "Hunley" on August 19th by General Jordan; his duties were described as torpedo expert. The above pay voucher lists his occupation as torpedo boatman and his pay as $3.00 a day. The Five Dollar bill with its fanciful depiction of a sailor is from the Author's collection. Voucher courtesy of the National Archives.

adventures shared by these two nineteenth-century divers have long since been forgotten. Hard-hat-diving during the Victorian period was still in it's infancy with virtually nothing known about the deadly bends or other dangers associated with breathing air under pressure. They were probably considered the astronauts of their day.

With negotiations completed and an agreement for the salvage of the *Hunley* signed, the two underwater adventurers gathered up their crew, air pumps, and diving helmets and set course with Payne for the wharf at Fort Johnson. Soon after Smith and Broadfoot arrived at their site of operations, it became clear that they would be conducting their salvage efforts practically under the very guns of the enemy. Fort Sumter, only a couple of hundred yards away, was under a slow continuous bombardment; with the sounds of the muffled explosions within her shattered walls quite clear at the divers' work site.

Several times during the first day, the men working at the air pumps would look skyward to see the faint smoke trail of yet another shell from nearby Morris Island arch slowly overhead only to disappear into the city followed by a faint flash and muffled boom. The two divers working forty feet below the surface were quite aware of the events taking place above them. As they felt around the now partially buried hull of the dormant submarine, it became clear that this small but bulky craft would require heavy chains and several large ships to free it from its murky resting place.

The problems associated with raising the hulk, now slowly sinking into the soft bottom were enormous. One must be aware of the fact that for a submarine to be successful, it must have the capability to displace its own weight in water exactly. If too heavy it will sink to the bottom like a rock; if too light it won't be able to leave the surface. Since the *Hunley* nearly displaced her own weight in water with her hull filled with air, she now weighed almost as much as she did on land with her cabin now flooded. How could two deep sea divers, ankle deep in muck, feeling around in the blackness, ever hope to raise a craft that had required many men and horses to move on land?

During the early 1980's, I myself worked with a commercial diving company, logging many hours of bottom time in modern hard-hat equipment. The constant flow of air through the helmet has a tendency of drying out your eyes. The lead boots often cause you to sink up to your knees in the

bottom, and the view seen through the small port holes in the helmet is practically zero. Having done the same sort of work myself, I can inform the reader that the task performed by Smith and Broadfoot in their nineteenth century diving gear was astounding. These two divers must have literally burrowed their way under the *Hunley*, passing heavy chains beneath the keel and up to the waiting ships. As we shall see shortly, this dangerous business would turn out costing the Confederate government quite a lot of money.

Within weeks after this accidental sinking of the *Hunley* had taken place, a curious letter describing the incident appeared in the *New York Herald*. The letter in question had been written by a union soldier on Morris Island who had apparently received this rather distorted account of the *Hunley* from a group of Confederate deserters, who had come into their lines shortly after the submarine was lost. After describing the current situation then taking place around Charleston, the fanciful letter continued as follows.

"Seven privates of the First South Carolina infantry came into our lines the other night from Fort Moultrie, in a pine boat belonging to their Colonel, which they appropriated, it is fair to presume, without his knowledge or consent. The men were well dressed and unusually intelligent. The majority of them were foreigners. They gave a good deal of valuable information, of interest only to the General Commanding, which I shall not repeat; but I may, without detriment to the cause, relate the other bits of news which I obtained from them.

They state that a submarine apparatus in Charleston harbor, which was invented by an ingenious fellow from the north, who found himself in the enemy's lines at the beginning of the war, and since then unable to effect his escape, has gone to the bottom, greatly to the regret of the rebel authorities, who hoped by its means to blow up the ironsides, and drive all the fleet from the coast. They report that the inventor of the machine took the liberty of cruising around with it when he chose, and frequently, unbeknown to the rebels, made submarine trips down the harbor.

By some means or other suspicions were excited in the minds of some of the enemy, that all was not going right, and a watch was placed on the Yankee's movements. The deserters report that he was caught one night at work clearing away the obstructions in the harbor, in order to give our

Wartime view of Fraser's Wharf, showing one of the Confederate earthworks that defended Charleston. The building in the right background is the United States custom's house, which was still under construction at the outbreak of the War. Photo courtesy of the U.S. National Archives.

This painting by Civil War artist Conrad Wise Chapman, shows the Confederate ironclads "Chicora" and "Palmetto State," is viewed from the dock at Fort Johnson where the "Hunley" was swamped. The fort to the right of the city is Castle Pinckney. U.S. Naval Historical Center photograph of the original at the Museum of the Confederacy, Richmond, Virginia.

Voucher to diver Angus Smith for payment of $300.00 charged "For removing Five Corpses of men drowned in Torpedo Boat." Note from Brigadier General R.S. Ripley stating that the "Hunley" had been brought up to the city and placed in charge of Lieutenant Payne, C.S.N. Documents from the U.S. National Archives.

ironclads access to the city. He was immediately deprived of his command, arrested, with all his crew, and thrown into Charleston jail, to be tried as a traitor. What has been done with him my informants could not state.

His machine was placed in charge of an officer and five men, and an attempt was made to operate it, but with partial success. The last time it was tried the Lieutenant and his crew of five men got into it, adjusted the machinery and opened the valves through which flowed the water necessary to sink the machine to the proper depth. It gradually disappeared from view, and up to the latest accounts had not come up again.

So the machine, the Lieutenant and five men found a grave together in ten fathoms of water, and have probably passed from the sight of men forever, and Commodore Ingraham is busy investing some other apparatus to drive the navy from its anchorage and from his sight."[86]

Since a copy of the Nassau letter warning the Union Navy Department about the *Hunley* did not reach Admiral Dahlgren until some days after the above testimony had been given, it appears obvious as to why the Admiral never issued a warning to the fleet.

For over a week both Angus Smith and David Broadfoot had groped around the cold dark bottom of Charleston harbor in their heavy lead diving boots, attaching numerous ropes and chains to the hull of the dormant submarine. While the two divers wallowed in the mud seven fathoms beneath the surface of the besieged harbor, one of the most extraordinary events of the Civil war took place within view of the men at the air pumps.

During a lull in the bombardment of Fort Sumter on the afternoon of September 8, a Charleston photographer named George Cook was granted permission to enter the battered fortifications and take some pictures of the damage that had been inflicted. While he was taking some photographs of the parade grounds, the enemy ironclads: *Weehawken*, *Montauk*, and *Passaic* approached nearby Fort Moultrie and opened fire. Rushing to the top of the ramparts, Cook saw what a unique photograph the scene would make and quickly set up his large tripod on the wall, focused his camera on the action; and captured one of only two known Civil War photographs taken during a naval assault.

Moments after this unique image was taken, one of the enemy ironclads turned his turret around and commenced to shell Fort Sumter. All who had been standing on the wall watching the action with Cook swiftly dove for cover. In the confusion that followed, Cook accidentally dropped the exposed plate in a crevice as exploding shells fell all around the crouching men. Knowing how unique the image was that he had just captured, Cook shouted that he would give five dollars (about two weeks pay to a Confederate private) to any man who could retrieve the missing plate. As the guns on the smokey ironclad were being reloaded, a soldier sprang from his hiding place, ran to the spot where the plate had been dropped, snatched it up and returned it to Cook.[87] Thanks to the reward offered by Cook, and the daring of a Confederate soldier, we have been granted a glimpse into a unique moment of history. (See photo middle of page 65.)

Within two or three days after this picture was made from the ramparts of Fort Sumter, the two exhausted divers freed the *Hunley* from the black mud. The water-filled vessel was gently hoisted to the surface, where a pump removed the sea water, thereby causing the ill-fated craft to slowly regain buoyancy and once again float at the Fort Johnson wharf. With the submarine once again tied up at the dock, the grisly task of removing the bodies of the unfortunate seamen had to be performed as quickly as possible.

The scene that met that first man to reenter the resurrected Hunley must have been quite shocking - for the bodies of the unlucky crew had been on the bottom of the harbor for over ten days with the hatches open to any sea creature that wished to enter the unfortunate craft. From a soon to be quoted bill to the Confederate Navy Department, evidence would suggest that some difficulty may have been encountered while removing the corpses though the *Hunley's* narrow hatches, for the document in question clearly states that the bodies had swollen considerably due to having "been a long time under water."

At about the same time that the late crew of the *Hunley* were being removed from their iron coffin, General Maury appears to have sent a telegram to Charleston military headquarters inquiring about the current status of the submarine boat he had sent them from Mobile. In response to his inquiry, Beauregard sent the following message: "CHARLESTON, SEPTEMBER 12, 1863, THROUGH ACCIDENT HAVE NOT BEEN ABLE TO TRY FISH TORPEDO (STOP) CAN GIVE YET NO OPINION (STOP) OWNERS

WOULD NOT TRY IT THEMSELVES."[88]
Among the hundreds of Confederate documents at the National Archives related to military activities around Charleston Harbor, is a letter from General Ripley indicating that the Smith and Broadfoot group had not only raised the small submarine, but had also cleaned and towed the craft to a city dock across the harbor. "Headquarters first military district Charleston, Sept. 14, 1863 - General: I have the honor to inform you that the torpedo submarine boat was brought up to the city this afternoon and is in the vicinity of the RR wharf, in charge of Lt. Payne CSN."[89]

The above document confirms that Payne had retained command of the ill-fated submarine throughout the salvage operation at Fort Johnson. The question of whether or not he could find another volunteer crew still willing to squeeze through the narrow hatches and re-man the submarine, was anyone's guess. Sailors during the Victorian Age were notoriously superstitious, and the fact that this mysterious vessel had already killed one of her crews would have weighed heavily on the minds of these seamen. In the numerous saloons on the Charleston waterfront, the friends of the dead sailors would have undoubtedly cursed this "infernal machine" as an underwater death trap, lethal to all who entered. It is no wonder that they thought of her as a traveling coffin, she certainly lived up to her reputation in many ways.

From September 14, when the submarine was towed across the harbor and tied up at the railroad wharf, to September 19, I could find no requisitions, invoices, or orders, regarding the *Hunley's* status. She may have done little more than rock gently in her slip, becoming something of a curiosity to those who dared stroll down by the waterfront whenever the "Swamp Angel" fell silent.

By now, all of Morris Island was under the complete control of the ever nearing enemy army. On the night of September 6, 1863, with all hope of holding out against the federal onslaught forsaken, the weary garrison of defiant Battery Wagner drove iron spikes in the touch holes of their worn cannons and abandoned the battered position.[90] Now Fort Sumter would be within point blank range of the enemy guns. If only more time had been allowed McClintock and his experienced crew from Mobile, perhaps the blockade fleet would be in confusion from the recent loss of an ironclad; Battery Wagner would continue to hold on, and the *Chicora* would

still have a full crew. Since the *Hunley* was now under the complete control of the Confederate government, the title of Confederate States Ship (C.S.S.) would have been bestowed by the Confederate Navy. Whether or not Payne was actively seeking another volunteer crew to re-man the small craft during this chaotic period is unknown. As stated previously, he may have had some difficulty finding willing volunteers brave enough to reenter the dangerous contraption. He also may have had some reservations about continuing in command of a vessel that had already cost the Confederate Navy five able seamen.

It seems that the answer of what to do with the accident-prone submarine was delivered to General Beauregard's headquarters on the afternoon of September 19, 1863. In a letter penned by an enthusiastic Horace Hunley earlier that morning, an offer to take charge and re-man the unlucky diving machine was put forth by the patriotic sea captain. The letter read: "Charleston, September 19th, 1863. General G.T. Beauregard Sir: I am part owner of the torpedo boat the 'Hunley.' I have been interested in building this description of boat since the beginning of the war, and furnished the means entirely of building the predecessor of this boat, which was lost in an attempt to blow up a Federal vessel off Fort Morgan in Mobile Harbor. I feel therefore a deep interest in its success. I propose if you will place the boat in my hands to furnish a crew (in whole or in part) from Mobile who are well acquainted with its management and make the attempt to destroy a vessel of the enemy as early as practicable. Very respectfully your servant, H.L. Hunley."[91]

It appears that the determined Hunley, who had remained in Charleston after the submarine had been seized by the government, and was undoubtedly aware of its accidental sinking, may have taken an active role in the recovery of the vessel. In Hunley's letter to Beauregard, he seems to have no reservations about putting the submarine back in action as soon as possible, with another crew. The group of men he had in mind were probably made up from the crew who, until a few weeks ago, had been under the command of James McClintock and the late Gus Whitney. With Morris Island now in the hands of the enemy, and the Charleston Naval Department unsure as to what to do with the unlucky craft; an anxious Hunley was summoned to military headquarters and given charge of this very important, yet highly dangerous

Charleston Septr 19th 1863.

General JT Beauregard.

Sir.

I am a part owner of the torpedo boat the Hunley. I have been interested in building this description of boat since the beginning of the war, and furnished the means entirely of building the predecessor of this boat which was lost in an attempt to blow up a Federal vessel off fort Morgan Mobile Harbor. I feel therefore a deep interest in its success. I propose if you will place the boat in my hands to furnish a crew (in whole or in part) from Mobile who are well acquainted with its management, & make the attempt to destroy a vessel of the enemy as early as practicable

Very Respectfully,
Your Obt servt,
H. L. Hunley.

Captain Hunley's letter to General P.T. Beauregard requesting command of the "Hunley," saying he will furnish a crew familiar with its operation and will attempt to destroy an enemy vessel as quickly as possible. Hunley states that he is a part owner of the vessel and describes his past involvement and interest in earlier submarine experiments.
Letter courtesy of the U.S. National Archives.

diving machine.

Three days after headquarters received Hunley's offer, General Jordan, Beauregard's Chief of Staff, issued the following order to Major Trezevant, commanding the city's arsenal: "Charleston, Sept. 22nd, 1863. Major: The submarine Torpedo Boat has been placed in charge of Capt. H.L. Hunley, with a view to prompt repairs all dispatches essential and vital, I am instructed to request you to have all work done for Capt. Hunley that he may require with the utmost celerity and to supply such material as he will requisition as the mechanics under his control can apply. His requisitions will be approved at these Head Quarters."[92]

To insure that all haste would be made in putting the submarine back into service as quickly as possible, the following communication was sent to Brigadier-General R.S. Ripley later that afternoon: "General: Captain H.L. Hunley having applied on behalf of himself and other owners to be allowed to assume the working of the submarine torpedo boat, you will please direct said boat to be cleaned and turned over to him with the understanding that said boat shall be ready for service in two weeks. The repairs to be made at the expense of the Confederate States."[93]

On the same day that the above orders were sent from military headquarters, a somewhat dismal requisition was at that time being issued to the Confederate Navy Paymaster Henry Myers. From that document we read the following.

"Confederate Navy Department. Charleston, September 22, 1863. (pay) To: Joseph Poulnot $135.00 for: 5 Coffins at $15.00 (each) $75.00, Transportation to Mariners Graveyard $20.00, Interment of 5 seaman from the torpedo boat $6 (each) $30.00, Drayage of coffins to R.R. Wharf $10.00. I certify that the above is correct, the amount is large but the body(ies) had been a long time under water and required larger coffins. John A. Payne, Lieut. C.S. Navy."[94]

While the five seamen who had drowned in the submarine boat were being laid to rest in the Mariners Graveyard, Horace Hunley was that very day arranging facilities for repairing and cleaning his ill-fated namesake.

Although Hunley had been granted control of the submarine, he was not necessarily granted command of the vessel. It's doubtful that General Beauregard and flag officer Tucker would have returned the torpedo boat to civilian command with the ineffective actions of James McClintock so well remembered. If the Hunley were to return to action, it was probably stipulated that the man at the helm should be a military officer, obligated to take orders from the Confederate commanders assigned to the defense of Charleston. As Captain Hunley stated in his letter to General Beauregard, "If you place the boat in my hands I will supply a crew (in part or in whole)." He never said he would command the vessel. Instead, it seems more likely that he was to fill the role of logistics officer in charge of maintenance, repairs, and supplies.

Whether or not Captain Hunley had ever taken command of the vessel in the past has not yet been determined. It seems logical that he would have had some experience in the craft, but whether or not he had actually been at the forward diving planes is not known. During the submarine's trial in the Mobile river, he had been in central Mississippi on military business. He arrived in Charleston soon after McClintock and Whitney had already launched the craft, so if he had indeed gained any experience at the helm, it would have been during the short period that the vessel was under McClintock's command. Since McClintock would have been denied a second command owing to past inaction, the only other non-civilian besides the inexperienced Payne to have had charge of the vessel was George E. Dixon, the army engineer on detached duty at the Park & Lyons shop in Mobile. As stated previously, Dixon had taken a keen interest in the submarine from its conception, and may have contributed to its design and construction.

According to the post-war writings of General Beauregard, it was generally understood by him that Dixon had commanded the submarine during her trials in the Mobile River. Writing from memory over a decade after the War had ended, we are informed that, "After the recovery of the sunken boat Mr. Hunley came from Mobile, bringing with him Lieutenant Dixon, of the 21st Alabama Volunteers, who had successfully experimented with the boat in the Harbor of Mobile, and under him another crew volunteered to work it."[95]

Whether or not Captain Hunley returned to Mobile to secure the experienced crew he had promised is unknown. He probably communicated with the far off city by telegraph - his messages given top priority due to the urgency of the situation. From a requisition for cleaning supplies dated September 28, and signed for by Hunley, it

1863

Charleston, September 22d 1863.

Confederate Navy Department,

For

To Joseph Poulnot   Dr.

To 5 Coffins @ 15.   √ 75 00
" Transportation to Mariners Graveyard   √ 20 00
" Interment of 5 seamen from Torpedo
  Boat @ 6   √ 30 00
" Drayage of Coffins to R.R. Wharf   √ 10 00 $135 00

I certify that the above is correct
the amount is large but the
body has been a long time
under water and require larger
coffins

                                    John W Payne
                                    Lieut C.S.Navy

Approved for _One Hundred thirty five_ Dollars, ——— Cents
ordered to be paid by Paymaster _Henry Myers_ ——— Confederate Navy.

                    DN Ingraham   Commanding Naval Station.

Received, _Sept 26_ 186 3 from _Henry Myers_ Paymaster
Confederate Navy, the sum of _One Hundred thirty five_ ———
——— Dollars, ——— Cents, in full of the above bill.

                                    Joseph Poulnot

Navy Department document regarding the burial of the "Hunley" crew that drowned at Ft. Johnson. National Archives.

Requisition for rope to be used in the raising of the "Hunley." Note: Rather than specifying length, the amount of rope is stated in pounds. Courtesy of the U.S. National Archives.

Requisition for six scrub brushes, giving the special circumstances as "The submarine boat was sunk in preparing to blow up a federal vessel & suffocated five men whose bodies remained within for several weeks. Said boat had been seized by Military authorities." Document courtesy of the U.S. National Archives.

appears that he remained in Charleston to oversee the repairs and cleaning of the vessel; sending instructions to his colleagues in Mobile by telegraph.

While Hunley waited in Charleston for the arrival of his fellow adventurers, he appears to have taken an active role in cleaning the small submarine. From the requisition referred to above, we read: "Charleston, September 28th, 1863: Special requisition for: Half box of soap (For cleaning the submarine boat the 'Hunley') and 6 brushes for scrubbing. Circumstances: The submarine boat was sunk in preparing to blow up a Federal vessel and suffocated five men whose bodies remained within for several weeks. Said boat had been seized by military authorities. H.L. Hunley."[96]   Noting that Hunley's crew had not yet arrived from Mobile, it's a good bet that the brushes to be used for scrubbing the hulls interior were issued to six slaves, appropriated from the many who had been seized from the numerous plantations around the city. On January 1, 1863, the Emancipation Proclamation had gone into effect, freeing all slaves residing in the "rebellious" states. Under United States law these men were now free; However South Carolina was not the United States, and two more years of fierce war would continue before this proclamation was realized. (It is interesting to note that slaves in the areas, such as Maryland, not "under rebellion" were not freed by Lincoln's proclamation, and had to wait until the Constitution was amended.)[97]

While an anxious Captain Hunley monitored the repairs to his namesake craft, the new crew that was to re-man the resurrected submarine was being selected from the men who had built and tested her in far away Mobile. Some of these men could have very well been part of the McClintock crew that had recently returned from Charleston, thereby knowing the perils that awaited them outside that besieged harbor. (Since the names of the first crew have not come to light, I can only speculate as to the possibility of this theory.) Fortunately we do have the names of this second Mobile crew from an article William Alexander wrote for Munsey magazine in 1903. Written forty years after the events described took place, an aged Alexander informs us as to the activities in the Park & Lyons shop in late September of 1863:

"General Beauregard then turned the craft over to a volunteer crew from Mobile known as the 'Hunley and Parks crew.' Captain Hunley and

Thomas Parks, a member of the firm in whose shop the boat had been built, were in charge, with Brockband, Patterson, McHugh, Marshall, White. Beard and another (Dixon) as the crew. Until the day this crew left Mobile, it was understood that I was to be one of them, but at the last moment Mr. Parks prevailed on me to let him take my place. Nearly all of the men had some experience in the boat before leaving Mobile, and were well qualified to operate her." Within a month Alexander would realize just how lucky he was not to have been part of this second crew of ill-fated adventurers.

While going through George Dixon's Confederate war record at the National Archives, I came upon an interesting entry dated October 1, 1863. It reads as follows: "1st. Lt. George E. Dixon, Co. 'A' 21st Regiment Alabama Infantry detached October 1st, 1863 (30 days) by order of General Maury." The optimistic Maury appears to have assumed that a month would be all that was needed for Dixon to accomplish his mission in Charleston. Since Dixon was an engineering officer, it may have been decided that his skills were too valuable to the defense of Mobile to be lent out for more than the brief period cited above.

Unfortunately very little is known regarding the background of George Dixon prior to his enlistment in the 21st Alabama Regiment. However judging from the surviving examples of his handwriting and few remaining letters, it would appear that Dixon had received a through Victorian education, for his writings reflect an individual who possessed an excellent command of the English language. From information gathered from several *Hunley* articles that have appeared in Alabama newspapers over the past century, come the following few tidbits regarding Dixon's background.

From 1861 enlistment records kept by Dixon's company commander comes the fact that Dixon was a 22 year old native of Campbell County, Kentucky prior to his enlistment in the "Mobile Grays" (later mustered into the 21st Alabama), stood nearly six feet tall, with blue eyes and fair hair.[98] Unfortunately the 1860 census of Mobile, Alabama fails to list George Dixon as a resident of the city, so it may never be known just what his educational and family background was, or even when he arrived in southern Alabama.

From a 1904 news article titled *Dixon builder of the submarine Hunley* comes the fact that Dixon was engaged to a young Mobile belle before his enlistment in the "Mobile Grays" and had been employed as a steam engineer aboard a Mobile River boat prior to the south's succession. [99] This one fact alone could account for Dixon not being mentioned on the 1860 Mobile census, for he may have lived on the river boat on which he was employed and was thereby over looked by city census takers.

The frustrations felt by early Hunley researchers trying to uncover Dixon's background can be seen in a few passages taken from an 1895 *Mobile Register* news article titled *The Submarine Boat Which is Believed to have been the first of its Kind*. From within the text of that article the following lines can be found. "In an effort to find out something concerning Lieutenant George E. Dixon a Register representative was referred to Major Palmer J. Pillans, now visiting his son. Major Pillans said that he remembered Lieutenant Dixon, who was a member of the Mobile Grays, organized by him. Major Pillans said he was doubtful as to whether or not Lieutenant Dixon was originator of the boat." The article then went on to state the following.

"The ladies of Mobile presented his company with a handsome flag, and the presentation took place at the residence of Major Pillans on Government street. Major Pillans received the flag and turned it over to young Dixon, whom he had chosen as color bearer. The "Mobile Grays" afterward became a part of the Twenty-first Alabama Regiment, and the flag became the regimental flag. Major Pillans said that Lieutenant Dixon was six feet tall and a splendid specimen of physical manhood."

From the above description it would appear that Dixon's dedication to duty was recognized early in his military career for its well known that the honor of being regimental color bearer was bestowed on only the bravest members.

Sometime during the first week of October, this second crew from Mobile arrived at the Charleston rail station and immediately set about reacquainting themselves with this vessel that had already cost the lives of five of their fellow countrymen. From the sparse information that exists relating to this first week of renewed operations, it appears that Dixon was in command of the submarine with Thomas Park (son of Mr. Park of Park & Lyons)[100] as his first officer manning the aft ballast pumps and sea valves.

The only member of the previous crew to have survived the sinking at the Fort Johnson dock, and return to duty aboard the *Hunley* was Charles Sprague.[101] As the reader will recall, Sprague had been assigned to the submarine as a torpedo expert after the Navy had taken charge of the vessel in late August. He was one of the two men who made their escape through the rear hatch while Payne and Hasker struggled to exit the doomed submarine by way of the forward opening. As an underwater explosives expert, Sprague would have been invaluable in repairing and maintaining the contact mine that would be used in the next nocturnal attempt against the enemy fleet. Although no documents have come to light indicating just where Sprague gained his experience with underwater explosives, it's a good bet that his education in the subject derived from experience gained in building and maintaining some of the numerous contact mines anchored at the entrance to Charleston Harbor.

With the *Hunley* once again in the hands of a crew well practiced in the operations of the unique invention, she was soon again seen diving about the harbor by the soldiers and sailors who had only a few weeks before cursed her and jeeringly christened her the "Peripatetic Coffin." To the spectators who watched the *Hunley* disappear and reappear amidst the numerous ships at anchor in the port, the following routine would have been witnessed before each excursion.

After the crew had entered the submarine and taken their places at the crankshaft, the fore and aft hatches were closed and bolted shut by the skipper and first officer. While the motionless vessel floated on the surface, the skipper would order the first officer at the rear of the craft to open his sea valve and allow water to enter the ballast tank. As sea water flowed into this rear tank, the skipper would open his own valve as he watched the iron hull slowly settle below the surface through glass view ports located in the conning tower. Once the small vessel's black hull was seen to be about three inches below the water, the fore and aft sea valves would be ordered closed. At this point, only the upper half of the two conning towers would remain visible, with their view ports appearing just above the water line.

Before the skipper would order the crew to turn the crankshaft, and thereby get underway, he would first light the candle located on a shelf attached to the forward ballast tank bulkhead. With the candle lit and the craft trimmed to near neutral buoyancy, the skipper would order the crew to begin cranking.

The Confederate States of America,

To *George E. Dixon* Dr.

ON WHAT ACCOUNT.	Commencement and Expiration.		Term of Service Charged.		Pay per Month.		Amount.		REMARKS.
	From—	To—	Months.	Days.	Dollars.	Cts.	Dollars.	Cts.	
Pay—	31st of May	31st of Aug	3	"	90.	00	270	00	
For myself.................									
For years service.........									
Forage for horses.........									
							$		

I HEREBY CERTIFY that the foregoing account is accurate and just; that I have not been absent without leave during any part of the time charged for; that I have not received pay, forage, or received money in lieu of any part thereof, for any part of the time therein charged; that the horses were actually kept in service and were mustered for the whole of the time charged; that for the whole of the time charged for my staff appointment, I actually and legally held the appointment, and did duty in the department; that I have been a commissioned officer for the number of years stated in the charge for every additional five years service; that I am not in arrears with the Confederate States, on any account whatsoever; and that the last payment I received was from *Capt A McIvoy* and to the *Thirty First* day of *May* 186 *3*.

I, at the same time, acknowledge that I have received of........ *Capt A McIvoy*

this *16* day of *Sept* 186 *3* the sum of *Two Hundred and Seventy* dollars, being the amount, in full, of said account.

Pay................$

Forage..............

Amount..$

[Signed Duplicates.]

George E. Dixon
1st Lieut Co A 21st Ala

Pay voucher for Lieutenant George E. Dixon, who commanded the "Hunley" on her final voyage. Courtesy of the U.S. National Archives.

Sinking torpedoes in Charleston Harbor by moonlight. Engraving from Harper's Weekly, June 13, 1863, courtesy of U.S. Naval Historical Center

Through the forward view port remaining about an inch above the water line, our man at the forward station would be able to sight in on a target; take note of the compass heading; depress the forward diving planes; and quickly disappear beneath the waves.

The *Hunley's* speed, while submerged, may have been significantly faster than the four knots she could obtain topside. In my own submarine I have found my speed when submerged to be almost twice as fast as when floating on the surface - even though the motor settings have not been changed. When running submerged a vessel is able to pass through the water much easier than on the surface due to the significant decrease in drag. For this reason, I feel that the *Hunley* in the hands of a capable pilot would have been quite a sight to see, quickly rising and descending along a straight line much like a dolphin momentarily breaking the surface for a quick look around. (As the reader will recall from the wartime diary of Emma Holmes, one of the nicknames given the submarine was "The Porpoise.") I have little doubt that our newly arrived Mobile crew under the command of Alabama Infantry officer George Dixon, was soon re-establishing General Beauregard's faith in this ingenious underwater weapon.

While newly-mounted batteries on Morris Island continued their slow bombardment of Charleston, the crew of the *Hunley* kept up their unique training by staging mock attacks against the *C.S.S. Indian Chief* anchored in the Cooper River.[102] Towing a small barrel or container of some kind, Dixon and his eager crew sharpened their attack skills by submerging beneath the *Indian Chief* and drawing their dummy mine against her hull several times a day. By now, the submarine was becoming a common sight to the sailors and soldiers who manned the gun boats and shore batteries scattered around the harbor. With renewed confidence in the destructive capabilities of the submarine growing daily, all who witnessed the trials of the strange contraption were sure that she would soon strike a death blow to one or more of the unwelcome enemy ships lying at anchor outside the harbor.

On October 10, just five days before the renewed confidence in the submarine would be irreversibly shattered Captain Hunley filed his last requisition with the Charleston quartermaster. To replace the tow rope that had been dragged so many times beneath the barnacle encrusted hull of the

C.S.S. Indian Chief; a replacement was ordered: "One hundred fifty feet of rope 3/8 inch diameter." Along with a fresh rope to tow the *Hunley's* explosive device to her target, was also requisitioned a new compass, apparently a superior model to the one that was currently attached to the forward bulkhead.[103] With the new rope and compass now in the possession of the *Hunley's* well practiced crew, it would appear that Dixon was planning a nocturnal visit to the heart of the enemy's fleet within a matter of days. Little could he have known that within a week he would be the only surviving crew member left to tell the tale of this unlucky Confederate diving machine. On the dreary overcast morning of October 15, 1863, the confident crew of the *Hunley* squeezed through the submarine's narrow hatches for the last time. At the rear of the vessel standing at his station was Thomas Park, who was now well acquainted with his duties at the ballast tank pumps and sea cocks. Standing in the forward hatch was Hunley, perhaps not an unfamiliar site at this post; after all he was part owner of the invention, and had taken part in the building of two other such vessels. The number of times Hunley actually commanded this crew has not come to light; however, it is unlikely that it was his first time at this position.

Just why Hunley was at the helm of his name sake that morning instead of Dixon may remain one of the many mysteries now associated with this unique invention. Perhaps he was going to test the new compass recently requisitioned through the Confederate quartermasters department. For whatever reason Hunley took the helm that day, only one thing is known for sure - when the heavy iron hatch covers were closed and bolted shut that morning, not one man aboard the ill-fated vessel would live to see them swing open again.

The exact events that transpired within the unlucky submarine's cramped hull after her hatches had been sealed will forever remain the subject of speculation. From the accounts given by the numerous witnesses standing on the Cooper River docks and aboard the *C.S.S. Indian Chief*, nothing was observed that morning that had not been seen many times before. All who saw the tragic event stated that the small submarine was seen preparing to make a typical dive under the *Indian Chief*. She approached the vessel in the normal fashion, depressed her diving planes a couple of hundred feet off the starboard side of the ship; disappeared beneath the surface; and was not seen again. The

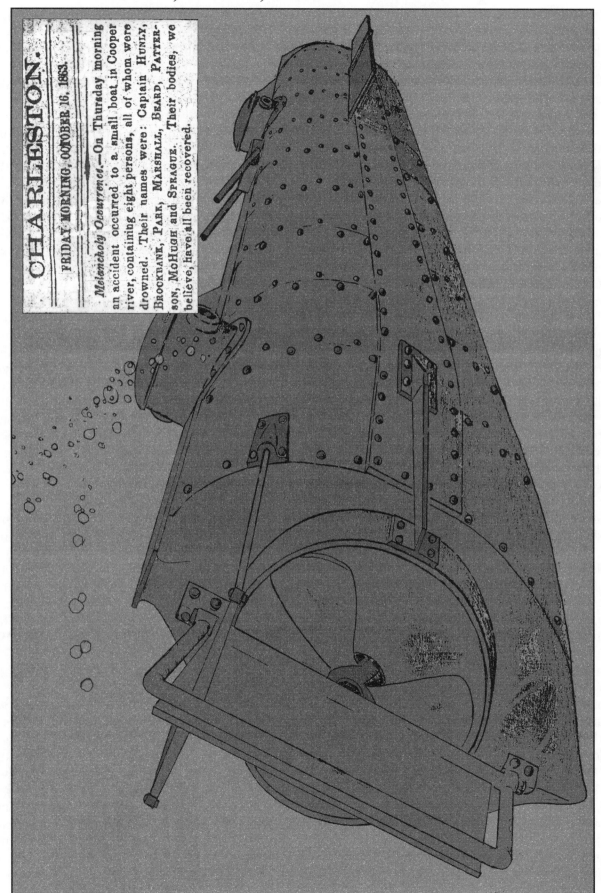

CHARLESTON.

FRIDAY MORNING, OCTOBER 16, 1863.

Melancholy Occurrence.—On Thursday morning an accident occurred to a small boat in Cooper river, containing eight persons, all of whom were drowned. Their names were: Captain HUNLY, BROCKBANK, PARK, MARSHALL, BEARD, PATTERSON, MCHUGH and SPRAGUE. Their bodies, we believe, have all been recovered.

Too deep and too fast, describes the "Hunley's" fatal dive of October 15, 1863. Sketch by Greg Cottrell.

sailors on the deck of the *Indian Chief* waited for the *Hunley* to re-appear on the port side as they had done many times before. After frantically scanning the surface for what must have seemed like hours, the harsh reality of the event was soon realized by everyone. The *Hunley* with her full crew was lost; for a second time the ill-fated submarine had taken her occupants on a fatal dive, and on this one, none would survive.

From an extract taken from the Journal of Operations kept at Confederate Headquarters in Charleston, we read the following entry dated October 15, 1863: "Raining again this morning, and too hazy to get report on the fleet. An unfortunate accident occurred this morning with the submarine boat, by which Captain H.L. Hunley and seven men lost their lives in an attempt to run under the navy receiving ship. The boat left the wharf at 9:25 a.m. and disappeared at 9:35. As soon as she sunk air bubbles were seen to rise to the surface of the water, and from this fact it is supposed the hole in the top of the boat by which the men entered was not properly closed. It was impossible at the time to make any effort to rescue the unfortunate men, as the water was some nine fathoms deep."[104] Of the event General Beauregard would latter write. "Lieutenant Dixon made repeated descents in the harbor of Charleston, diving under the navy receiving ship which lay at anchor there. But one day when he was absent from the city, Mr. Hunley, unfortunately, wishing to handle the boat himself, made the attempt. It was readily submerged, but did not rise again to the surface, and all on board perished from asphyxiation."[105]

Even though the submarine had now cost the lives of two crews, a search and salvage operation to locate and raise the missing *Hunley* was put into motion the following day. Since the underwater vessel had obviously proven herself a formidable weapon in the capable hands of Dixon, no time was lost in recruiting the services of Smith and Broadfoot to once again don their diving gear and return to the black, muddy bottom of Charleston Harbor in search of the submarine and her crew of dead men.[106]

On the same day that our two divers started to explore the cold bottom around the keel of the *C.S.S. Indian Chief*, the following orders were issued by General Ripley: "October 16th, 1863. Major: Give transportation to Lieut. Dixon 21st Regiment Alabama Volunteers, and Henry Dillingham to Mobile and return, on business

connected with the submarine torpedo boat."[107]

From the above order, it could be assumed that the determined Dixon had not yet given up on the unlucky *Hunley*; even though the cause of the accident was a mystery to him; and the location of the submarine was still unknown. It seems that this only surviving crew member was returning to Mobile to extend his detached duty in Charleston and, as we shall see shortly, draft the services of his friend and fellow engineering officer William Alexander.

In the course of my research, I have found the name Henry Dillingham to appear only one time in connection with the *Hunley*. The above order shows that he was obviously associated with the submarine, but as to what his duties were I am at a loss. On researching the identity of this individual, I was stunned to find him to be a full fledged Confederate Secret Service Agent whose duties were to destroy federal property behind their lines. Whatever connection Dillingham had with Dixon and the crew of the *Hunley* remains a mystery to me, Perhaps some future researcher will be able to answer this intriguing question. A very interesting fact came to light during my investigation of the mysterious Dillingham. It would appear that he was so competent in his duties at destroying enemy property behind their lines, that even after the war had ended, federal authorities were still actively pursuing this Confederate saboteur.[108]

Although Singer's group of engineers were primarily engaged in the manufacture and deployment of underwater contact mines, some evidence does in fact exist confirming the fact that at least some members of the group were engaged in the type of sabotage attributed to Henry Dillingham. Proof of this activity can be found in an 1864 letter sent by *Hunley* investor R.W. Dunn to General Magruder (Military commander of the District of Texas). From that communication we read the following excerpt.

"In a few days I will lay before you our propositions for forcing the Enemy's Fleets, lying off our Bars and Harbors to take some of our medicine. In Tennessee we have blown up eight railroad trains. Successes show conclusively the certainty of explosion of our torpedoes."

From the above evidence it would appear that at least some of Singer's group were engaged in railroad sabotage, and it could be assumed that perhaps Dillingham himself may have been involved in the destruction of some, if not all, of the

Vanderhorst's Wharf in Charleston, served for both incoming and outbound vessels of all rigs and sizes. This vessel was probably used as a coastal trader rather than a blockade runner. Castle Pinckney can be seen through the rigging. Photo courtesy of Massachusetts Commandery Military Order of the Loyal Legion and the U.S. Army Military History Institute.

This 1844 woodcut shows the type of diving gear in common use during the 19th century.
From "La Nauigation Sous-Marine," 1906.

.WE HAVE RECEIVED from Captain CHISOLM, his check for $250, for the benefit of the families of the five men who lost their lives in the submarine boat with Captain HUNLEY.

Artist's conception of Angus Smith and David Broadfoot salvaging the "Hunley" after she plowed into the mud and drowned her crew in Charleston Harbor. Among the dead was her captain and namesake, Horace L. Hunley.
Illustration adapted from a sketch by Greg Cottrell.

8 Union trains mentioned in Mr. Dunn's letter.[109]

While Dixon and Dillingham slowly made their way to Mobile, the underwater search conducted by divers Smith & Broadfoot continued beneath the keel of the *C.S.S. Indian Chief.* On October 17, 1863, the following request was made of Flag Officer Tucker: "Captain Angus Smith engaged in raising the submarine torpedo boat which was unfortunately sunk a few days ago, requires the assistance of several boats and crews to endeavor to raise the vessel. I therefor request that you will give him the necessary aid in this matter, and also that the receiving ship under which the torpedo boat is thought to lie, may be moved from it's present position, so as not to interfere with the operations of dragging for the boat."[110]

With the request obeyed and the *Indian Chief* moved away from the search area, the following entry can be seen the next day in the journal of operations: "Oct. 18th Mr. Smith provided with submarine armor, found the sunken submarine boat today in nine fathoms of water. The engineering department was instructed to furnish Mr. Smith all facilities in the way of ropes, chains, etc., that an attempt might be made to recover the boat."[111]

It would appear that the Charleston Engineering Department had some reservations regarding the lending of equipment to divers Smith and Broadfoot, for within 48 hours after the resting place of the little submarine had been discovered, the following letter was being sent to General Jordan, Beauregard's Chief of Staff.

"Office Chief Engineer. Charleston, October 20, 1863. Brig-General Jordan, Chief of Staff, Sir: In reply to your communication of this date I have the honor to state that there is no indisposition on the part of the Engineering Department to afford Captain Smith all the assistance in its power in raising the submarine boat. I am desirous however that the material to be used for this purpose should be properly cared for, and with this view I proposed to send an employee of the Department with Captain Smith, who would not be in his way, to look after it. Captain Smith refused to take the material under this arrangement, and left the office saying he could do without it. I have the honor to refer you to the enclosed report from Lt. Young. Yours very respectfully, Colonel D.B. Harris."[112]

In response to this letter (and report from Lt. Young outlining how divers Smith and Broadfoot had lost a government owned chain and anchor at Fort Johnson through carelessness), General Jordan

sent the following response. "Colonel: The Commanding General wishes the instructions contained in a letter from Head Quarters of Yesterday detailing you to turn over to Capt. Smith certain tools, ropes chains etc., complied with without delay."[113] From the forceful way the above communication was worded, there can be little doubt as to whether Smith and Broadfoot received the specified equipment that very day.

From a soon to be cited letter received by Captain Hunley's sister shortly after the accident, we find that within hours after Angus Smith had located the hull of the derelict submarine, a severe weather front moved in, postponing salvage of the unlucky vessel for several days. During this period of inactivity (from October 19 through about the 25th), I found filed with several requisitions for supplies needed to raise the *Hunley*, a letter sent to military headquarters from Smith and Broadfoot. On the very day the ill-fated *Hunley's* resting place had been discovered, our two divers notified headquarters that they were now ready to discuss the amount of salvage they would receive for raising the submarine after her first accident. With the two men holding a virtual underwater monopoly in Charleston harbor, they must have realized that this would be the best time to talk money. The letter reads "Charleston, October 18th, 1863. Sir: We are now prepared to name a referee on our part to confer with a referee on the part of the government, that they may determine the value of the submarine boat, and the amount of salvage to be awarded to us for raising the said submarine boat from the place where she sunk off Fort Johnson wharf, and delivering her at a wharf in Charleston. We would respectfully propose Chief Engineer Freeman of the Navy department as referee on our part.. We are respectfully your obedient Servants Smith and Broadfoot - Divers."[114]

With the weather clearing, and salvage negotiations underway, Smith and Broadfoot once again donned their heavy copper diving helmets and plunged to the cold muddy bottom of the Cooper River. Much to our two divers' surprise, the unlucky submarine was not found resting on the river bed as had been the case at Fort Johnson; instead she was discovered with her bow buried deep in the mud with her hull protruding at about a 30° angle. It looked to the two divers as though the *Hunley* had literally plowed nose first into the black mud nine fathoms beneath the hull of the *C.S.S. Indian Chief.*[115] Upon further investigation it was found that the hatches remained bolted shut from the inside, with the emergency drop weights still attached to the bottom of the keel. At no point was a hole found in the vessel, so it appeared that the cabin had not flooded, and therefore was still filled with air. If this was the case, why hadn't the trapped and suffocating crew men turned the bolts that would have released the emergency drop weights? It was obvious that the mystery to this tragic sinking would not be solved until the small submarine was once again hoisted to the surface and her narrow hatches forced open.

At about the same time that Smith and Broadfoot were pondering the mystery as to why the little *Hunley* had plunged to the bottom of the harbor, military head quarters were sending a blistering message to the editors of the *Augusta Constitutionalist*, severely reprimanding them for printing a letter they had received from their Charleston correspondent known as "W."[116]

As we shall see the letter in question had reported many details regarding the testing of the *Hunley*, as well as important facts concerning Charleston's harbor defenses. In the communication sent from Charleston Head Quarters, it was stated that the informative article might be read by the enemy and thereby cause a severe breach of security. Towards the end of this letter, the identity of their correspondent "W" was requested, as well as a warning not to print such sensitive information again. From the Augusta news article that so infuriated Charleston Head Quarters we read the following excerpt.

"Torpedo or submarine boats are so far as beneficial results, mere experiments. They have been tried, and found not to accomplish the end proposed. The crews are generally unacquainted with the working of the boats. On experimenting it has happened on one or two occasions that the lives of the men have been lost. These crafts have been more injurious to our people than to the enemy, and thus far have proved to be a humbug."[117]

Although the Confederacy, like the United States, had a free press, it would seem that military leaders in the blockaded city had decided that it was best not to allow the news papers within their jurisdiction to print stories about Charleston's new secret weapon. In reporting both sinkings of the *Hunley*, the two Charleston newspapers purposely failed to mention that the vessel accidentally sunk was the submarine boat (it was probably common knowledge throughout the city anyway).

Turning once again to the diary of Emma Holmes, we read her entry concerning the *Hunley's* first sinking at Fort Johnson and her comments as to how vague the papers had been in reporting the facts: "Sept. 23, 1863. A month since I left town and what important events have taken place there. Daily the most furious bombardment was kept up, each day seeming to increase in fury and for nineteen or twenty days it was most particularly directed to Fort Sumter. The Yankees thought they had completely demolished it and flaming announcements appeared in the northern papers of its surrender as well as that of Charleston. But though it is in ruins and fourteen times the flag shot down, it still flaunts a proud defiance to the foe. About the time I was taken sick, The *Porpoise* or cigar shaped boat, with four or five men on board, was accidentally sunk and of course the men were drowned. From some recent allusions in the paper, however, very carefully worded, I think and hope it has been recovered."

While divers Smith and Broadfoot groped around in the muddy darkness at the bottom of Charleston harbor, trying to salvage the Hunley a second time, a Captain M. P. Usina, on duty in the Battery at the southern tip of the city, was examining a curious note he had removed from a bottle that had washed to shore with the morning tide. In 1885, at the May meeting of the Georgia Historical Society (where this marvelous artifact still resides), Captain Usina presented his glass bottle and its amazing contents to the groups secretary. As we shall see the note contained within this unique trophy is a testament to both Civil War espionage and history of the *Hunley*. Excerpts of this secret correspondence, accidentally intercepted from a union spy by a fluke change of the tides read.

"Charleston November 2, 1863. My Dear Friends on Morris Island: There is at present in Fort Sumter 500 troops with 200 negroes for working parties. There is a most powerful bomb proof in Sumter covered with railroad iron, however the railroad iron did not save them in the fort. You buried 13 in one pile on Saturday the 31st of last month. If you be right smart you can have Fort Sumter in less than thirty days. They are going to renew the fort with fresh troops if possible very soon, so keep a sharp look out and bag them.

I wish to let you know that you have nothing to fear from the Submarine battery that was to blow up the Ironsides, is nearly two weeks at the bottom,

*Memorial to the men of the "Hunley,"
located in Mobile, Alabama.*
Photo from Eustice Williams Collection.

THE MERCURY.

BY R. B. RHETT, JR.

OFFICE NO. 484 KING-STREET, CHARLESTON.

THE DAILY MERCURY, ten cents per copy, $20 per annum.

THE TRI-WEEKLY MERCURY, issued on Tuesdays, Thursdays and Saturdays, ten cents per copy, $10 per annum.

ADVERTISEMENTS, Two Dollars per square of 18 lines.

MONDAY, NOVEMBER 9, 1863.

LAST HONORS TO A DEVOTED PATRIOT.—The remains of Captain HORACE L. HUNLEY were yesterday interred in Magnolia Cemetery. His body was followed to the grave by a military escort, and a large number of citizens.

The deceased was a native of Tennessee, but for many years past has been a resident of New Orleans.

Possessed of an ample fortune, in the prime of manhood—for he was only thirty-six at the time of his death—with everything before him to make life attractive, he came to Charleston, and voluntarily joined in a patriotic enterprise which promised success, but which was attended with great peril. Though feeling, as appears from the last letter which he wrote to his friends, a presentiment that he would perish in the adventure, he gave his whole heart, undeterred by the foreboding, to the undertaking, declaring that he would gladly sacrifice his life in the cause. That presentiment has been mournfully fulfilled. Yet who shall call that fate a sad one, which associates the name of its victim with those of his country's most unselfish martyrs?

Although Hunley and his crew were publicly buried with full military honors, the secrecy that surrounded the venture precluded any direct mention of his experimental submarine in the news articles about his death and burial.

with eight souls in her, never more to rise. No more at present. I am yours truly U.S."

The identity of this union spy who referred to him/her self as "U.S." will probably never be known, however as we shall see shortly, their confident statements that "you have nothing to fear from the Submarine Battery" and that she was "never more to rise" were less than accurate.[118]

On November 7, just over three weeks after the *Hunley* had disappeared beneath the keel of the *C.S.S. Indian Chief*, the black iron hull of the mysterious invention once more broke the surface of Charleston Harbor.[119] After many days of work on the cold dark bottom, Smith and Broadfoot had once again been successful in salvaging this ill-fated vessel that might still prove to be of service to the downcast and ever-shrinking Confederacy.

From a news article that appeared in the *Charleston News and Courier*, July 29, 1916, we read a first hand account of the jubilation felt round the city when news of the *Hunley's* recovery swept through war-weary Charleston: "Mr. R.M. Haddon, of Abbeville, one of the best known merchants in upper South Carolina, has been spending a few days in Charleston and on Sullivan's Island, on his annual pilgrimage to the seacoast and he was especially interested yesterday, in strolling about Charleston, in the monument to the brave men who lost their lives in the submarine exploits in Charleston harbor during the War Between the States.

The inscription on the monument recalled to Haddon a very interesting experience of his own boyhood. he was in Charleston during part of the war, as a boy of 16, and recalls well the excitement which ran through the city in the Fall of 1863, when the word flew about that the *Hunley*, which had gone down several weeks before and for which a vigilant search had been made, had been discovered and raised to the surface.

Haddon was off duty when he heard the *Hunley* had been raised and he hurried at once to the wharf at the foot of Calhoun Street. He thinks it was there that a great crowd had gathered. He was close by when the hatch was lifted.

It is interesting to know that Haddon recalls vividly that even before the inventor and his crew had been removed from the wharf, it was generally understood in the crowd that seven or eight others had already volunteered on the spot to take the *Hunley* out again."

Years after the war, General Beauregard still

TRIPLE SHEET.

New York, Wednesday, Sept. 30, 1863.

CHARLESTON.

News from Morris Island to the 26th Instant.

The Siege Progressing Favorably.

Reception of the News of Gen. Gillmore's Promotion.

ENTHUSIASM OF THE TROOPS.

GRAND ARTILLERY DUEL

Rebel Submarine Machine Sunk.

NAVAL NEWS.

LIST OF CASUALTIES, &c., &c., &c.

Announcement from the September 30, 1863 edition of the New York Herald regarding the siege of Charleston and the sinking of a "Rebel Submarine clearly remembered his reaction to the scene that met his eyes as the hatches on the submarine were raised. In his own words we can get a good idea as to the horror that must have been felt by all those who were witness to the unhappy event. "When the boat was discovered, raised and opened the spectacle was indescribably ghastly; the unfortunate men were contorted into all kinds of horrible attitudes, some clutching candles, evidently endeavoring to force open the man-holes; others lying in the bottom, tightly grappled together, and the blackened faces of all presented the expression of their despair and agony."[120]

The exact cause of this unfortunate accident that had cost the lives of yet a second *Hunley* crew would undoubtedly remain a complete mystery to us today if not for the post war writings of William Alexander. Carefully composed from memory some forty years after the events in Charleston Harbor had taken place; Alexander was able to leave to future generations the most complete history of this Confederate submarine ever likely to come to light. In an article he wrote for the *New Orleans Picayune*, June 29, 1902, we are told in great detail the exact reasons why the *Hunley* plunged to the bottom of Charleston harbor on that October morning in 1863.

"The position in which the boat was found on the bottom of the river, the condition of the apparatus discovered after it was raised and pumped out, and the position of the bodies in the boat, furnished a full explanation for her loss. The boat, when found, was lying on the bottom at an angle of about 35 degrees, the bow deep in the mud. The bolting-down bolts of each cover had been removed. When the hatch covers were lifted considerable air and gas escaped. Captain Hunley's body was forward, with his head in the forward hatchway, his right hand on top of his head (he had been trying, it would seem, to raise the hatch cover). In his left hand was a candle that had never been lighted, the sea-cock on the forward end, or 'Hunley's' ballast tank, was wide open, the cock-wrench not on the plug, but lying on the bottom of the boat. Mr. Park's body was found with his head in the after hatchway, his right hand above his head. He also had been trying to raise the hatch cover, but the pressure was too great. The sea-cock to his tank was properly closed, and the tank was nearly empty. The other bodies were floating in the water. Hunley and Parks were undoubtedly asphyxiated, the others drowned. The bolts that had held the iron keel ballast had been partly turned, but not sufficient to release it.

In the light of these conditions, we can easily depict before our minds, and almost readily explain, what took place in the boat during the moments immediately following its submergence. Captain Hunley's practice with the boat had made him quite familiar and expert in handling her, and this familiarity produced at this time forgetfulness. It was found in practice to be easier on the crew to come to the surface by giving the pumps a few strokes and ejecting some of the water ballast, than by the momentum of the boat operating on the elevated fins. At this time the boat was under way, lighted through the dead-lights in the hatchways. He partly turned the fins to go down, but thought, no doubt, that he needed more ballast and opened his sea cock. Immediately the boat was in total darkness. He then undertook to light the candle. While trying to do this the tank quietly flooded, and under great pressure the boat sank very fast and soon overflowed, and the first intimation they would have of anything being wrong was the water rising fast, but noiselessly, about their feet in the bottom of the boat. They tried to release the iron keel ballast, but did not turn the keys quite far enough, therefore failed. The water soon forced the air to the top of the boat and into the hatchways, where captains Hunley and Parks were found. Parks had pumped his ballast tank dry, and no doubt Captain Hunley had exhausted himself on his pump, but he had forgotten that he had not closed his sea cock."

From the above description it would appear that the cause of this second accident can be attributed to what we call today "pilot error." If Captain Hunley had been able at any time to close the forward sea valve, the cold water that had already entered the ballast tank and spilled over the top could have been bailed back into the compartment and pumped back into the sea. In the blackness and confusion that followed the great jolt that took place on impact with the muddy bottom, the valve handle must have fallen off the stem and become lost beneath the bodies that had been hurled into the forward area.

As sea water started to spill over the top of the ballast tank bulk head and slowly fill the darkened hull, the blinded crew must have desperately scrambled away from the cold rising water towards the stern area that remained higher than the bow. With the icy water and internal pressure steadily

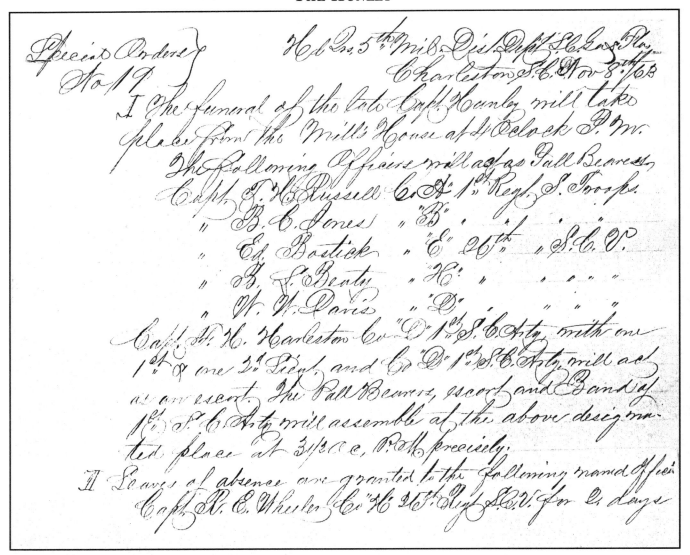

Orders regarding Captain Hunley's funeral. National Archives.

Civil War sketch of funeral procession. Copied from the collections of the U.S. Library of Congress.

This Confederate war memorial in Charleston's historic Magnolia Cemetery, is one of many still maintained in the South. Photo by Mark K. Ragan.

Captain Horace L. Hunley and the men who died with him were buried with full military honors in Magnolia Cemetery. Photo by Mark K. Ragan.

rising within the doomed vessel, panic and despair would have soon taken hold as the terrified crew men realized that there would be no escape. Beneath nine fathoms of water, with their bow hopelessly stuck in the mud, their desperate shouts for help were soon silenced by the frigid water at the dark bottom of Charleston Harbor.

Three weeks later, as divers Smith and Broadfoot were making final adjustments to the numerous chains that would hoist the silent submarine back into the world of the living, the following orders were being issued from Charleston headquarters to Colonel Alfred Rhett:

"November 6th, 1863. Colonel: The commanding general desires that you have the remains of Captain Hunley buried with the military honors due to an officer of his rank. He was drowned in the submarine torpedo boat some weeks since, and you will be notified by his friends when his remains are ready for interment."[121]

Two days after this order was issued, the remains of Captain Horace L. Hunley and his brave crew of adventurers from Mobile were laid to rest in Magnolia Cemetery on the banks of the Cooper River. From a letter received by Hunley's sister shortly after the funeral, we can form a faint picture of the ceremony surrounding the burial of what the Charleston papers called "The last honors to a devoted patriot."[122]

"Mrs. V.W. Barrow, New Orleans, Louisiana. Madam: It becomes my painful duty to address you in relation to the decease of your brother Horace Lawson Hunley. He had delegated me at Mobile to come to Charleston, S.C. I started and arrived on the 18th of October. He was drowned on the 15th - three days previous. I immediately telegraphed Mr. Leovy and other of his friends.

Mr. Leovy came to Charleston and remained a few days. It took several days to make arrangements to raise the boat to enable us to produce the bodies. When the raising tackle and hoisting boats were ready, a strong north east wind blew for many days. We could not work at the raising of the boat, only in smooth weather and slack water of the tide, therefore the great delay. We succeeded in raising the boat and recovered the body of Captain Hunley on Saturday evening, the 7th on November. I had a fine lined coffin ready. The funeral took place on Sunday the 8th at four o'clock pm - General Beauregard ordered a military escort, two companies and a band of music. The funeral service was solemn and impressive, performed by the Rev: W.B. Yates - 'Episcopal.' On Sunday evening the remaining seven bodies were recovered. and on Monday I had them buried with funeral services by the same clergyman and in a lot adjoining the one of Captain Hunley. I then selected a tombstone, it is small but appropriate, merely to mark the place, with the following inscription: Captain Horace Lawson Hunley, aged 39 years. A native of Tennessee, but for many years a citizen of New Orleans, who lost his life in the service of his country.

At the grave I could not refrain from tears as the casket of the spirit of a noble and generous man was being lowered, 'earth to earth' - to its final resting place. I lost in him my best friend. My wife had also become much attached to him. He was so gentlemanly and kind. When I came home and related the death and burial, she wept though it had been a dear relative. And said - Oh! That I could have been with you to have wept at the grave for an only sister whose heart must bleed for a brother lost and buried among strangers. But here I assure you, not without friends, for he was beloved by all who knew him. I remain Madam, very respectfully Gardner Smith."

Captain Horace Hunley's grave marker in Magnolia Cemetery. Photo by Mark K. Ragan.

CHAPTER THREE
Salvaged Submarine Remanned

"The common name given her is murdering machine." – Augustine Smythe (crew member, *C.S.S. Palmetto State*)

On or about October 18, 1863, at about the same time that Angus Smith was groping his way around the partially buried Hunley, Dixon and Confederate agent Dillingham walked through the doorway of the busy Park & Lyons shop. The loud hammering commonly heard in the factory must have slowly died out as the shop's workers took note of the visitors. Less than three weeks before, the familiar Dixon had departed for Charleston with several of their friends as well as the shop-owner's son Tom. Why, they must have wondered, had he returned so soon after leaving, and why was there a distressed expression on the young officer's face?

As the mechanics and engineers gathered around Dixon, they were sadly informed of the tragic and mysterious accident that had recently taken the lives of Captain Hunley and many of their comrades. After answering the many questions put to him by the clearly shaken men, Dixon took his old friend and fellow engineering officer William Alexander to one side to reveal the reason why he had returned to Mobile before the little vessel had even been found.

As the reader will recall, Dixon and Dillingham were given transportation to Mobile immediately after the loss of the *Hunley*, "on business connected with the Submarine Torpedo Boat." This business, in all probability, had to do with recruiting a replacement crew of men experienced in the operation of the unique invention. As George Dixon had proven over the past couple of weeks, the *Hunley* was indeed a very formidable weapon in the hands of a capable pilot and well-practiced crew.

Shortly after relating the news of the tragic accident to the friends of the missing crewmen, Dixon, in all likelihood, hastened to the home of his long time sweetheart Miss Queenie Bennett, the daughter of a steamboat captain whom he had met while working as engineer aboard a steamship which operated along the Mobile River.[123] By now their romance was in it's second year, and they had vowed to marry as soon as the war ended.

From an article that appeared in the November 15, 1904 edition of the *Mobile Daily Herald*, we are told about a good luck piece Miss Bennett had given Dixon as he departed with his regiment for the front. The article headlined *Dixon, Builder of the Submarine Hunley* read: "When the Twenty-first Alabama left Mobile the ladies of Mobile came out in full force to bid the boys adieu and say their loving farewells (for some would never return). Among those present was the sweetheart of George Dixon. Just before the departure of the train she handed him a $20 gold piece, bidding him to keep it for her sake. Not long after, in a hot corner of the battle of Shiloh, he was felled by a bullet in the thigh. The wound would have been mortal had not the ball first struck the gold piece and carried it into the flesh. When removed it was found that the coin was doubled up into such a shape as to form a bell, the bullet being firmly imbedded in the metal."

The article went on to say that Dixon highly prized the mangled good luck piece given him by his fiance, and always carried it in his pocket.

At first glance the article appears to be somewhat fanciful and too outlandish to be totally true. The idea of a lover's good luck charm stopping an enemy bullet in the heat of battle is just too fantastic to be believed. For the longest time I considered the story to be little more than a southern yarn about parted lovers in time of war. This belief would probably have persisted if it had not been for a collection of letters sent to me by Caldwell Delaney.

The letters were written by Lt. James J. Williams, a friend of Dixon's. Both were attached to a seven man group known as "The Battering Ram Mess." From the following letter written in April of 1862, shortly after the bloody battle of Shiloh, Tennessee, we are given an independent verification concerning the good luck gold piece.

"Dear Lizzie: I telegraphed you today that I am well and safely through the two days of battle. I have not time nor disposition to attempt a description - when I get home it will take me months to describe what I saw on that terrible Field. I commanded Company 'A' the whole battle. The wounded are being brought into camp and they claim all my attention. John Herpin was killed early in the action, John King is shot in the mouth and, I fear, mortally wounded. George Dixon came down a minute later, shot in the hip, the ball striking a gold piece; he will probably recover if he can be

Lieutenant Dixon's war record shows he was severely wounded in the thigh during the Battle of Shiloh. Courtesy of National Archives.

well cared for. I send you as trophies of the field a brass eagle from a Yankees hat, and a button off a coat. - Williams."

Many short accounts regarding Dixon appear in these early war letters. From the way that George is described to William's wife Lizzie, it would seem that he was something of a practical joker, who enjoyed the camaraderie of his friends, and always shared the "Boxes of good things," sent to him by his sweetheart Queenie Bennett.

Thanks to the efforts of Caldwell Delaney, I was able to meet with Queenie Bennett's great-granddaughter, who lives near Richmond, Virginia. She showed me a newspaper clipping describing a post-war incident Queenie had instigated. From the following lines we can catch a glimmer of her independent and defiant spirit.

"This patriotic feeling was evidenced by an incident described by Mrs. Frohlichstein which occurred in 1865 following the surrender of Mobile. Five young Mobile girls, the leader being Miss Queenie Bennett, daughter of George Bennett, marched to the Provost Marshal's office where the Federals were. Here they cut the halyard and allowed the United States flag to drop to the ground. The young girls were ordered arrested by the Provost Marshal and detained at headquarters for a little while, but were later permitted to leave. In her declining days, whenever Mrs. Frohlichstein heard any one speak of patriotism she proudly recalled the deed of her four young companions and herself."

To interest a lady of such spirit Dixon probably had a bit of a flamboyant and independent personality of his own.

After relating the tragic accident that had taken place in Charleston harbor to his beloved, and reassuring her that the same fate would not happen to him, Dixon and his traveling companion, Dillingham, presumably reported to General Maury at military headquarters to give him a full report regarding the situation at Charleston and an account of the sinking.

While in this urgent meeting, Dixon would have undoubtedly stated his reasons for returning to the city, as well as request permission to extend his detached duty in South Carolina. Although no specific order for extended duty in Charleston appears in George Dixon's Confederate War record, General Maury would probably have issued one. (Or, perhaps the mysterious Dillingham with his unique government connections may have had

The "Hunley" practiced mock attacks by diving under the Confederate ironclad "Palmetto State" in Charleston Harbor. Illustration from Official Records of the Union and Confederate Navies in the War of the Rebellion.

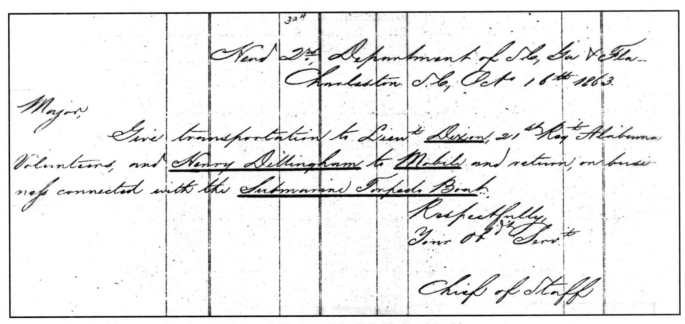

Order sending Lt. Dixon and Agent Dillingham back to Mobile. U.S. National Archives.

some influence in this matter.)

Confederate documents regarding activities in and around Charleston are fairly plentiful, those relating to events around the Gulf and city of Mobile are very fragmented.

Much of what I have discovered relating to the history of the *Hunley* was obtained by reading each hand-written order issued by Charleston military headquarters during the time of her activities around the harbor (those records are now located in the National Archives). Unfortunately no such similar documents are known to have survived from General Maury's headquarters in Mobile. The lack of such records causes great difficulty.

While in Mobile, as Dixon presumably arranged to have his detached duty extended in far away Charleston, a very interesting telegram (datelined: "CHARLESTON, S.C. NOVEMBER 5TH, 1863") was sent to the young officer from a greatly discouraged General Beauregard. It read "LIEUTENANT DIXON: I CAN HAVE NOTHING MORE TO DO WITH THAT SUBMARINE BOAT. IT'S MORE DANGEROUS TO THOSE WHO USE IT THAN THE ENEMY."[124] Whether Dixon received this message while he was still in Mobile is not known. After searching the Charleston military files relating to messages received during this period, I was unable to locate any response to this interesting telegram. In any event, it appears obvious that the general, during the absence of the capable Dixon, had lost faith in the strange invention, and wished nothing more than to wash his hands of the whole affair.

From post-war writings of William Alexander, we are told that Beauregard did indeed have grave reservations regarding the continued use of the small submarine. Regardless of the fact that Dixon had proven the *Hunley* to be a formidable engine of war, Beauregard must have decided the contraption to be too dangerous for continued use after taking the life of Captain Hunley - a man who had been involved with such machines since the beginning of the war, and who had requested that the craft be put under his control.

Civil War photograph of Miss Queenie Bennett and her sister. The paper money in the background was issued by the State of Alabama during the Civil War, and, like virtually all of the South's currency, was worthless after the War.
Photo by Mark Ragan, courtesy of Miss Bennett's great-granddaughter, who wishes to remain anonymous.

Miss Queenie Bennett was Lt. Dixon's sweetheart. A gold piece she gave him took the main force of an enemy bullet that struck Dixon in the thigh at the battle of Shiloh. The gold piece saved his leg and possibly his life. Photo courtesy of Miss Bennett's great-granddaughter, who wishes to remain anonymous.

By all surviving accounts, it would seem that everyone who knew George Dixon considered him to be a very brave and dedicated officer. As the reader will recall, he had entered Confederate service in the spring of 1861 as a private, been severely wounded at the Battle of Shiloh, and had risen to the rank of first lieutenant by the fall of 1863. His one-time company commander John Cothran later said of him "Dixon was very handsome, fair, nearly six feet tall, and of most attractive presence. I never knew a better man; and there never was a braver man in any service of any army."[125]

It was probably this air of self-confidence, dedication to duty, and unyielding faith in the destructive capabilities of the *Hunley*, that enabled Dixon (upon his return from Mobile) to convince Beauregard to grant him a final chance to command the submarine in action against the enemy fleet.

Returning once again to the post-war writings of Alexander, we find that he returned to Charleston with Dixon to take over as the *Hunley's* first officer, manning the rear ballast tank pump and sea valves. Although the orders given Dixon and Dillingham were to go to Mobile and return, whether Dillingham actually did so is not known. A very interesting passage from Alexander's 1903 Munsey magazine article (to be quoted later) indicates that there was indeed an important member of this final crew who was mysteriously reassigned later.

At about the same time Dixon was bidding his Alabama sweetheart a tearful farewell, and boarding a crowded Charleston bound railroad car with Alexander, the referees assigned to the salvage case of divers Smith and Broadfoot were coming to a decision regarding the amount of money to be paid the two adventurers:

"Charleston, S.C. November 9th, 1863. General: The undersigned referees appointed to ascertain the salvage due Messrs. Smith and Broadfoot (divers) for raising the 'submarine Torpedo Boat' sunk off Fort Johnson, in consideration of the difficulties in raising said boat - i.e. Depth of water, number of days employed and loss of submarine armor and from the best information we can obtain that the said boat could not be replaced for less than twenty-seven thousand five hundred ($27,500) dollars, therefor we do award to Messrs. Smith and Broadfoot (divers) the sum of thirteen thousand seven hundred + fifty ($13,750) dollars, being 50 percent of the salvage of the boat."[126]

Although this document clearly states that the amount to be paid Smith and Broadfoot for salvaging the *Hunley* was $13,750, a receipt from early January, 1864, found within the divers' file of business dealings with the Confederate government shows that the amount actually paid was only $7,000. A book of endorsements sent by General Ripley (First Military District of S.C.) shed a bit more light on the subject:

"Report of board of survey appointed to ascertain the salvage due Smith and Broadfoot for raising Submarine Boat. The circumstances of the case are as follows: The crew of the submarine torpedo boat not being all willing to go out with her. Lt. Payne of the Navy volunteered with a number of seaman to take charge. The remaining portion of the crew consented. Lt. Payne CSN found after some days they would not obey his directions, with the approval of the Commanding General induced him to take possession which he did.

The first accident occurred soon after. The command of Gen. Beauregard directed that the boat should be raised. The light ship, derrick and crew were furnished to Lt. Payne, but the boat (submarine) having got away, Smith was called in by himself and Major Pringle (Chief Quartermaster), the amount being paid being left open to success and value. Lt. Payne had charge of the matter and I considered it as being a naval matter, although under the directions of the commanding general.

I consider the charge and reward excessive, as the light ship, most of the hands employed, steamers and coal were furnished by the government. The services of Smith were very valuable in proportion to the value of the boat, but I do not think to the extent of one half the present exaggerated estimate. The stores, the light ship, and the hands employed by the government were equally as necessary as the services of the divers.

The risk (to our men) was greater, as the steamer and light boat had to be exposed for a week or more to the enemy's fire, and I think that one half the award of the referees would be ample should the boat be successful."[127]

From the communication just cited, evidence would suggest that Smith and Broadfoot were induced to accept just $7,000 of the $13,750 awarded them by the referees, and at some point in the future, if the submarine proved successful, they could still lay claim to the remainder. Further evidence (to be discussed shortly) indicates that

This picture was discovered tucked behind the cover of a photo album kept by Queenie Bennett. The man in the picture seems to match a description of Lt. Dixon (Miss Bennett's wartime sweetheart) as given by his commanding officer.
Photo courtesy of Queenie Bennett's great-granddaughter, who wishes to remain anonymous.

Broadfoot, after raising the *Hunley* a second time, may have taken an active roll in the operations of the submarine.

By the afternoon of November 12, Dixon and those who had accompanied him from Mobile were undoubtedly back in Charleston.[128] With the submarine having been raised and emptied of her dead crew, Dixon would have sought out the sub to assess any damage sustained in the sinking and subsequent salvage. It was presumably during this inspection of the craft, and associated interviews of those who had removed the bodies, that the cause of the accident was determined. With this information in hand, Dixon and Alexander most likely reported to military headquarters to reveal their findings, as well as request permission to continue diving operations.

While searching through the index book of letters received at Charleston military headquarters during this period, I happened on an interesting entry summarizing a communication from Dixon. It read: "Charleston, S.C., November 12th, 1863. Lt. George E. Dixon Co. A. 21st Alabama Volunteers requests to be put in charge and command of the submarine torpedo boat." Without Dixon's original letter, we can only wonder as to what patriotic pleadings the young engineering officer raised to secure command of a vessel that most others believed was doomed to failure.

From post-war writings of General Beauregard, we are informed that only after much discussion with his Chief of Staff General Jordan was permission to continue operating the unlucky craft granted to the persuasive Dixon.[129] Beauregard further stated that the *Hunley* was not to dive again, and was instead only to be used as a surface vessel. Whether the general was mistaken in his recollection of this meeting may never be known, for it's well documented that the refitted *Hunley* not only continued to dive, she and her new volunteer crew, under the command of Dixon and Alexander, did so with far greater vigor and determination than ever seen before.

With permission granted for Dixon to once again ready the small submarine for action, it was apparently decided that the length of the detached duty already authorized by Mobile headquarters was insufficient. In the book of telegrams sent by Charleston headquarters during this period we find the following entry: "TO: COL. G. GARNER, CHIEF OF STAFF, MOBILE, ALABAMA. NOVEMBER 14, 1863. PLEASE EXTEND DETAIL OF LIEUTENANT GEORGE E. DIXON TO END OF YEAR. (SGN.) THOMAS JORDAN, CHIEF OF STAFF CHARLESTON, S.C."[130]

With permission apparently granted from far off Mobile, we find Dixon sending the following communication (written in a very legible, bold Victorian hand) to General Jordan: "Charleston, November the 14th, 1863. Brig. General Jordan, Chief of Staff, Sir: Before I can proceed with my work of cleaning the Sub-Marine boat, I shall have to request of you an order on the Quartermaster or Engineer Department for ten Negroes, also an order on the Commissary Department for soap, brushes, and lime, and an order on the Arsenal to have some work done at that place. In order to make all possible haste with this work, I would be pleased to have those orders granted at your earliest convenience. I am Yours with Respect Lt. Geo. E. Dixon, Commanding Sub-Marine Boat."[131]

From the way in which Dixon signed the above letter, there can be little doubt as to his having been granted complete control of the *Hunley* by November 14th. Judging from his request that some work be done at the arsenal, it would appear that the small submarine had sustained some damage to the bow or forward diving planes upon impacting the bottom on the 15th of October. In response to Dixon's request the following order was sent to the Charleston Arsenal later that day. "Headquarters, Charleston, S.C. November 14, 1863. Major Trezevant: Please afford Lieutenant Dixon all possible facilities for repairing the Submarine Torpedo Boat again. The Commanding General will give his official sanction to any repairs that may be further necessary. Respectfully General Thomas Jordan."[132]

Evidence indicating that Dixon was planning a complete overhaul of the unlucky craft can be ascertained from the large number of men (Negroes) he requested from the Engineering Department. As we shall see shortly, these men were used to help hoist the *Hunley*, and place her on the wharf for maintenance and repairs. After spending some three months in the water as well as several weeks on the bottom, it was apparently decided that it was about time to repack the numerous stuffing boxes and re-equip the submarine for the dangerous underwater adventure that lay before her.

On the day after sending the above letter to Jordan, Dixon filed the following requisition with the Quartermasters Department: "Quartermaster

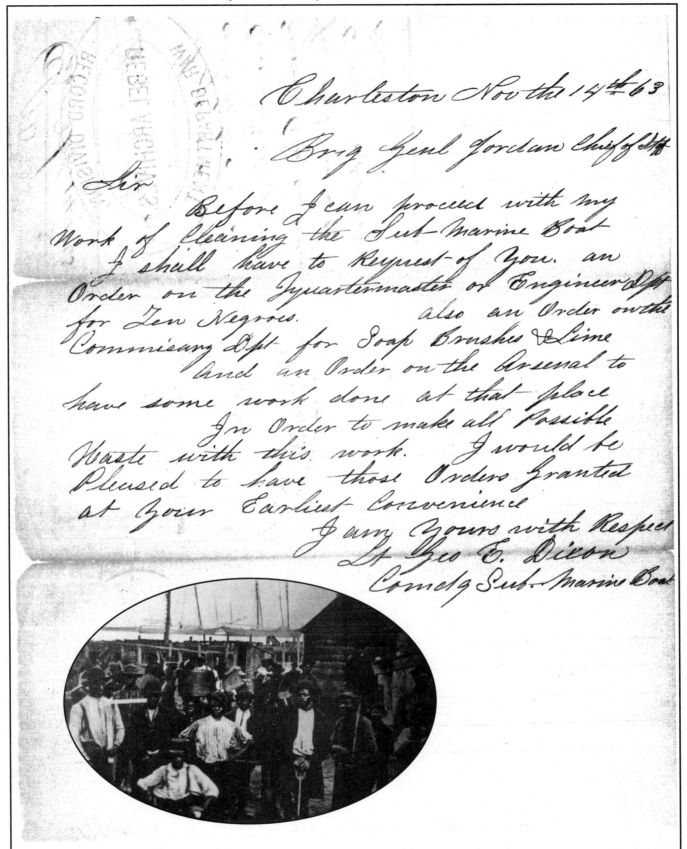

Charleston Nov the 14th 63

Brig Genl Jordan Chief of Staff

Sir

Before I can proceed with my Work of Cleaning the Sub-Marine Boat I shall have to Request of You. an Order on the Quartermaster or Engineer Dpt for Ten Negroes. also an Order on the Commisary Dpt for Soap Brushes & Lime

And an Order on the Arsenal to have some work done at that place

In Order to make all Possible Haste with this work. I would be Pleased to have those Orders Granted at Your Earliest Convenience

I am Yours with Respect
Lt Geo E. Dixon
Comdg Sub-Marine Boat

Lt. Dixon's letter of November 14, 1863 with depiction of slave labor as requested. National Archives.

(No 40.)

SPECIAL REQUISITION.

For *Sub marine Torpedo Boat H L Hunley*

Nov 17th   5 Scrubbing Brushes

1 Bble of Lime

1 Box of Soap   25 pounds

" 23d   2 pound of Cotton Rope

Dec 7th   18 " " " "

1 " of Cotton "

One Compass for Boat

Two Paint Brushes

18 feet of 2½ Rope 5 ℔

One Bucket

One Brass Sieve

I certify that the above Requisition is correct; and that the articles specified are absolutely requisite for the public service, rendered so by the following circumstances:

Lt Geo. E. Dixon

Appd By Genneral Beauregard

Quartermaster, C. S. Army, will issue the articles specified in the above requisition.

Lt Geo E. Dixon Commanding.

RECEIVED at *Charleston* the 15th of November 186 3 of

Maj. M. A. Pringle Quartermaster, C. S. Army, the above articles

in full of the above requisition

(SIGNED DUPLICATES.)

Lt Geo E. Dixon

Requisition made by Lt. Dixon for supplies to clean, paint and refit the "Hunley" after the sinking of October 15, 1863. Courtesy of the U.S. National Archives.

C.S. Army, November 15th, 1863 SPECIAL REQUISITION: For Submarine Torpedo Boat *H.L. Hunley* : Five scrubbing brushes, One barrel of lime, One box of soap (Several lengths of rope, quoted in pounds), One compass for boat, Two paint brushes, One bucket, One brass shieve" (probably sheave for a pulley). [133]

From the dates on the above letter and requisition, it could be assumed that within a week after burying Captain Hunley and his brave crew of volunteers, work was once again underway to ready the small submarine for renewed action. The list of supplies requested by Dixon seem to have been primarily for cleaning the vessel. After spending over three weeks at the bottom of the harbor, manned by a crew of dead men, it's no wonder a barrel of lime appears towards the top of the list.

Since Dixon ordered another compass, along with the cleaning supplies and rope, one can assume that the compass, previously requisitioned by Captain Hunley, had been damaged or was thought inadequate for the job. A working compass was an absolute necessity to their operations, but none were truly sufficient for the job.

As mentioned in McClintock's post-war letter to Matthew Maury (cited in the first chapter) "The boat was steered by a compass which at times acted so slow, that the boat would at times alter her course for one or two minutes before it would be discovered, thus losing the direct course and so compel the operator to come to the top of the water more frequently than he otherwise would."

Not until the invention of the gyroscopic compass years later would the problems associated with the use of a compass inside of a ferrous hull be satisfactorily resolved. I myself have given up trying to use a magnetic compass aboard my own submarine; they simply don't work inside the steel casing. It's a mystery to me how Dixon was able to get any sort of accurate reading within the submarine.

Shortly after Dixon had received the supplies ordered in his requisition of November 15, 1863, the submarine was hoisted from the water and placed on a Mount Pleasant wharf. With the *Hunley* cradled, it would have been an easy task to turn the bolts that held the emergency drop weights attached to the bottom of the vessel. With these keel weights removed, the stuffing boxes that prevented the water from entering the vessel through the bolt holes could be repacked, as well as the boxes that kept water from entering by way of the propeller shaft, diving planes, and snorkel assembly.

This snorkel assembly, although ingenious in design, appears never to have come up to expectation. From William Alexander's 1902 *New Orleans Picayune* article, we are informed that "There was an opening in the top of the boat for an air box, a casting with a close top 12 by 18 by 4 inches. made to carry a hollow shaft. This shaft passed through stuffing boxes. On each end was an elbow with a 4 foot length of 1 1/2 inch pipe, and keyed to a hollow shaft; on the inside was a lever with a stop-cock to admit air."

In theory, the *Hunley* would rise to just beneath the surface, the air shafts would be raised above the water, the stop-cock would be opened and the stale air would be quickly refreshed (possibly with the aid of a bellows). In practice, the arrangement was either insufficient or otherwise unsatisfactory, and it was found best to simply surface the submarine, open the rear hatch for a few moments, then re-submerge. According to Alexander, this was the standard procedure used to replenish the air supply during his tour of duty in the *Hunley*. It was probably also discovered during trials, that the two pipes protruding from beneath the water (while the submarine continued on course) were too obvious and would have served to alert the enemy sentries. Besides, it would have been extremely difficult if not impossible to obtain and maintain the exact depth required to keep the vessel submerged at exactly the right level. If too deep the air pipes would flood, if too shallow the sub's raised hatches and upper hull would be exposed. In view of the problems, this system of air replacement was probably used only when the vessel was forced to run on the surface with her hatches closed due to rough water.

Shortly before the *Hunley* had been removed from the harbor to undergo her much needed repairs, Confederate soldiers stationed on Sullivan's Island made a very interesting discovery. While walking down the beach following a storm that had taken place the night before, a canvas bag was found washed up on the beach. Upon investigating the contents of the satchel, it was found that the bag contained dozens of letters recently written by enemy sailors on blockade duty. Three were subsequently published on the front page of the *Charleston Mercury*. They were described by the editor as having been "written in defiance of Webster's spelling book." One letter read as follows: "Dear Mother: Old Fort Sumter looks quite bad now, and they have throwed (sic) a few shells over into Charleston City, to just stir them up a little by way of a change, and though the British Consul does not appreciate it much and furthermore, he does not seem to think it quite right, but I don't see any way he can help himself, as they have been told to remove the women and children from the city - for we was going to shell the city, and he can stay and take the contence (sic) or leave just as he chooses about it.

The fleet is getting along quite well, only the other night the monitors went up near Fort Sumter to make a night attack and the *Passaic* got aground and we came very near coming out without her, but at last she got off and came out all right. We have throwed from the gunboat (*Ottawa*) 80,000 Lbs. of shot and shell at the Rebs, and used almost 11,000 Lbs. of powder, that is 5 1/2 tons of powder 40 tons of iron. That was about one week ago, but our guns will not stand to throw as much more without bursting - that's what the matter is."[134] This letter sums up fairly well the situation around Charleston Harbor while Dixon and Alexander readied the *Hunley* for renewed action.

Sometime after the submarine had been hoisted from the water; our two Alabama Infantry officers once again reported to military headquarters to request yet another crew for the unlucky diving machine. From Alexander's 1903 article in Munsey magazine, we are informed as to how the two officers were received by the reluctant Beauregard. "We soon had the boat refitted and in good shape, reported to General Jordan that she was ready for service, and asked for a crew. After many refusals and much discussion, General Beauregard finally assented to our going aboard the Confederate receiving ship *Indian Chief* and calling for volunteers. He strictly enjoined upon us to give a full and clear explanation of the desperately hazardous nature of the service required."

Although Beauregard authorized Dixon and Alexander to call for volunteers to re-man their boat, surviving documentation would suggest that he first had to clear his decision with the Navy Department, for in the book of endorsements kept at headquarters we find the following short note to Commodore Ingraham: "Lieutenant Dixon is thoroughly conversant with the management of the 'Fish Boat' and maintains it offers little danger when properly handled. The destruction of the enemies ironclads would warrant in my opinion the approval of Lt. Dixon's application (for a crew)

when men are found still willing to accompany him with a full knowledge of the accidents which have already happened to the crews of that boat. General Beauregard."

With permission apparently granted from Ingraham, Dixon and Alexander walked down to the Cooper River docks, boarded a skiff, and were rowed out to the harbor-bound *C.S.S. Indian Chief.* After presenting Beauregard's orders to the vessel's captain, the entire ship's company was called to assemble on the quarter deck. Since Dixon and Alexander had just come from their meeting at Confederate military headquarters, they were probably dressed in their finest uniforms. The two young officers must have been quite a sight to the unshaven, barefoot sailors. Some of the ship's company may have recognized Dixon from his previous practice diving operations around the hull of their vessel. They would have had numerous opportunities to have seen him opening the forward hatch of the torpedo boat after mock attacks on their ship.

It was probably no accident that the *Indian Chief* was selected as the ship from which to choose the new volunteer crew. Most of the ship's company had undoubtedly seen the *Hunley* successfully dive beneath their vessel's hull. Although this crew was certainly aware of the submarine's tragic past, it appears that Dixon gave a speech that inspired sufficient men to put aside their fears and step forward to re-man the little diving machine. Turning again to Alexander's post war writings, we are informed that "We had no difficulty in getting volunteers to man her. I don't believe a man considered the danger which awaited him. The honor of being the first to engage the enemy in this novel way overshadowed all else."

Due to the rigorous nature of the duty that would be expected of this new crew, Dixon and Alexander probably chose only the most able-bodied seamen from the group that had stepped forward. Dixon knew that the men selected would have to propel the submarine for hours on end, miles out to sea, several feet beneath the surface, night after night. It was obvious that this duty was not for the weak or faint of heart.

From the numerous volunteers who apparently stepped forward that day, the two Alabama engineering officers selected five seamen. The first to be selected was Boatswain's Mate James A. Wicks, a Virginia native, and father of four, who had been assigned to the Charleston Station at

General Thomas Jordan, Chief of Staff for General Beauregard, CSA, met with Lieutenants Dixon and Alexander many times during the fall of 1863 and early winter of 1864. Photo courtesy of the U.S. Library of Congress.

The "Hunley" was pulled from the water and placed on a Mount Pleasant dock where she was scrubbed, painted and refitted. The docked submarine then became a classroom as the volunteers sat inside and were lectured on its operation.

SPECIAL REQUISITION

For *Lt. Geo. E. Dixon Comdg Sub Marine boat.*

1 | *One Camp Kettle*
1 | *One Mess Pan*

I certify that the above requisition is correct; and that the articles specified are absolutely requisite for the public service, rendered so by the following circumstances :

Lt Geo E. Dixon
Quartermaster, C. S. Army, will

Capt W. G. Vardell A

will issue the articles specified in the above requisition.

RECEIVED at *Mount Pleasant* the 28th of *Dec* 1863 of *Capt W. G. Vardell*
A Quartermaster, C. S. Army, *The articles*
in full of the above requisition.

(SIGNED DUPLICATES.)

Geo. E. Dixon
Lt Comdg Sub-Marine Boat

The crew had to cook their own food as reflected by this requisition for a camp kettle and mess pan.
Copied by permission of the U.S. National Archives.

about the same time that the *Hunley* had arrived from Mobile. The second crew member to be selected was Seaman Arnold Becker, a Louisiana chef who until late August, had served as the captain's cook aboard the Ironclad *C.S.S. Chicora*. The third man to join Dixon's crew of adventurers was Seaman Joseph Ridgeway, another Virginia native who had been attached to the Quartermaster Corps since his enlistment at Richmond in the summer of 1862. The fourth Seaman selected was Frank J. Collins another apparent Virginian who's service before being assigned to Charleston is unknown due to his war record being somewhat fragmented. The last name to appear on Dixon's list of volunteers was Seaman C. Simkins, a man who's service record in the Southern Navy is regrettably unknown, for his name has long since faded from the tattered Confederate Navy muster rolls now on file in the National Archives.[135], [136]

After clearing the five sailors' transfers with the captain of the *Indian Chief*, Dixon and Alexander, accompanied by their new crew of volunteers, set course for the Mount Pleasant docks where repairs to the submarine were almost complete. Dixon wished to waste no time in acquainting his new crew with the inner workings of this unique vessel.

With the *Hunley* still out of the water, Dixon's task of explaining the various components and features of the vessel would have been greatly simplified. Beauregard, upon granting Dixon and Alexander's request to seek out yet another crew, had ordered the young officers to explain fully to each volunteer the "desperately hazardous nature of the service required," and that a full history of the boat be given to each man. To comply with these orders, Dixon undoubtedly explained in great detail the causes of each of the two accidents, pointing out how each could have been easily avoided. After the unfortunate history of the submarine had been fully explained, the five volunteers would then have taken turns squeezing through the *Hunley's* tiny hatches to get their first glimpse inside the vessel in which they would soon be gambling their lives.

While Dixon and Alexander explained how their boat worked, each man would have taken a turn at the skipper's station and been briefed as to the function of the diving planes and ballast tanks. Each would have turned the wheel that caused the long rods over the crew's heads to move in and out the stern stuffing boxes causing the vessel's rudder to turn. The function of the mercury gauge would

have been explained; as to how it enabled the helmsman to regulate the depth of the submarine. The men would then have taken their places for a mock dive while still safe on the wharf. Since earlier crew members were presumably self taught and would not have actually received formal group instruction, it could be said with some confidence that the world's very first school for submariners was founded on a wind swept dock on the Mount Pleasant shore of Charleston Harbor in the fall of 1863. That school was founded by a Confederate engineering officer who, along with his brave crew, would usher in the dawn of underwater warfare.

With the death of Hunley, and both McClintock and Watson then engaged in mining Mobile harbor with Singer's group of engineers; no one who had originally been part of the daring scheme first hatched in New Orleans, was still associated with the adventure. The project that had started as a small privateering experiment in 1861 had now grown into an important military operation, hundreds of miles from Louisiana, managed by two Alabama Infantry officers, crewed by untrained Confederate sailors, and under the command of a reluctant General. Many men had died along the way, and it was hoped by all who were currently involved with the small submarine, that the future actions of the *Hunley* would in some way make up for her tragic past.

From an 1899 letter written by William Alexander to Colonel J.G. Holmes (an army historian who was then seeking information about the history of the *Hunley*), we discover that at about the same time that Dixon and Alexander were acquainting their new crew with the inner workings of the *Hunley*, a visit was paid them by an Episcopal Clergyman named Dr. Johnson. From that letter to Colonel Holmes (now on file at the South Carolina Historical Society) we read the following lines.

"Dr. Johnson, the rector of Saint Phillips Episcopal Church came to the wharf while we were refitting the boat. He talked to us about the risks of the undertaking and gave us a pressing invitation to attend services at his church, which we did, meeting him before service." From this short passage it could be assumed that this final crew of the *Hunley*, may have occasionally met with Reverend Johnson in special prayer services prior to, and perhaps during, their nocturnal operations. Although this bit of information adds little to the history of the *Hunley*, I feel it is worthy of note in

A Confederate soldier on guard duty at Fort Sumter looks towards the enemy gun emplacements on nearby Morris Island. The blockade fleet, consisting of warships and ironclads, lines the horizon. Used courtesy of Massachusetts Commandery Military Order of the Loyal Legion and the U.S. Army Military History Institute.

This drawing by wartime artist Conrad Wise Chapman, shows the extensive damage inflicted on Fort Sumter by the constant shelling from enemy guns. Despite the terribly battered condition of the fort, the Confederates held on knowing that if it fell Charleston would quickly follow. Reproduced from the collections of the Library of Congress.

A BALL

WILL BE GIVEN AT THE MASONIC HALL ON THIS EVENING, 8th Inst., at half past 8 o'clock. No Tickets can be got in consequence of all the Printing Offices being removed.

Admittance, **TWO DOLLARS.**

MANAGERS.

T. O. McDONOUGH.	P. T. MURPHY.
W. CLAIR.	W. ADDISON.

December 8

1w

As evidenced by this announcement of a ball to be given at the Masonic Hall, the enemy's continual bombardment of Charleston did not stop the city's social life. The proceeds from the ball would undoubtedly have been used to care for wounded soldiers, the relief of needy families, and/or other causes related to the war.
Taken from the Charleston *Mercury.*

This sketch of a nighttime bombardment of Fort Sumter shows Fort Sumter illuminated by a calcium light shining from an enemy fort on Morris Island. Drawn by Conrad Wise Chapman, and used courtesy of the Massachusetts Commandery Military Order of the Loyal Legion and the U.S. Army Military History Institute.

view of the fact that William Alexander considered it worth mentioning some three decades after the war had ended.[137]

From evidence presented it would appear that at about the same time that Reverend Johnson was making his "*pressing invitation*" to the crew of the *Hunley* to attend his Sunday services, Augustine Smythe was sending the following letter to his father informing him of the current situation at Charleston.

"*C.S.S. Palmetto State* November 18th, 1863. Dear Father: I do not believe that the Yankees will ever take Charleston, nor Ft. Sumter either, certainly not with their *Ironsides*. As to their destroying the city, they may do that, though in a measure only, for shelling from Morris Island is rather dangerous on their guns.

They commenced yesterday about ten a.m. And kept it up to two p.m., throwing 15 of 20 shells. They fell mostly in the neighborhood of Elliott Street and Broad. One knocked down a house on the corner of that and East Bay. Another entered the Telegraph office, another struck the city hall, or two in fact, not doing much damage, another fell on the North Wharf, though I don't know how much hurt it did, if any. The Greek Fire part was all humbug, as they did not set fire anywhere. The people were much frightened and ran all about the streets hunting for some safe place. There is one consolation, and that is their guns can't stand firing at such range.

They still keep up their firing on Sumter, though now principally from mortars, and seem to be saving their heavy guns. The old fort still stands, waving her flag in triumph, though it is over ruins, and firing her evening gun in defiance.

The Yankees have a powerful calcium light with which they throw a ray on the very wharf, and hinder our safe passage considerably. Fort Moultrie, the other night, put it out twice with her guns. I was on James Island this morning and went up into the lookout at the Battery Martello Tower, and had a magnificent view of the harbor. I could see the Yankees walking about on both Gregg and Wagner, watching the effect of their shot on Sumter. One of the Monitors lies around the point all the time as a lookout, and I could see the men walking on her turret and decks."

Just three days after Smythe sent the above letter to his father, a very interesting acknowledgment appeared in the *Charleston Mercury* under the column heading "THE SIEGE - ONE HUNDRED AND THIRTY THIRD DAY" and reads as follows: "Saturday, November 21, 1863. We have received from Captain Chisolm, his check for $250, for the benefit of the families of the five men who lost their lives in the submarine boat with Captain Hunley." Unfortunately this brief statement makes no mention as to how this money may have been raised, however judging from numerous advertisements in the cities two newspapers, its quite possible that some form of city wide fund raising activity may have transpired.

The Charleston newspapers Mercury, and Daily Courier reported several examples of fund raising activities. A good example of this can be seen in the form of a ball having been given just four days earlier in the Masonic Hall, for the benefit of Thomas McNeil of Charleston, who had lost both his eyes and an arm during the bombardment of Battery Wagner.

Although I was unable to find any mention of a similar affair having been staged for the benefit of the families related to the crew men who died with Captain Hunley; the mere fact that $250 had been received by the Mercury is a good indication that donations had been collected by some patriotic organization for that purpose.

At this point in our story, the reader may be wondering why Dixon and Alexander selected only five seamen from the *C.S.S. Indian Chief*, instead of seven, the number required to make up a full crew of nine. It seemed highly unlikely that the two officers would choose to go into action with less than a full crew. While reading each order issued in and around Charleston for the month of January 1864, the answer to this small mystery was revealed in the form of an order to the Chief Quartermaster. "January 10th 1864. The Chief Quartermaster will cause Lt. G.E. Dixon to be refunded his actual expenses for lodging and subsisting for four men in Charleston attached to the Sub-marine Torpedo Boat or Engine of War, from the 12th of November to the 16th of December 1863. being the sum of six hundred and thirty one (631) dollars.

It would appear that while the Charleston garrison continued to hold out against the ever-nearing enemy army, Dixon Alexander and two unidentified associates (perhaps the elusive Dillingham being one) were hastily given accommodations in a Charleston hotel. Judging from the above order, it would seem that the reason Dixon had only selected five men from the *Indian*

Chief had to do with the fact that he already had three volunteers with him. Although I was not able to learn the names of these associates, it would appear that they had accompanied Dixon from Mobile to assist him in the continued operation of the submarine. With these three men (of which Alexander was one), and the five sailors from the *C.S.S. Indian Chief*, Dixon would have had his full crew of nine.

From William Alexander's 1899 letter to Colonel J.G. Holmes (cited earlier), we find that Lt. Dixon, his three Mobile associates, "and several men of the torpedo Corps" were roomed at the Oldebeck boarding house (also known as the Victoria House) near the market at the corner of King and Princess Streets. In his letter Alexander stated that their lodgings were located *"in the shelled district"* and that Mrs. Oldebeck ran the house by herself for *"her husband had been engaged in blockade running and had been captured and was then in prison"*.

Since Alexander explicitly stated that their quarters were located in *"the shelled district"* it could be said with some confidence that Dixon, Alexander and their two unknown associates were within range of the federal guns throughout their stay in the city; and for this reason it may be no mystery as to why Dixon penned the following line in a letter to a friend written several weeks later. *"For the last six weeks I have not been out of the range of the shells"*.[138]

With repairs and maintenance to the *Hunley* proceeding well, it was not long before the small submarine was returned from her makeshift cradle to the cold, green water of Charleston Harbor. As the submarine gently rocked in her narrow slip, Dixon would have entered the vessel to personally inspect all the recently packed stuffing boxes to make absolutely sure that no water would enter his craft by way of the numerous iron shafts that passed through her hull. With the inspection complete, our young engineering officer would have then ordered his new crew to enter the dark interior of the vessel, and man their stations at the crankshaft.

As the nervous sailors took turns squeezing through the narrow hatches, the *Hunley* slowly bobbed and rolled under the weight of the men standing on her floating hull. After the anxious crew had awkwardly made their way to their positions, Alexander, the last to enter the vessel, would have cast off from the dock and closed his heavy iron hatch cover.

With the uneasy crew now at their stations, all eyes would have turned to their skipper at the forward hatch. After a short speech reaffirming the important nature of their duty and the critical importance of breaking the blockade that strangled the Confederacy, Dixon would have ordered the men to turn the crankshaft as he set course for the open harbor. The crew, bobbing intermittently up and down, turning the shaft in unison, kept the three-bladed propeller[139] whirling within its protective iron band.

This first excursion was probably no more than a familiarization or shakedown cruise. With thirteen men having already died within the very hull that was now being propelled across the harbor, Dixon would have allowed his new crew time to gain confidence in this contraption that they would soon be risking their lives in miles out to sea.

Throughout this period of instruction and training, Lieutenants Dixon, Alexander, and their two unidentified associates would return nightly to their hotel room in Charleston to discuss tactics and strategy. As the four men talked into the night, the muffled booms of far off explosions could be heard. Perhaps an unlucky blockade runner had been spotted by the Union fleet, and now desperately tried to run herself aground under the protective guns on Sullivan's Island.

During this period of intermittent bombardment, Charleston was alive with activity. Judging from the numerous advertisements in the cities two newspapers, announcing charity balls and concerts, it would appear that Charleston in many ways mirrored London during the second world war. Ragged Confederate soldiers on leave, who had never seen a city before, crowded the waterfront saloons, rubbing elbows with the many pick pockets and ladies of dubious reputation. Rowdy English blockade runner crews who had recently beaten the odds reveled in the streets, eagerly spending their newly acquired wealth. One Confederate naval officer described these temporary visitors as "A reckless lot who believed in eating, drinking and being merry for fear they would die on the morrow. Their actions reminded me of the stories of pirates in the West Indies."[140]

The crews and officers of such crews could be considered both patriots and adventurers, but above all they were entrepreneurs. A captain could make as much as $5,000 on just one trip from Nassau.[141] This was today's equivalent of $100,000. Those, like the fictional Rhett Butler in Gone With The

These giant mortars were used to lob explosive cannon balls into Fort Sumter from Morris Island.
Photo courtesy of the Library of Congress.

This sketch of the "Hunley" was made by Conrad Wise Chapman on December 2, 1863.
Used by permission of the Valentine Museum, Conrad Chapman Collection, Richmond, VA.

Wind, who headed combines with multiple ships, became rich beyond their wildest dreams.

One of these English blockade runners would later write "Hunting, Pig-sticking, steeple-chasing, big-game shooting, polo - I have done a little of each - all have their thrilling moments, but none can approach running a blockade."[142]

Against this backdrop of a city under siege, Dixon and his three associates would return nightly, passing the scattered rubble from blown out walls that now littered the streets. With training going well, Dixon, Alexander, and their two unnamed comrades may have occasionally attended one of Charleston's numerous concerts or charity balls advertised alongside the column containing the city obituaries. With the two officers both being in their mid twenties, the opportunity of wearing their best military attire to an event frequented by finely dressed Charleston belles may have been a welcome diversion from the drudgeries of the war. Such balls were undoubtedly attended by high-ranking military officers and their wives, thus making it an ideal setting to discuss the future of the *Hunley* over a glass of fine wine recently run through the blockade.

Dixon knew if he and his crew could sink just one enemy ship, headquarters would realize what they had, and build other submarines better and faster. They could then be shipped to the various ports currently under siege and blast them free of enemy ships. The blockade would be broken and perhaps independence won. This was the speech the young lieutenant most likely gave over and over again to any officer who cared to listen.

While Dixon and Alexander returned to the city on those nights that were seen as unsuited for training, the recently acquired *Indian Chief* crew was probably given quarters near the dock where the *Hunley* was moored. As this crew became more confident with the workings of their submarine, she could once again be seen diving around the harbor by the numerous Confederate sailors who had recently taken to calling her "The murdering machine."[143] With Dixon's confidence in his new crew growing daily, it was not long before he and Alexander once more returned to Confederate military headquarters to report that the *Hunley* was once again ready for action.

At about the same time that the two engineering officers were reporting for duty, Smythe was writing another letter to his father from the lower end of the city. "December 11th, 1863 My dear father: The yankees shelled again last night at three intervals: 8 pm, 2am and 4: 30 am, again this morning, and they even threw one just now. I have heard where only a few went. One corner of Pitt & Beaufain, one corner of Rutledge & Beaufain, one in Elliott street near Church, and one on Vendue range. They all pass over me here, and I hardly stop writing when they pass over. It is a horrible thing, this shelling the city at night, and with pauses between, as if to catch us unaware, when they know there are women and children in the city.

This morning there was quite an excitement down the harbor. Fire and smoke was seen issuing from Sumter, and the Yankees were firing at her with a vengeance, while our batteries replied with equal vigor. - (Dinner) - I heard afterwards from a boat that had been sent there that the ammunition for small arms had taken fire and exploded, but not seriously injuring the fort. Several were killed and wounded by it though! The Yanks did pour in the shots when they saw the smoke. Augustine."

Two days after Smythe had sent the above letter to his father, the following order was issued by Confederate military headquarters. "Charleston, S.C., December 14, 1863, Special Orders, Number 271. First Lieut. George E. Dixon, Twenty-first Regiment Alabama Volunteers, will take command and direction of the Submarine Torpedo-Boat *H.L. Hunley*, and proceed to-night to the mouth of the harbor, or as far as capacity of the vessel will allow, and will sink and destroy any vessel of the enemy with which he can come in conflict.

All officers of the Confederate army in this department are commanded, and all naval officers are requested, to give such assistance to Lieutenant Dixon in the discharge of his duties as may be practicable, should he apply therefor. By command of General Beauregard."[144]

With the posting of these orders, Dixon and his newly trained crew of underwater raiders were at last to be unleashed on the unsuspecting enemy fleet. Tension must have run high that afternoon as the *Hunley's* anxious crew readied their diving machine for her first nocturnal excursion outside the harbor. The last time the craft had ventured past Sumter's shattered walls was in late August under the command of James McClintock. With the nocturnal positions of the ironclad's constantly changing, no one knew what to expect once the *Hunley* had passed beyond the relatively safe waters of the harbor. If the submarine accidentally ran aground on a shoal or hidden sandbar and was

Union Army battery during the bombardment of Charleston. Note the spare gun tube sitting on chocks in the foreground.
Photo courtesy of the Library of Congress.

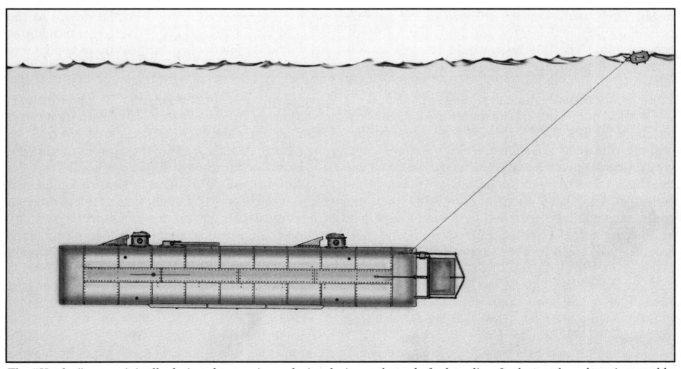

The "Hunley" was originally designed to tow its explosive device at the end of a long line. In theory, the submarine would dive under an enemy ship drawing the mine against the hull. This worked well in tests in the protected waters of Charleston Harbor, but it quickly became clear that it was not practical in the strong currents and heavy seas found offshore.
Illustration adapted from a drawing by Caldwell Whistler.

This receipt shows that David Broadfoot was paid $50.00 for a marine compass to be used on the 'Submarine Boat.' This was probably the compass requisitioned by Dixon on November 15, 1863. Dixon's requisition is shown on page 123 of this book. Receipt courtesy of the U.S. National Archives. $50.00 Confederate note from the author's collection.

captured by an enemy picket boat, what would be their fate?

From William Alexander's post-war writings, we are informed that both he and Dixon constantly sought out the older coast pilots around Charleston to get as much information as possible regarding the winter currents and sandbars that lay beyond Fort Sumter. With their charts marked with the compiled information on the currents carefully stowed aboard their submarine, Dixon and his brave crew of adventurers pushed off after dark to seek out and destroy any enemy vessel that could be observed through the sub's tiny view ports.

This first nocturnal patrol was probably an awkward experience plagued by mistakes and uncertainty. William Alexander informs us that the strong currents at the harbor entrance caused great difficulty with the line which towed the torpedo. From his 1903 Munsey magazine article we are told, "The torpedo was a copper cylinder holding a charge of ninety pounds of explosive, with percussion and primer mechanism, set off by triggers. It was originally intended to float the torpedo on the surface of the water, towed by the boat, which was to dive under the vessel to be attacked. In experiments made with some old flat boats in smooth water, this plan operated successfully, but in a seaway the torpedo was continually coming too near our craft."

Along with the drifting torpedo and strong currents that severely hindered navigation, the enemy picket boats that patrolled around the ironclads would also have presented a constant source of danger. With enemy calcium lights continually scanning the surface of the black water, Dixon would have surfaced his craft for air and observations only when absolutely necessary. That first awkward night out amongst the enemy ironclads must have been an unforgettable experience.

During the course of this long chaotic night, it would seem that Dixon discovered that the prolonged cranking from Mount Pleasant to the mouth of the harbor had caused too much additional fatigue on his crew. For following this first unsuccessful attack, it was decided that the *Hunley* should be towed to the mouth of the harbor whenever possible by a steam vessel, so that the men within the craft would not exhaust themselves while still in safe waters.

From the dates previously cited in Dixon's lodging refund from the Chief Quartermaster (November 12th through the 16th of December), we can say with some certainty that within 48 hours after General Beauregard had ordered the *Hunley* back into action, Dixon and his three associates moved from their room at the Victoria House Hotel to join their crew on the Mount Pleasant side of the harbor. From the 1899 letter written by Alexander to Colonel J.G. Holmes we know that for much of December and January the crew was quartered in "*an old abandoned house*" near the Mount Pleasant docks.[145]

With Morris Island now under the complete control of the enemy army, it would seem that The Cove behind Fort Moultrie (the assumed mooring used by the McClintock crew in late August), was now considered unsatisfactory. Possibly the currents at the nearby entrance to the harbor were simply too great or the anchorage was too shallow and thus too limited by the tide. Another explanation would be that there were simply too many federal pickets at the harbor's main entrance for the submarine's activities to go unobserved. Mount Pleasant, although much further from the harbor's entrance, appears to have been the *Hunley's* base of operations for several weeks following the orders issued by headquarters on December 14, 1863.

Hopefully her new compass would do its job. With the submarine once again moving against the Union fleet her crew didn't need compass problems compounding the difficulties already associated with towing the deadly torpedo. The last thing they needed was to become disoriented while diving beneath the keels of the blockading fleet in the middle of the night. With ninety pounds of gun powder rigged to explode at the slightest touch, floating less than 200' from their hull, the thought of surfacing for air while the device floated above them must have been a source of constant dread.

From a receipt dated December 18, that was filed with the Charleston Quartermaster, surviving evidence suggests that the Confederate States of America paid $50.00 for a marine compass sold to them by David Broadfoot on December 7, 1863.[146] The receipt may be an indication that Broadfoot, after raising the ill-fated Hunley twice with his partner Angus Smith, had taken an active role in re-outfitting the diving machine, and was involved in trying to resolve the difficulties Dixon was experiencing with the vessel.

Shortly after locating this receipt for the marine compass, I was lucky enough to stumble upon yet another army requisition dated to within ten days of Broadfoot's purchase. It would seem that Dixon and Alexander were slowly settling into their accommodations in Mount Pleasant and required utensils in which to cook their ever dwindling army rations: "SPECIAL REQUISITION for Lt. George E. Dixon, Commanding Sub-Marine Boat. One camp kettle, one mess pan, Received at Mount Pleasant, December, 1863."[147] Based on the requisition, the crew of the *Hunley* probably cooked their own rations (which typically included salt pork and hardtack, some rice and/or greens) around a common fire, while they uneasily joked about the numerous dangers they would be facing when they took their craft to sea.

The camaraderie shared by this group of underwater pioneers must have been even more intense than the much celebrated friendships found among the bomber crews during World War II. Although bomber crews developed fierce loyalties that grew from shared dangers (past, present and future), they knew that the crews of other planes were facing similar risks every day. Although they faced awesome dangers, they could see the successes of others. The *Hunley's* men could not take such comfort. They were alone. There was no one around who could say "I did it, you can too." Instead the only ones who had tried before had died. They were training to be the first men in history to move against an enemy ship from a vessel that attacked from beneath the surface. Well meaning comments from people who had no first hand knowledge of the risks and problems involved would have done little to relieve the fears each crew member would have felt. These first sub-mariners would have been forced to turn to each other for encouragement, and a bond like no other would have developed.

The invisible barrier that separates an officer from his subordinates could have presumably blurred aboard the submarine; all within the vessel's tiny hull knew that the fate of one was in fact the fate of all. Either they would sink an enemy ship together or be killed together in the attempt. With the enemy grip on Charleston tightening daily, this small group of undersea warriors was well aware that they were the city's best hope of breaking free of the terrible blockade that was slowly bringing the Confederacy to its knees.

At this point, I would like to remind the reader as to what William Alexander wrote about the character of this crew forty years after the War:

"I don't believe a man considered the danger that awaited him. The honor of being the first to engage the enemy in this novel way overshadowed all else."

From existing evidence, it would appear that shortly after Dixon had decided that a nightly tow from a steam vessel would greatly reduce fatigue, he reported to military headquarters with his request, and was in turn directed to the skipper of the small steam powered torpedo boat *David*.[148]

Although legend, encouraged by the wife of one of the David's owners has it that the craft was named after the biblical story of David and Goliath, her builder, David Ebaugh, later wrote that he had named the first boat for himself.[149] She was the namesake of an entire class of about twelve of these cigar shaped torpedo boats. According to Ebaugh's post-war letters, some of the *Davids* were steam powered and some were hand cranked. This probably explains why many contemporary records refer to the *Hunley* as a *David*.

On the night of October 5th, 1863 this semi-submersible vessel had attacked the Goliath of the blockading fleet: the U.S.S. *Ironsides*. With an explosive device attached to the end of a long spar, and her narrow hull hidden beneath the dark surface, she had been able to approach the massive vessel undetected. Upon impacting the vessel's thick iron hull with her contact torpedo, a huge geyser was thrown high into the air, sending some of the water into the *David's* tiny smoke stack. With the fires extinguished and the vessel swamping badly, Lieutenant Glassel, the torpedo boat's skipper, ordered his three-man crew to abandon ship. Within minutes he and the fireman were both captured and taken aboard the slightly damaged *Ironsides*. From the following letter filed by the *Ironsides* Commanding Officer, Captain Rowan we read his official report of the incident.

"*U.S.S. New Ironsides*. Off Morris Island, S.C. October 6, 1863. Rear-Admiral J.A. Dahlgren, Sir: I have the honor to report the circumstances attending the explosion of a torpedo against the side of this ship last night at quarter past nine o'clock.

About a minute before the explosion, a small object was seen by the sentinels and hailed by them as a boat, and also by Mr. Howard, Officer of the Deck, from the gangway, receiving no answer, he gave the order 'fire into her', the sentinels delivered their fire, and immediately the ship received a very severe explosion, throwing a column of water upon the Spar deck, and into the engine room. The object

This photo was taken by Matthew Brady shortly after the fall of Charleston, and shows one of the "David" class torpedo boats abandoned by the Confederates. Davids were ballasted so they had a low silhouette, but were not true submarines. Photo courtesy of the U.S. Library of Congress.

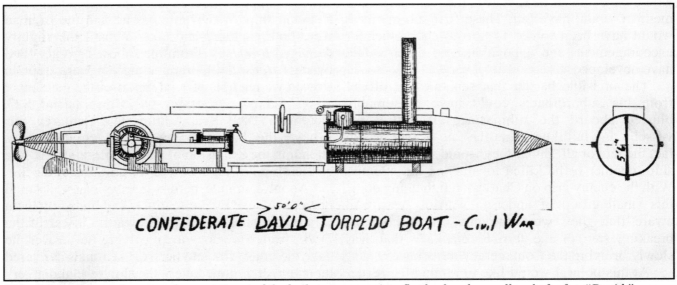

This diagram shows the general arrangement of the boiler, steam engine, flywheel and propeller shaft of a "David." Photo courtesy of Dr. William J. Morgan and the U.S. Naval Historical Center.

The "David" at Charleston, South Carolina in 1863. Painted by Conrad Chapman. U.S. Naval Historical Center photograph released.

fired at proved to be, (as I subsequently learned from one of the prisoners), a Torpedo Steamer, shaped like a cigar, fifty feet long by five feet in diameter, and of great speed, and so submerged, that the only portion of her visible was the combings of her hatch, which were only two feet above the waters edge, and about ten feet in length.

The Torpedo boat was commanded by Lt. Commander Glassell, formally a lieutenant in our navy, and now our prisoner. He states that the explosion threw a column of water over the little craft, which put out the fires and left it without motive power, and it drifted past the ship.

Nothing could be seen from the gun deck and to fire at random would endanger the fleet of transport and other vessels near us. The Marine guard and musketeers on the Spar deck saw a small object at which a very severe fire was kept up, until it drifted out of sight. Two of our cutters were dispatched in search of it, but returned without success.

I hope our fire destroyed the Torpedo steamer. Lt. Commander Glassel acknowledges that he and Engineer Tombs, and Pilot, who constituted the crew at the time of the explosion, were compelled to abandon the vessel, and being provided with life preservers swam for their lives. Glassel hailed one of our coal schooners as he drifted past, and was rescued from a grave he designed for the crew of this ship."[150]

Unbeknown to Captain Rowan at the time, it would seem that as the little *David* had slowly drifted away from her victim, Assistant Engineer Tomb had swum back to the crippled vessel and found the pilot, who could not swim, clinging to the rudder of the lifeless craft. Together the two men were able to climb back aboard the vessel, relight the fire, and limp back into Charleston harbor. Upon inspecting the craft the following day, her hull was found to contain no less than 13 bullet holes, undeniable proof of the two men's narrow escape.

Of the event Admiral Dahlgren would write. "Among the many inventions with which I have been familiar, I have seen none which have acted so perfectly at first trial. The secrecy, rapidity of movement, control of direction, and precise explosion indicate, I think the introduction of the torpedo element as a means of certain warfare. It can be ignored no longer."[151]

As luck would have it, Lt. Commander Glassel and his fireman were both found to have detailed diagrams of the little *David* in the pockets of their uniforms. Within hours, the entire blockading fleet had drawings of the vessel, along with a full description of her capabilities.

Publicly Admiral Dahlgren was furious over the attack and stated that both prisoners should be taken to New York harbor, tried and hung, "for using an engine of war not recognized by civilized nations." [152]

However, privately the Admiral was truly impressed with the design of the *David* and considered the craft to be quite ingenious. Upon reporting the *David's* attack to Charleston military headquarters, and the story of the two men's narrow escape, Assistant Engineer Tomb became an instant local hero; was promoted to Chief Engineer and given full command of the torpedo boat.

From a 1908 letter written by James Tomb (in the collection of Charleston Maritime Historian Dr. Charles Perry) comes proof that Dixon and Tomb were well acquainted prior to their meetings to discuss the nightly towing of the *Hunley*. This should not be a surprise for both men commanded similar vessels and would have been interested in the other's opinion regarding their craft's attack efficiency. From post-war writings of Tomb we are informed of the following:

"There was a submarine torpedo boat, not under the orders of the navy, and I was ordered to tow her down the harbor three or four times by Flag-officer Tucker, who also gave me orders to report as to her efficiency as well as safety. "Tomb went on to say: " Lieutenant Dixon was a very brave and cool headed man, and had every confidence in his boat, but had great trouble when under the water from lack of air and light. She was very slow in turning, but would sink at a moment's notice and at times without it."[153]

From the 1908 Tomb letter in the collection Dr. Perry comes the following short passage regarding Dixon's apparent pursuit of an alternative light source.

"At the time we met him (Dixon) he was trying to secure a light that would not impair the air in the boat while submerged, he said it was very disagreeable at times when below the surface." From the above passage it could be assumed that the crew of the *Hunley* may have experimented with various forms of phosphorescent algae or other luminous materials as a secondary light sources when the candle flickered out from lack of oxygen.

Soon after the start of the two men's joint

Attack on the U.S.S. Ironsides by the Confederate torpedo boat David. Harper's Weekly

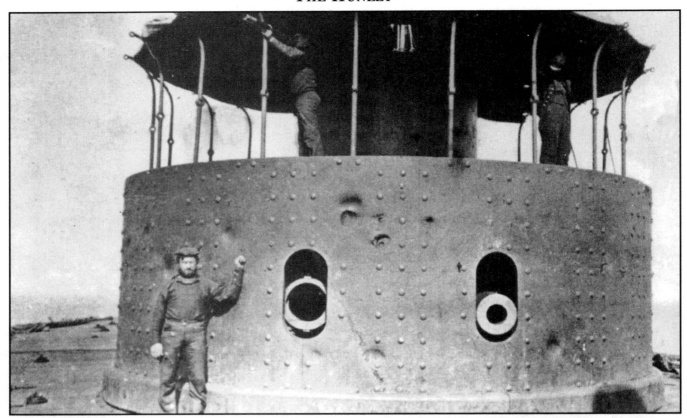

Photos taken off Charleston, Summer, 1863. Note the numerous deep dents made by Confederate cannon balls in the turret of this monitor, and the large caliber of its formidable guns. Reproduced from the Collections of the Library of Congress.

In early January, 1864, the "Hunley's" base of operations was moved from the harbor to Breach Inlet, where it went out an average of four nights a week, often going six or seven miles offshore. This map clearly shows Breach Inlet and the creeks and marsh between Sullivan's Island and Mount Pleasant.
Courtesy of the U.S. National Archives.

operation, it would appear that Tomb became highly critical of the way in which the submarine was to attack her victims. He seems to have felt that the suction caused by a sinking ship filling with water, might draw the *Hunley* inside the hull through the gaping hole caused by the explosion. Turning once again to his post-war writings we are told "In my report to him (Flag-officer Tucker) I stated that the only way to use a torpedo was on the same plan as the '*David*' - that is, a spar torpedo - and to strike with his boat on the surface, the torpedo being lowered to 8 feet. Should she attempt to use a torpedo as Lieutenant Dixon intended, by submerging the boat and striking from below, the level of the torpedo would be above his own boat, and as she had little buoyancy and no power, the chances were the suction caused by the water passing into the sinking ship would prevent her from rising to the surface."

In spite of Engineer Tomb's objections concerning the manner in which the *Hunley* was to deliver her death blow, towing operations from Mount Pleasant to the mouth of the harbor began immediately. As the weary citizens of Charleston prepared to celebrate their third war-time Christmas under the very guns of the enemy army, Dixon and his dedicated crew readied their submarine for yet another night among the ironclads.

Based on harbor charts, the *David* probably towed the *Hunley* about one or two miles on nights that the weather permitted. As the submarine gently rocked from side to side at the end of her tow line, nervous laughter probably echoed from the small sub's damp iron walls. With nothing to do during their monotonous tow, the crew would have undoubtedly talked and joked among themselves, trying to free their minds of the numerous dangers all knew awaited them at the mouth of the harbor. Standing at his station in the rear of the vessel was Alexander, straining his eyes in the darkness trying to catch a glimpse of the deadly torpedo that followed in their wake.

Dixon stood at the forward hatch, his head and shoulders above the rim, occasionally catching bits of spray while he watched the long rope attached to the stern of the *David* strain under the weight of his submarine. As the two strange vessels slowly made their way to the mouth of the harbor, his thoughts may have wandered to his sweetheart in far off Alabama who was anxiously awaiting his return. If the Confederacy's luck changed, and all went well with the war, perhaps this time next year they would be married, and he could once again return to the life he loved as a steamboat engineer along the Mobile River.

With the ruins of Fort Sumter hazily coming into view, he would have quickly returned to the present and retreated further into the dark faintly lit hull to inform his crew of their progress. As the small candle flickered next to their newly acquired compass, all on board probably took a moment for a silent prayer, and hoped that the war would not last until the following Christmas.

As the two vessels slowly passed the shattered walls of Fort Sumter, the sentries standing guard paused a moment to watch the strange pair pass by on their way out to sea. Soon after the two war machines had left the fort far behind, talking turned to whispers. The soft vibration from the pulse of the *David's* steam engine, felt through the *Hunley's* hull, suddenly slowed as the torpedo boat prepared to cast the *Hunley* free. While the submarine drifted in the moon light, Dixon leaned over the rim of the conning tower and slipped the tow line into the sea. With a wave to the crew of the *David* and a whispered thanks, Dixon quietly sealed his hatch while his anxious crew readied themselves for the long night in enemy waters that lay before them.

With both hatches dogged, Dixon pulled his watch from the pocket of his grease stained uniform to check the time. If luck were with them, they would return to the relative safety of the harbor before the sun rose in nine hours. As the flickering candle cast eerie shadows on the wet walls of the submarine, Dixon nodded his orders to the crew. With a groaning lurch, the crankshaft started turning in its iron braces, sending a squeaking echo throughout the cramped, dimly lit hull. As Tomb slowly headed his torpedo boat towards the safety of the harbor, he saw the rear hatch of the tiny submarine gently vanish beneath the dark waves. With her deadly torpedo following in her wake, the *Hunley* once again set out to do battle with the unsuspecting iron ships of the enemy fleet.

Its known from the post-war writings of James Tomb that the scene just described was repeated several times during late December and early January of 1864. Surviving documentation would suggest that the order issued on December 14, 1863, directing the *Hunley* to "proceed to the mouth of the harbor and sink any vessel of the enemy which comes in conflict" was in fact a standing order granting Dixon a sort of roving commission to be acted upon whenever the weather permitted. It was soon found during one of these nocturnal excursions, that the enemy navy had deployed an elaborate system of chain booms around their ironclads, designed to defend their hulls against a torpedo attack by a *David*-class vessel. Much to Dixon's dismay, this same system would also have been a very effective defense against the type of torpedo employed by the *Hunley*.

With Dixon's detached duty in South Carolina quickly coming to an end, it would seem that his unique services were considered too valuable to the defense of Charleston to allow him to return to his post with the 21st Alabama; for on the morning of January 5, 1864, the following message was telegraphed to Colonel Garner (General Maury's Chief of Staff). "PLEASE EXTEND LIEUTENANT DIXON'S DETAIL 30 DAYS LONGER."[154]

Within hours a response was received from Maury's headquarters granting permission for Dixon to remain in Charleston until the end of January. In spite of the disturbing discovery that the ironclads were well defended against all sorts of contact mines, Tomb, and the crew of the *David* continued to tow the *Hunley* past Fort Sumter whenever weather conditions allowed. This arrangement continued until one night in early January when near disaster forced an end to the operation.

It would appear that while the *David* paused at some point during her towing of the *Hunley*, the torpedo line that towed the explosive device drifted along side the *David* and became entangled in her rudder assembly. Under the very guns of the nearby enemy fleet, Tomb and Dixon watched in horror as the deadly explosive slowly drifted alongside their two vessels. One can only imagine the terror felt by everyone present as the ninety pound cylinder, brisling with contact detonators, gently tapped the wooden hull of the helpless torpedo boat. Immediately someone was dispatched into the icy water to fend off the lethal device that threatened to destroy the *David* as well as the *Hunley*. While both crews held their breath, this unnamed hero shivering in the freezing water, somehow managed to clear the tow line from the rudder and push the deadly device back to where it belonged.

Though the candle consumed oxygen and would flicker out after about 25 minutes, it was found that the "Hunley" could remain submerged for 2 1/2 hours. Used by permission and courtesy of the City of Mobile Museum.

ORDER, No. 2.

Flag Steamer Philadelphia,
OFF MORRIS ISLAND, S. C., Jan. 7, 1864.

I have reliable information that the Rebels have two Torpedo Boats ready for service, which may be expected on the first night when the water is suitable for their movement. One of these is the David which attacked the Ironsides in October, the other is similar to it.

There is also one of another kind, which is nearly submerged, and can be entirely so; it is intended to go under the bottoms of vessels and there operate.

This is believed by my informant to be sure of well working, though from bad management it has hitherto met with accidents, and was lying off Mount Pleasant two nights since.

There being every reason to expect a visit from some or all of these Torpedoes, the greatest vigilance will be needed to guard against them.

The Iron Clads must have their fenders rigged out, and their own boats in motion about them.

A netting must also be dropped overboard from the ends of the fenders, kept down with shot, and extending along the whole length of the sides; Howitzers loaded with Canister on the decks and a Calcium for each Monitor.

The Tugs and Picket Boats must be incessantly upon the look out when the water is not rough, whether the weather be clear or rainy.

I observe the Iron Clads are not anchored so as to be entirely clear of each other's fire if opened suddenly in the dark. This must be corrected, and Captain Rowan will assign the Monitors suitable positions for this purpose, particularly with reference to his own vessel.

It is also advisable not to anchor in the deepest part of the channel; for by not leaving much space between the bottom of the vessel and the bottom of the channel, it will be impossible for the diving Torpedo to operate except on the sides, and there will be less difficulty in raising a vessel if sunk.

JOHN A. DAHLGREN,
Rear Admiral, Commanding
South Atlantic Blockading Squadron.

Orders to the South Atlantic Blockading Squadron advising them of three Confederate torpedo boats, two being surface bound vessels, and the third (the "Hunley") being capable of going under vessels "and there operate." Dahlgren then outlines steps to be taken to protect the vessels of the fleet.
Courtesy of U.S. National Archives.

From the post-war writings of Tomb we are informed as to the consequences of this near tragic event. "The last night the *David* towed him (Lt. Dixon) down the harbor, his torpedo got foul of us and came near blowing up both boats before we got it clear of the bottom, where it had drifted. I let him go after passing Fort Sumter, and on my making report of this, Flag-Officer Tucker refused to have the *David* tow him again."[155]

At about the same time that Tucker was putting an end to the nightly towing operations from Mount Pleasant, Admiral John A. Dahlgren, commanding the United States South Atlantic Blockading Squadron, was being briefed as to the description and present location of a small Confederate diving machine known as the *H.L. Hunley*. On the night of January 5, 1864, seaman Shipp and Belton of the *C.S.S. Indian Chief* had stolen a small skiff and deserted to the Union fleet. When questioned about Charleston Harbor defenses and the latest location of the *David*, they told a tale that quickly sent shock waves through the blockading fleet. The stunned naval officers were told that the Confederacy not only possessed a torpedo boat that could be submerged up to her smoke stack, they were also informed as to the existence of an iron submarine boat that could deliver a death blow to any ship afloat without ever coming to the surface.

The lengthy reports taken from these two deserters[156] are filled with detailed descriptions about harbor defenses, shore batteries, ironclads, life in the city, and military morale. From the several pages of testimony (now on microfilm at the National Archives), I would like to share the following extracts with the reader.

"She is about 35 feet long, height about the same as the *David* (5 1/2 feet). Has a propeller at the end, she is not driven by steam, but her propeller is turned by hand. Has two man heads on the upper side about 12 or 14 feet apart. the entrance into her is through these man heads, the heads being turned back, they are all used to look out of.

She has had bad accidents but was owing to those in her not understanding her. She can be worked perfectly safe by persons who understand her. Can be driven 5 knots an hour without exertion to the men working her. When she went down the last time, was on the bottom 2 weeks before she was raised. Saw her when she was raised the last time. They then hoisted her out of the harbor, refitted her and got another crew. Saw her after that submerged, Saw her go under the *Indian Chief*, and then saw her go back under again. She made about 1/2 mile in the dives. Saw her go under the *Charleston* - went under about 250 feet from her and come up about 300 feet beyond her, was about 20 minutes under the water. Believes she is at Mount Pleasant. One of her crew who belongs to his vessel came back for his clothes and said she was going down there as a station." Within hours after this testimony was given, Dahlgren issued the following orders to the fleet:

"ORDER No. 2, January 7, 1864. I have reliable information that the Rebels have two torpedo boats ready for service, which may be expected on the first night when the weather is suitable for their movement. One of these is the *David* which attacked the *Ironsides* in October, the other is similar to it.

There is also one of another kind, which is nearly submerged, and can be entirely so; it is intended to go under the bottoms of vessels and there operate. This is believed by my informant to be sure of well working, though from bad management it has hereto met with accidents, and was lying off Mount Pleasant two nights since. There being every reason to expect a visit from some or all of these torpedoes, the greatest vigilance will be needed to guard against them. The ironclads must have their fenders rigged out, and their own boats in motion about them. A netting must also be dropped overboard from the ends of the fenders, kept down with shot, and extended along the whole length of the sides; howitzers loaded with canister on the decks and a calcium (search light) for each monitor.

The tugs and picket boats must be incessantly upon the lookout, when the water is not rough, whether the weather is clear or rainy. I observe the ironclads are not anchored so as to be entirely clear of each others fire if opened suddenly in the dark. This must be corrected, and Captain Rowan will assign the monitors suitable positions for this purpose, particularly with reference to his own vessel.

It is also advisable not to anchor in the deepest part of the channel; for by not leaving much space between the bottom of the vessel and the bottom of the channel, it will be impossible for the diving torpedo to operate except on the sides, and there will be less difficulty in raising a vessel if sunk."

By a strange twist of fate, it would seem that at precisely the same time that Dahlgren learned of the existence and location of the *Hunley*; issued orders to the inner circle of ironclads to increase their defenses, by hanging nets from their fenders, and anchor in shallow water after dark, plans were being made by Dixon and Alexander to relocate the submarine from Mount Pleasant and turn their attention towards the less protected wooden hulls of the vessels anchored further out to sea.

With the towing services from the *David* abruptly canceled by Tucker, our two officers had to find another mooring from which to strike out at the enemy fleet. From the now well-quoted post-war writings of William Alexander we are informed of the following "On account of chain booms having been put around the *Ironsides* and the monitors in Charleston harbor to keep us off these vessels, we had to turn our attention to the fleet outside."[157]

On the morning of January 10, just 72 hours after Dahlgren had been informed as to the existence of the *Hunley*, Dixon and Alexander crossed the marshes between Mount Pleasant and Sullivan's Island to seek out a new mooring closer to the open sea and the blockading fleet. In Dixon's pocket was the following order from Confederate headquarters to Brig. General W.S. Walker commanding the third military district:

"Charleston, S.C. January 10th, 1864 General: I am instructed by the commanding General to inform you that Lieutenant Dixon, the bearer of this, goes to your district for the purpose of monitoring the several positions of the enemy in your front with a view to operations (by water) against the enemy. The commanding General directs that you furnish Lt. Dixon with every possible facility for carrying out his plans."[158]

Of all the orders, requisitions, letters, and dispatches I have been fortunate enough to locate during the course of my investigation, I feel that this order is one of the most significant. With the ironclads at the mouth of the harbor well-defended against any sort of contact mine, and the towing services of the *David* now denied, Dixon, instead of canceling the operation, decided that the *Hunley's* new objective would be the main fleet lying further out to sea. Evidence to be presented shortly indicates that Dixon's commanding officer Captain John Cothran (who later wrote of Dixon: "I never knew a better man, and there never was a braver man in any service of any army.") was constantly requesting him to return to his post with the 21st Alabama in Mobile.

Like everyone else connected with the ill fated *Hunley*, Dixon himself was a volunteer. With the situation appearing hopeless, and Dixon's commanding officer requesting him to return to Mobile, it would have been quite easy to abandon the operation. Instead, it was decided that the submarine would be relocated away from the harbor and start operations against the ships located several miles out to sea. Up to this point, the *Hunley* had only ventured a mile or two past the mouth of the harbor. Now they would be attempting to attack ships that would require several hours of hard cranking to reach.

Again from William Alexander's post-war writings, we are informed as to the course of action taken by Dixon and the crew of the *Hunley*: "We were ordered to moor the boat off Battery Marshall, on Sullivan's Island. The nearest vessel which we understood to be the United States Frigate *Wabash*, was about twelve miles off, and she was our objective point from this time on." [159]

As luck would have it, while searching through the numerous faded Confederate documents at the National Archives, I happened on a hastily written requisition that would have been meaningless if not for the date. "January 14th, 1864 Major: It is the wish of the Commanding general that you shall furnish Lieutenant Dixon with a light row boat such as one he may select."[160]

It would seem that Dixon had decided that Battery Marshall, located on the northern tip of Sullivan's Island, was indeed a suitable mooring from which to strike out at the enemy fleet. He appears to have requested the rowboat so that he and his crew could locate a navigable route by which to float the submarine through the thick marshes and shallow water ways that connected the harbor with Breach Inlet.

From the Charleston Headquarters Journal of Operations we find that during those awkward days of re-deployment a severe winter cold front had moved into the Charleston area, accompanied by a thick fog that lingered for several days. From the period in question we find journal notations reading (January, 14) "rainy and foggy" and (January, 18) "The fog is so great that it is hard to obtain observations".

On January 13, 1864, (just 24 hours before Dixon and his crew received their "light row boat" and presumably found a navigable route through the foggy rain swept marshes behind Sullivan's Island), Admiral Dahlgren had sent an urgent

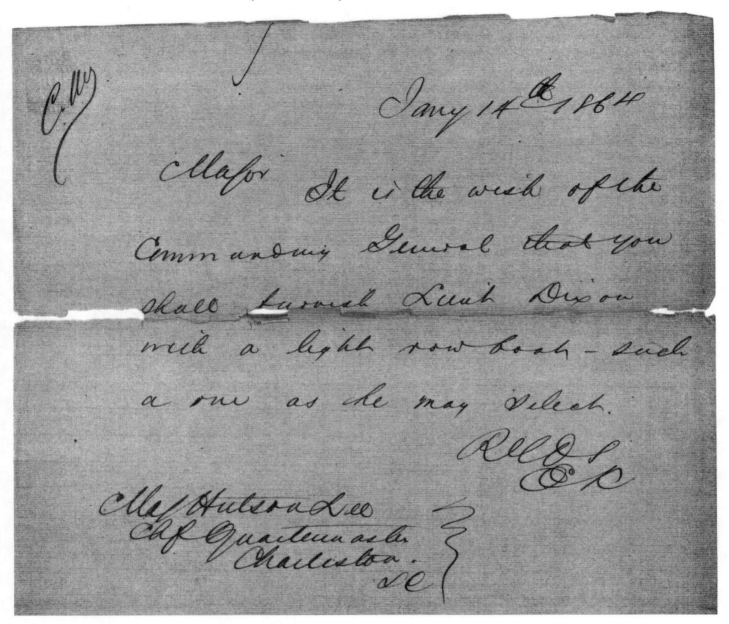

Short note regarding a row boat that was to be given to Lt. Dixon. National Archives.

communication to Secretary of the Navy Gideon Welles, informing him as to the existence of a diving machine that the Confederates had stationed at Mount Pleasant. After reacquainting the secretary with the description of the *David* class torpedo boats, Dahlgren penned the following information regarding this new threat to the fleet.

"The *Diver* as she is called is also ready, and with the original *David* is now at Mount Pleasant on the lookout for a chance. The action of the *David* has been of course pretty well exemplified on the *Ironsides* - That of the *Diver* is different, as it is intended to submerge completely, get under the bottom, attach the torpedo, haul off and pull trigger.

So far the trials have been unlucky, having drowned three crews of seventeen men in all. (The admiral was misinformed as to the number of accidental sinkings.) Still she does dive, as one of the deserters saw her pass twice under the bottom of the vessel he was in, and once under the *Charleston*."[161]

While Dixon and Alexander prepared to move the submarine from the harbor to Breach Inlet, surviving evidence indicates that they were also redesigning the means by which the *Hunley* would deliver her explosive device. Instead of towing her deadly cargo at the end of a long tow line, miles out to sea in unpredictable currents, she would now attack the wooden ships utilizing an explosive

Union sailors pose for a photograph while on blockade duty. Reproduced from the Collections of the Library of Congress.

These captured blockade runners would have been tried before a United States prize court before being sold at auction, or pressed into service as part of the ever expanding Union blockade. U.S. Navy photo courtesy of the U.S. National Archives.

charge attached to a harpoon like spar extending from the bow.

From an article by Lt. Harry Von Kolnitz, USN, titled "The Confederate Submarine" that appeared in the October, 1937, issue of U.S. Naval Institute Proceedings, we are given a good description as to how this new method of torpedo delivery functioned. "A torpedo was designed which could be mounted on a short pole and which would delay it's explosion until the attacking vessel could back off to a safe position. It consisted of a steel head which fitted as a thimble over the end of the ten foot spar or pipe projecting from the bow. This was driven into the enemy's wooden hull by ramming and was retained there by saw-toothed corrugations when the fish boat backed off. As it slipped off the spar, it would keep with it the torpedo, which was a simple copper can of powder fitted with a trigger. This trigger was attached to a cord lanyard carried on a reel on deck and after the boat had backed a safe distance, 150 yards, the rope was to tighten and would trip the trigger." (Based partially on Dixon's requisition of October 10, 1863, I feel it was 150 feet, not 150 yards.[162])

Unfortunately the author of the above article failed to give the source of his information. In the course of my own research regarding this new form of torpedo delivery, I was fortunate enough to find a news article written just five years after the end of the War from which Von Kolnitz may have derived his intriguing description of the delivery system used by the *Hunley* after early January 1864.

From an article that appeared in the Charleston Daily Republican of October 8, 1870, headlined "The Remarkable Career of a Remarkable Craft" we read "General Beauregard changed the arrangement of the torpedo by fastening it to the bow. It's front was terminated by a sharp and barbed lance-head so that when the boat was driven end on against a ship's sides, the lance head would be forced deep into the timbers below the water line, and would fasten the torpedo firmly against the ship. Then the torpedo boat would back off and explode it by a lanyard."

Contemporary writings would suggest that this new form of torpedo delivery was introduced at about the same time that the *Hunley* was being relocated to Sullivan's Island; however, this type of torpedo configuration may have been regarded as a secondary means of attack since the beginning. With the water in Mobile Bay so shallow, a spar torpedo may have been considered as a method of attack before the *Hunley* ever came to Charleston. Since a lance-headed torpedo could not be used against the metal armor of the ironclads, this method of attack may have been abandoned after the submarine was brought to South Carolina.

A very interesting scrap of evidence, suggesting that the spar torpedo had always been considered a potential mode of attack, comes from the Chapman sketch dated December 2, 1863. In this drawing the reel spindle behind the forward conning tower can be clearly seen; cocked off to the side so that the line running from it would not interfere with the forward diving planes.

From a 1916 news article that appeared in the *San Antonio Express* entitled *Texan Gave World First Successful Submarine Torpedo*; we learn that E.C. Singer (and at least part of his staff of underwater explosives designers), had by late December returned to Charleston. From the pages of this fascinating news story relating the adventures shared by The Singer Submarine Corp during the war years, it is stated by the author that Singer torpedoes were used exclusively with the little submarine boat, and that Captain E.C. Singer had personally fabricated the explosive device that was to be used at the end of the *Hunley's* spar.

From the following evidence found within the faded pages of the Confederate Engineering Departments letter book, we find undeniable proof that Mr. Singer had indeed returned to Charleston, for the Engineering Department in Richmond seemed to want detailed information regarding the design of the groups little torpedo boat. From the collection of letters sent from the Capital in late December of 1863, we read the following.

"December 23, 1863. Mr. E.C. Singer and Company, Care of Colonel Harris, Chief of Engineers, Charleston, S.C. Gentlemen: Please furnish this Bureau as promptly as possible with the plans of a torpedo boat best adapted in your opinion for the purpose of harbor defense. Yours Very Respectfully, A.L. Rives, Lt. Col. and Acting Chief of Bureau."[163]

Although Mr. Singer and several of his associates had been ordered to join General Kirby Smith's forces operating west of the Mississippi (September 15, 1863),[164] it would appear from the above communication that revised orders had been drawn up sending Mr. Singer and staff back to Charleston to assist in mining of the Harbor (It was during this period that he apparently reconfigured the *Hunley's* torpedo system).

With so much time and money having been spent on building and testing of their submarine boat, it seems logical to assume that the plans presumably sent the Richmond Engineering Department, would have been for the torpedo boat they were then working on. Since all inventions developed by Singer's group were protected by Confederate Patent laws, the Singer Submarine Corps. would have had nothing to fear in presenting the government with detailed plans of the *Hunley*, or any other inventions developed by the organization.

By coincidence, it would seem that Smythe had lived on Sullivan's Island with his family before the war. From a letter sent to his father at about the same time that the *Hunley* was being moved to

Battery Marshall, we can form a good picture as to what Dixon and his crew found at their new base of operations:

"Since my last letter they have continued to shell the city daily, throwing in about 10 or 20 daily. They do not shell constantly, but for an hour or so in the morning and then again in the P.M. Today they have thrown in quite a number, so far I have heard of but one man killed. They are quiet now but will probably commence again in the A.M.

I went down to the east end of Sullivan's Island, to Trucedell's place, but was not very successful, only being able to get some racoon (sic) oysters. Our house has been pulled down, and all the others on the front beach, from the cove up to the fort, have shared the same fate, while their place is

A Union war ship closes in on a Confederate blockade runner in this Frank Leslie wood cut. Naval History Center.

supplied by batteries. I did not have time to land, but only took observations while sailing past. The church is down. The Episcopal one is used for a commissary, and the Catholic one stands, but is shut up. The whole island, or rather, that part of it comprising the village, looks desolate and rather the worst for wear.

The Moultrie House stands, but no longer a house. All the weather boarding, floors, piassas (sic) and roofs have been taken away, most probably by the soldiers for fire wood, or to build their shanties, and there now remains only the gaunt framework. It looks so deserted, and made me so sad to look at it, and then think of its former days, when it was the gay, fashionable resort. many of the houses are riddled with cannon balls, and but very few I fear will ever be habitable again. The island is full of soldiers, and the whole face from the fort to the cove is one long battery mounting the heaviest guns. I do not think now that I shall ever live there again since the dear old house is gone, but it was a plan of mine to live there one of these days when I was rich.

Battery Marshall, at the end of the island, where I went for the oysters, is a splendid fortification. It is to protect the end of the island from an advance from Long Island, which you know is only separated from it by a narrow creek, Breach Inlet. It also protects the entrance to the creek that run in back of the island. It is a mixture of breastwork and battery, and a fine work it is."[165]

From the post-war writings of William Alexander, we are told that even after the submarine had been relocated to Breach Inlet, the crew of the *Hunley* remained quartered at Mount Pleasant several miles away. It would appear that this awkward arrangement continued at least until the end of January, when quarters for Dixon's men were finally provided on Sullivan's Island. During this period of re-deployment (about January 14 - 20), the crew of the *Hunley* apparently practiced their new method of attack in an area described by Alexander as the Back Bay behind Battery Marshall. From Alexander's 1902 Picayune article, we are informed as to the crew's routine during this awkward period: "Our daily routine, whenever possible, was about as follows: Leave Mount Pleasant about 1 P.M., walk seven miles to Battery Marshall on the beach (this exposed us to fire, but it was the best walking), take the boat out and practice the crew for two hours in the Back Bay."

This "practice" presumably consisted of mock attacks with their new torpedo system against the hull of an old flat boat anchored behind Battery Marshall.

This new form of attack required the crew of the *Hunley* to literally ram an enemy vessel with the harpoon mounted on the bow of the submarine. With the barbed steel lance head of the torpedo driven deep into the vessel's wooden hull, the crew would then reverse the propeller and back away, leaving the harpoon head and explosive device attached to the ship. (A similar arrangement had been used by whalers for over a century.) When the line, or lanyard carried in a reel outside the hull reached the end, the trigger would be pulled and the explosive detonated. It was a risky system, but far safer than towing a contact mine miles out to sea in the dark of night.

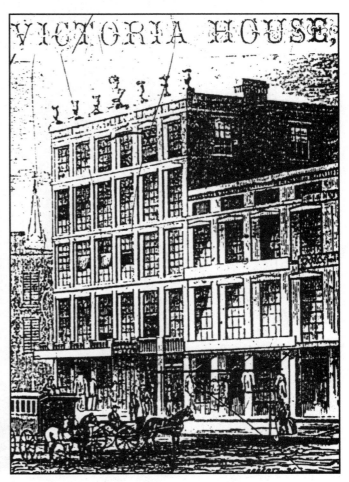

The Victoria House Hotel at the corner of King and Princess streets was Lt. Dixon and Alexander's headquarters for much of November and December 1863. From the 1859 Charleston City Directory.

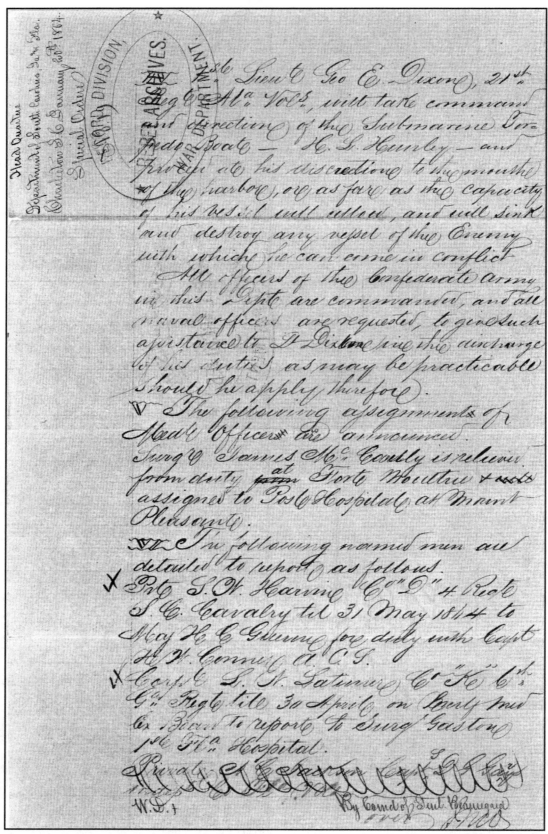

Special orders dated January 20, 1864, directing Lt. Dixon to take command of the "Hunley" and proceed 'at his discretion to the mouth of the harbor, or as far as the capacity of his vessel will allow, and will sink and destroy any vessel of the enemy with which he can come in conflict.'
Reproduced by permission of the National Archives.

CHAPTER FOUR
Breach Inlet Becomes Submarine Base

"My headquarters are on Sullivan's Island and a more uncomfortable place could not be found in the Confederacy." – Lt. George E. Dixon (final commander, *H.L. Hunley*)

While Admiral Dahlgren and the crews of the various ironclads prepared their vessels for a nocturnal visit from the *Hunley*, Dixon and Alexander, unaware that the existence of their submarine had been compromised to the Union fleet only days before, finalized their plans of attack from Breach Inlet 2 1/2 miles up the coast.

By night the federal sailors standing watch on the ironclads strained their eyes in the darkness, nervously scanning the surface for any sign of the "diving torpedo" of which they had been warned. The occasional piece of drift wood that came into view must have come close to causing heart failure, as the tense sailors slowly scanned the dark surface with their bright calcium lights. The sounds of a school of porpoises surfacing for air undoubtedly sent numerous beams of light and musket barrels to bear on the area from which the sound originated. Within their hammocks below deck, the sleepless crews listened restlessly for any unfamiliar sound that vibrated through the thick hull. As they stared into the gloomy darkness, they must have wondered how this invention was able to operate underwater, and what type of defense, if any, could be used against such an infernal machine. Those first few weeks in January must have been filled with many sleepless nights for those uneasy Union sailors on blockade or picket duty near the mouth of the harbor.

While the sailors on duty aboard the ironclad's tossed and turned through the night, fearing at any second to be hurled from their hammocks and scramble through cold rising sea water to the nearest hatch, the crews on the wooden ships far out to sea slept comfortably, content in the knowledge that the diving torpedo boat was at Mount Pleasant and would only be attacking the ironclads that anchored close to shore.

As rumors of this new underwater menace spread throughout the Union fleet, Dixon continued to sharpen his crew's attack skills in the brackish bay behind Battery Marshall. William Alexander described the method by which he and Dixon were to move against the enemy ships in the outer circle of the blockade. "The plan was to take the bearings of the ships as they took position for the night, steer for one of them, keeping about six feet under water, coming occasionally to the surface for air and observation, and when nearing the vessel, come to the surface for final observation before striking her, which was to be done under the counter, if possible."[166] By January 19, 1864, Dixon had decided that his crew was proficient enough with their new attack plan to make another try. Dixon and Alexander once more reported to Confederate military headquarters to inform Beauregard as to their intentions and request orders.

On January 20, just ten days after the two officers had first gone to Sullivan's Island to arrange a new base of operations for the submarine, the following orders were issued by military headquarters: "1st Lt. George E. Dixon, 21st. Regiment Alabama Volunteers, will take command and direction of the Submarine Torpedo Boat - *H.L. Hunley* - and proceed at his discretion to the mouth of the harbor, or as far as the capacity of his vessel will allow, and will sink and destroy any vessel of the enemy with which he can come in conflict.

All officers of the Confederate Army in this Department are commanded, and all naval officers are requested, to give such assistance to Lt. Dixon in the discharge of his duties as may be practicable, should he apply therefore. By order of General Beauregard."[167]

As the reader may have noticed, the wording of this order is practically identical to the one issued on December 14, 1863. The only difference in the two can be seen in the directive following the words *H.L. Hunley*. Instead of ordering Dixon to "Proceed tonight to the mouth of the harbor," he has instead been ordered to "Proceed at his discretion to the mouth of the harbor." With the hazardous nature of the duty aboard the submarine well known at headquarters, it was apparently decided that it was best to put the entire operation of the *Hunley* in the capable hands of Dixon. This arrangement may have been implied in the past; However, with the issuing of this order, it would appear that from that point forward, Dixon would have total control over the operations of the submarine, with power to decide when and where the *Hunley* would strike out at the enemy fleet.

Federal gun crew standing next to one of the U.S.S. "Wissahicken's" big guns.
Photo courtesy of the United States National Archives.

Admiral Dahlgren and the officers of his fleet, aboard his flagship, U.S.S. "Wissahicken."
Photo courtesy of the United States National Archives.

From both the above order, and post war recollections of Engineer James Tomb, we can presume that the *Hunley* was under the direction of the Army, not the Charleston Naval squadron, following the accidental sinking on August 29th. Since the above order states that "all naval officers are requested" (not ordered), to lend assistance, it would appear that Confederate naval personnel had little or nothing to do with the operations of the vessel.

Although the Navy Department seems to have had no involvement with the *Hunley*, evidence suggesting that the five sailors from the *Indian Chief* crew (then attached the submarine) were still drawing navy pay, can be found in a 1918 article about the *Hunley* written by an old Confederate Naval veteran who had served in the Charleston Squadron. Within this short article a 78 year old, W.B. Fort (then living in Pickville, North Carolina), stated that he had been personal friend with Lt. Charles Hasker (survivor of the Fort Johnson sinking), and that he had served in the Navy Paymasters Department, where, along with his other duties, had been personally responsible for paying the crew of the submarine boat.[168] (Since Mr. Fort's brief history of the *Hunley* appeared during the opening month of World War One, its interesting to note that he purposely mentioned that five of Charles Hasker's grandsons were then serving in the French trenches.)

While Dixon and Alexander practiced their crew in Back Bay behind Battery Marshall, Seaman Belton, one of the deserters from the *C.S.S. Indian Chief*, had been busy constructing a model of the innovative submarine for Dahlgren.[169] Before Belton had been conscripted into the Confederate Navy, he had worked in a Mobile shop near where the *Hunley* was built, as well as on the railroad connecting Mobile and Charleston. After examining Belton's model in great detail, Dahlgren sent it to the Secretary of the Navy in Washington for further study.

While searching through the letters sent to the Navy Department by Dahlgren, I was very fortunate to find the communication that accompanied this model, dated to within 48 hours after Dixon had received his revised orders from Confederate Headquarters: "January 22, 1864 The Honorable Gideon Welles, Secretary of the Navy Washington, D.C. Sir: I transmit by the *Massachusetts*, a model of the *Diver* which is said to have been built at Mobile by the rebels, and brought to this place for use against the vessels in this Squadron.

The Department will find a brief description of her in my communication of the 13th (quoted in Chapter Three). The model was made by E. C. Belton who is a mechanic, and ran an engine on the Montgomery and Mobile Railroad for some time. He worked in a building near where it was built and claims to understand fully its construction. It has been very unlucky in the trials made with it, and is stated to have drowned at different times three crews of seventeen men."[170]

Upon learning that a model of the *Hunley* had once existed, and been sent to the Navy Department in 1864, my imagination soared as I envisioned a small image of the submarine sitting on some forgotten shelf in the Naval Archives; with a dusty label "The *Diver*, Charleston, S.C., 1864" attached to the forward diving planes. After numerous telephone calls to various archivists attached to the Washington Navy yard, I was finally informed by the curator in charge of all antique ship models that although he was familiar with at least two modern models of the *Hunley*, he was unaware of any that had been built during the Civil War. Perhaps some future Hunley researcher will have better luck in tracking down this model of the *Hunley*, fashioned by a Confederate deserter in the Winter of 1864.

At about the same time Dahlgren was examining Belton's model of the *Hunley* and forwarding it to Washington for further study (January 22, 1864), Dixon and Alexander were preparing to lead their crew on the first nighttime run against the wooden fleet from their new base at Breach Inlet.

As the flickering light from numerous camp fires started to appear behind the sloping walls of Battery Marshall, the crew of the *Hunley* could be seen preparing their submarine for that first night that lay ahead of them far out to sea. At the bow of the vessel, Dixon and Alexander checked the reel and line that would trip the trigger of the torpedo, making absolutely sure that nothing could accidentally snag the cord and detonate the device while it was still attached to the spar. Nearby, Seaman Becker and Collins, formally of the *C.S.S. Indian Chief*, stamped their feet on the dock trying to keep warm while talking to some soldiers from Battery Marshall who had come over to wish them luck.

While the last faint rays of sunlight slowly disappeared behind the far off church steeples of

near where
claims to un
struction.
It has
the trials
stated to
times

The
a vessel,
to the bottle

Afte
ed him
the office

C.R.W.R.

Despatch No. 33

Flag Steamer Philadelphia
Off Morris Island
January 22d 1864.

Honorable Gideon Welles.
Secretary of the Navy
Washington DC

Sir:

I transmit by the Massachusetts, a model of the "Diver", which
is said to have been built at Mobile
by the Rebels, and brought to this
place for use against the vessels
of this Squadron.

The Department will find a
brief description of her in my communication of the 13th — No. 16.

The model was made by E.C.
Betton, who is a mechanic, and
ran an engine on the Montgomery
and Mobile Rail Road for some
time. He worked in a building

*Letter from Admiral Dahlgren, commanding the Federal fleet off Charleston to the Honorable Gideon Welles,
Secretary of the Navy, USA, enclosed with a model of the "Diver" ("Hunley"). The model has not been located.*
Courtesy of the U.S. National Archives.

Charleston, Dixon asked Seaman Ridgeway to open the hatches and make ready for the rest of the crew to enter. As the young sailor stepped onto the *Hunley's* slick iron hull, the submarine gently bobbed and rolled under his weight. While reaching down to pull open the heavy hatch cover, he requested a lantern from one of his comrades. As he climbed down into the cold clammy interior of the submarine, he noticed that the flickering light given off by the small flame shimmered on the thin streaks of ice that covered the walls.

While Alexander talked to Dixon at the bow, Wicks passed four or five canteens of water down through the rear hatch to Ridgeway, along with some hardtack and dried beef. Since the submarine would remain at sea until dawn, food and water would have been very important in helping the men get through the long winter night. As the crew slowly started to climb down into the cramped, icy hull, a distant boom from Morris Island notified everyone that the new batteries recently mounted on the point had come to life for their evening harassment of Charleston. As Dixon squeezed through the narrow hatch, he found the rest of the crew already at their stations, talking softly amongst themselves. Wicks was saying something about his wife, Catherine, and their four daughters. The oldest daughter, Eliza, was just eleven years old.[171]

By now, the ceiling around the forward hatch would have been blackened with soot from the dozens of candles that had been burned there. The floor of the hull beneath the tarnished compass that had been sold to them by Broadfoot would be speckled with small piles of melted wax that had run down the bulkhead.

While the crew prepared themselves for the long night that lay ahead, Dixon lit one of the candles he had brought on board and wiped the frost from the view ports and mercury gauge with an old rag.

At the rear hatch, Alexander lifted the lantern through the narrow opening and handed it to a soldier who stood nearby. As he squeezed through the small opening and took his place at the rear ballast tank pump, Dixon asked if every one was ready. In the shadowy candle light he at once saw each man nodding yes to his question. Within moments the order to move forward was given. As the long cold propeller shaft started turning in the capable hands of Dixon's crew, our young engineering officer stood with his head above the

hatch rim, steering his submarine toward the open sea and the twinkling lights of the Union fleet that lay at anchor several miles off shore.

It's known from the post-war writings of William Alexander that this scene just described was repeated many times during the nights that followed. After practicing the crew in the Back Bay for a couple of hours in the late afternoon, Alexander informs us "Dixon and myself would then stretch out on the beach with the compass between us and get the bearings of the nearest vessel as she took her position for the night; ship up the torpedo on the boom, and when dark, go out, steering for that vessel, proceed until the condition of the men, sea, tide, wind, moon and daylight compelled our return to the dock; unship the torpedo, put it under guard at Battery Marshall, walk back to quarters at Mount Pleasant and cook breakfast."[172]

From the above description, it could be assumed that the physical drain on the crew of the *Hunley* during this period must have been tremendous. After making the seven-mile hike from their quarters at Mount Pleasant, the weary seamen would then take the submarine into the Back Bay and practice for a couple of hours, keeping their skills sharp for the attack that could take place later that night. With the coming of early evening, the men may have been allowed to nap while Dixon and Alexander surveyed the horizon for a potential victim.

All through the long cold night at sea, the crew would most certainly have been in a constant state of paranoia. Each of the many surfacings for air would have caused great uncertainty; if an enemy picket boat spotted them as they opened their hatch for air, a well placed shot from anyone of her small deck guns would send the *Hunley* to the bottom forever. If the line to the torpedo accidentally snagged on a piece of drift wood and pulled the detonating trigger, the explosion from 135 pounds of gun powder in front of the bow could easily rip open the hull of their vessel. From the time that the men took their places until the following dawn, nothing could be seen but the dripping condensation running down the *Hunley's* dark iron walls. During the monotony of the long night, one can only wonder as to how many times each man must have contemplated the tragic history of the diving machine, as cold and fatigue started to numb their bodies. While Dixon knelt in front of the candle monitoring the dimly lit compass, trying to

The Honorable Gideon Welles, Secretary of the Navy, USA, was kept closely informed of all new information relating to the "Hunley." Photo courtesy of the U.S. National Archives.

Conrad Wise Chapman's sketch of Battery Marshall as seen from the far side of Breach Inlet. From a vantage point on the ramparts of this fortification, Lieutenants Dixon and Alexander were able to monitor the activities of the ships of the federal blockading squadron on the horizon. Courtesy of the Massachusetts Commandery, Military Order of the Loyal Legion and the U.S. Army Military History Institute.

A modern view from Breach Inlet looking out into the calm waters of the Atlantic. The rotting pilings in the fore-ground are visible only at low tide, and may well have been part of the dock from which the "Hunley" embarked on her moonlit patrols. 1995 photo by Mark Ragan.

keep his submarine on course, the rest of the crew continued to turn the crankshaft hour after hour in near total darkness.

After traveling offshore for several hours, Dixon would have checked his pocket watch for the time. With only five hours till sunrise it was decided that the *Hunley* would surface for one final observation. If no enemy ships were spotted nearby, he would rest his tired crew before starting the long journey back to Breach Inlet. As he slowly pulled back the lever connected to the forward diving planes, the narrow hatch of the submarine gently rose above the surface. Quickly he blew out the candle and wiped the condensation from the view ports for a quick look around. It was pitch black in all directions. As his weary crew continued to turn the shaft, Dixon began pumping out the forward ballast tank. He ordered Alexander at the rear of the vessel to do the same with the aft tank. As the water from both tanks was pumped back into the sea, the iron hull of the *Hunley* slowly rose in the water until her deck was several inches above the surface.

Immediately Dixon pushed open his heavy hatch cover and scanned the horizon for any sign of an enemy picket boat. As he brought his telescope to his eye, he could see the lights of an enemy frigate twinkling through the light fog a mile and a half in front of them. From the south, about three quarters of a mile away, he could make out the faint beam of a calcium light, scanning the dark water from a picket boat. With no hostile ships in the area, Dixon ordered Alexander to stop cranking, open his hatch and light some candles. With this order, the crew ceased cranking and took a much needed rest. With no apparent danger lurking nearby, and a cool breeze passing through the hull between the two open hatches, the mood of the crew quickly changed as canteens of water and parcels of food were passed between the men. While the crew talked and joked in the now well lit cabin, Dixon and Alexander stood in the hatches whispering between themselves while watching the dim light of the picket boat that lay to the south.

As the *Hunley* slowly drifted in the gentle current, Dixon stood with his head above the hatch rim taking a much needed breath of fresh air. He peered at the far away lights of an enemy frigate as he reached over to check the line in the reel, making sure that nothing had jarred or snagged it's mechanism. While his weary crew talked and rested, Dixon noticed a faint flash of lightning over the horizon. He knew from past experience that a rain storm would severely hinder his visibility, and winds may cause the surface of the water to become too turbulent for any sort of sighting at all. Without proper sightings they could not safely find their way back. With this disturbing thought in mind, he advised his crew that, considering the weather and the distance they still had to the nearest enemy ship, they had best return to shore.

With his crew now refreshed and ready to continue their duties, he ordered the crankshaft to once again be turned. As the iron shaft once more spun inside its metal braces, Dixon turned the forward wheel, which caused the rudder to turn to starboard. As the needle on the compass slowly came to bear on the proper heading, he straightened the wheel and told the crew to stop for a moment. At once, all the candles were blown out except Dixon's. With the bow of the *Hunley* now pointing towards Sullivan's Island, Dixon ordered the hatches sealed and Alexander to open the rear ballast tank sea valve. As the submarine slowly settled beneath the dark surface, Dixon held his candle to the view port to monitor the water level through the thick glass pane. When the hull was seen to be three inches below the surface, both sea valves were closed and the submarine ordered to get underway. With a slight push on the heavy diving planes, the submarine once again disappeared into the sea. With the sun rising in about five hours, Dixon hoped he could guide his tiny vessel back to Breach Inlet before the dawn found him still in enemy waters.

From Alexander's 1902 Picayune article, we are informed in vivid detail as to the many dangers faced by the crew of the *Hunley* during those cold January nights in 1864. "It was winter, therefore necessary that we go out with the ebb and come in with the flood tide, a fair wind and a dark moon. This latter was essential to success, as our experience had fully demonstrated the necessity of occasionally coming to the surface, slightly lifting the after hatch-cover and letting in a little air. On several occasions we came to the surface for air, opened the cover and heard the men in the Federal picket boats talking and singing. During this time we went out on an average of four nights a week, but on account of the weather, and considering the physical condition of the men to propel the boat back again, often, after going out six or seven miles, we would have to return. This we always found a task, and many times it taxed our utmost exertions to keep from drifting out to sea, daylight often breaking while we were yet in range."[173]

At about the same time that the crew of the *Hunley* was moving against the wooden ships in the outer circle of the blockade, Captain Joseph Green of the *U.S.S. Canandaigua* appears to have sent a communication to Dahlgren requesting further information about the "Diving Torpedo" mentioned in his orders of January 7. In response to this inquiry, Dahlgren sent Capt. Green a letter from which I quote only a few lines pertaining to the subject: "I can hardly think that the design would extend beyond the Iron Clads that constitute the inner Blockade, for the outer vessels are distant and difficult of access. Still it would be unwise to omit any proper precautions and I therefore advise that you will take such measures as may suffice to defeat any attempt of the kind. I enclose for your information the directions prescribed for the Iron Clads."[174]

After receiving this communication, Captain Green, and the other captains of wooden vessels, decided that it would be wiser to anchor further off shore at night just in case the diving torpedo chose to come after them one evening, instead of the ironclads anchored closer to the mouth of the harbor.

From a soon-to-be-quoted order from Charleston military headquarters, it could be assumed that shortly after the *Hunley* started her nightly operations from Breach Inlet, it was found that a boat of some kind would be needed as a support vessel for the submarine.[175] It's highly unlikely that Dixon would have been able to guide the *Hunley* back to her mooring at Breach Inlet (only about 80 yards wide) night after night from several miles out to sea.

The boat in question may have been used to retrieve the submarine on those mornings where Dixon had been unable to reach Breach Inlet and been forced to run the *Hunley* aground somewhere along Sullivan's Island or Long Island (now the Isle of Palms). Although no information currently exists to support this theory, I can see no other reason for a support vessel to have been requested.

The rigorous nature of the duty required aboard the *Hunley* must have quickly taken its toll on the men who propelled the submarine night after night miles out to sea. The crew would have been required to sleep during daylight hours several miles from Battery Marshall, perhaps stuffing their ears with cotton so as to muffle the sounds of sporadic cannon fire from Forts Sumter and Moultrie. In the afternoon, they would walk the seven miles to Breach Inlet, sharpen their attack skills for a couple of hours in the Back Bay, then guide their submarine to the mouth of the inlet, and go to sea until the following dawn.

If all went according to plan, and the weather had not forced them to beach the submarine somewhere along the coast, the crew of the *Hunley* probably returned to their dock at Battery Marshall sometime around 5 o'clock in the morning. As the submarine slowly maneuvered next to her slip, a weary William Alexander climbed out onto the cold iron hull and threw a line to one of the shivering sentries. While the ragged guards pulled the *Hunley* to her place at the dock, Dixon stood in the forward hatch, watching their progress. As the *Hunley* was once again tied up in her slip, a vaporous steam could be seen rising from the two open hatches. Dixon and Alexander slowly climbed out onto the dock and checked the ropes that would restrain their submarine until nightfall. As the exhausted crew men sluggishly emerged from the now relatively warm interior of the dark hull, their gaunt and flushed faces displayed the fatigue each had suffered from working the crankshaft throughout the night. As they gathered around the guard's small fire, talk of the recently ended patrol soon filled the frigid pre-dawn air.

While the first hint of sunlight slowly started to appear on the Atlantic horizon, the weary crew of the *Hunley* dried their sweat soaked jackets around the fire, and joked about the bad quality of the singing heard through the open hatch the night before. As a pot of hot coffee (or at least a reasonable substitute) was passed around the small circle, Alexander and Seaman Wicks unshipped the deadly torpedo and gently lifted it onto the dock. By now, the pre-dawn talking of the *Hunley's* crew would have been a common sound to the soldiers quartered near the Breach Inlet dock. As the first rays of sunlight appeared on the horizon, several soldiers wrapped in tattered blankets walked over to talk with the recently arrived crew. With the submarine once again gently rocking in her slip, and her crew now ready for the long hike back to Mount Pleasant, Dixon and Alexander lead their weary men down the beach past the numerous fortifications starting to stir for the day. As Dixon's weary crew walked by, the men of the various batteries waved their hats and shouted encouragement to the brave crew of the *Hunley* as they slowly moved past. When they reached their

(No. 30.)

commanded by Lt. G. E. Dixon

REQUISITION FOR FUEL for *Crew in charge of Submarine Boat,* stationed
at *Mount Pleasant S.C.* for the month of *February* 1864

	WOOD.			COAL.		REMARKS.
	Cords.	Feet.	Inches.	Bushels.	Pounds.	
For myself,						
For private servant,						
For Crew in charge of Submarine Boat commanded by myself consisting of Eight Men	1 2/6					
						Approved by command of Brig. Genl. R. S. Ripley *Henry Bryss Capt & A A A G*
Total,	1 2/6					

I Certify, on honor, that the above Requisition is correct and just, and that I have not drawn
Fuel for any part of the time above charged.

Geo. E. Dixon
Lt Comdg Sub-Marine Boat

RECEIVED at *Mount Pleasant, S.C.* the *1* of *February* 1864
of *Capt W. G. Vardell* A Quartermaster C. S. Army.
One & two sixth cord s ~~feet~~ ~~inches~~ of Wood
~~of Coal~~, in full of the above Requisition.

[SIGNED IN DUPLICATE.]

Geo. E. Dixon
Lt Comdg Sub-Marine Bout

Requisition for firewood to be used by the crew of the "Hunley" to heat and cook.
Courtesy of the U.S. National Archives.

quarters, all flopped on their sandy blankets for a few hours sleep before they would once again rig the torpedo and return to sea.

As a result of their numerous close encounters with the enemy's steam powered picket boats, and the unavoidable dilemma of occasionally being caught at sea after sunrise, Dixon and Alexander decided that a test should be conducted to determine just how long the crew could remain beneath the surface without exhausting their air supply. From Alexander's 1902 Picayune article we are informed in vivid detail how he and Dixon conducted this unique and highly dangerous experiment: "This experience, also our desire to know, in case we struck a vessel (circumstances required our keeping below the surface), suggested that while in safe water we make the experiment to find out how long it was possible to stay under water without coming to the surface for air and not injure the crew.

It was agreed to by all hands to sink and let the boat rest on the bottom, in the Back Bay, off Battery Marshall, each man to make equal physical exertion in turning the propeller. It was also agreed that if anyone in the boat felt that if he must come to the surface for air, and he gave the word 'up,' we would at once bring the boat to the surface.

It was usual, when practicing in the bay, that the banks would be lined with soldiers. One evening, after alternately diving and rising many times, Dixon and myself and several of the crew compared watches, noted the time and sank for the test. In twenty-five minutes after I had closed the after manhead and excluded the outer air the candle would not burn. Dixon forward and myself aft, turning on the propeller cranks as hard as we could. In comparing our individual experience afterwards, the experience of one was found to have been the experience of all. Each man had determined that he would not be the first to say 'up!' Not a word was said, except the occasional, 'How is it,' between Dixon and myself, until it was as the voice of one man, the word 'up' came from all nine. We started the pumps. Dixon's worked all right, but I soon realized that my pump was not throwing. From experience I guessed the cause of the failure, took off the cap of the pump, lifted the valve, and drew out some seaweed that had choked it.

During the time it took to do this the boat was considerably by the stern. Thick darkness prevailed. All hands had already endured what they thought was the utmost limit. Some of the crew almost lost control of themselves. It was a terrible few minutes, 'better imagined than described.' We soon had the boat to the surface and the manhead opened. Fresh air! What an experience! Well, the sun was shining when we went down, the beach lined with soldiers. It was now quite dark, with one solitary soldier gazing on the spot where he had seen the boat before going down the last time. He did not see the boat until he saw me standing on the hatch combing, calling to him to stand by to take the line. A light was struck and the time taken. We had been on the bottom two hours and thirty-five minutes. The candle ceased to burn in twenty-five minutes after we went down, showing that we had remained under water two hours and ten minutes after the candle went out.

The soldier informed us that we had been given up for lost, that a message had been sent to General Beauregard at Charleston that the torpedo boat had been lost that evening off Battery Marshall with all hands.

We got back to our quarters at Mount Pleasant that night, went over early next morning to the city (Charleston), and reported to General Beauregard the facts of the affair. They were all glad to see us.

After making a full report of our experience, General Rains, of General Beauregard's staff, who was present, expressed some doubt of our having stayed under water two hours and ten minutes after the candle went out. Not that any of us wanted to go through the same experience again, but we did our best to get him to come over to Sullivan's Island and witness a demonstration of the fact, but without avail."[176]

After reading Alexander's account of this submerged endurance test, I was quite tempted to conduct a similar experiment with my two-man submarine on the very spot that Dixon and his crew had staged theirs in late January of 1864. The longest I've had my submarine underwater without adding air from one of the cylinders I carry on board is about an hour and a half. Although I did not conduct such a test while diving at Breach Inlet with my mini-sub, I can assure the reader that Alexander's description of the first breath of fresh air taken after a long dive is right on the money. After breathing an atmosphere that is steadily being contaminated by carbon dioxide, fresh air literally tastes as though it's laced with sugar.

While conducting diving operations with my K-250 submarine at the end of Sullivan's Island (during the summer of 1994), I was quite surprised

This tranquil scene of fishermen on the stone grillage at Sullivan's Island, showing a view of Fort Sumter, was typical of the lulls in the siege of Charleston. A scene like this could erupt into a bloody bombardment of bursting bombs, smoke, and death in a matter of seconds. Conrad Wise Chapman sketch courtesy of the Massachusetts Commandery, Military Order of the Loyal Legion and the U.S. Army Military History Institute.

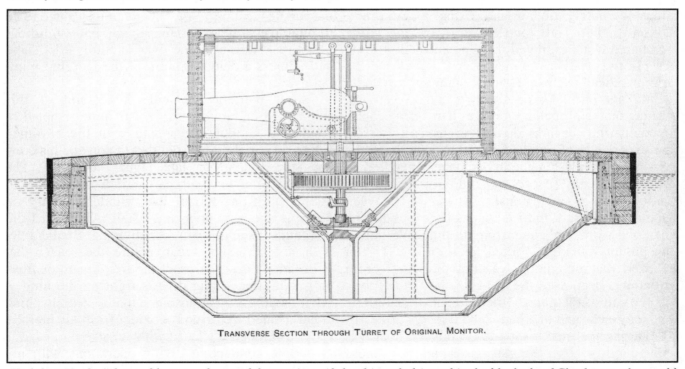

TRANSVERSE SECTION THROUGH TURRET OF ORIGINAL MONITOR.

Had the "Hunley" been able to reach one of the monitors (federal ironclads) used in the blockade of Charleston, she would have struck at the more vulnerable, undersides of the otherwise heavily armored war vessel.
Illustration from the *Official Records of the Union and Confederate Navies in the War of the Rebellion.*

Interior of Battery Marshall as sketched by Conrad Chapman during the Winter of 1864. This scene would have been very familiar to the crew of the "Hunley." Courtesy of the Massachusetts Commandery, Military Order of the Loyal Legion and the U.S. Army Military History Institute.

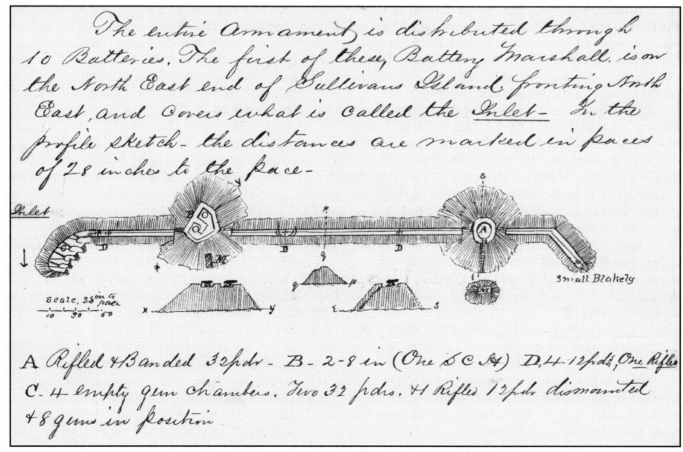

Diagram of Battery Marshall on the Breach Inlet end of Sullivan's Island. Courtesy of the U.S. National Archives.

to discover just how powerful the underwater currents that flow through Breach Inlet actually are. While running submerged, my two thrusters were continually fighting the strong currents with little or no effect. After several attempts we found it to be much easier to glide with the current's flow (regardless of direction), rather than try and maneuver the sub against it. If Dixon and his men ever missed the incoming tide in the early morning hours, I can't imagine how they would ever have been able to get back to shore.

From a letter to be cited shortly, it would appear that sometime during the final days of January, or first days of February, Dixon was able to secure quarters at Battery Marshall and move his crew from far away Mount Pleasant to Sullivan's Island.[177] It is probable that the long daily hike back and forth from their quarters was viewed as too much of a drain on the men's strength to be continued.

During the course of my research in the National Archives, I located an old box of daily reports filed by each encampment scattered along Sullivan's Island for January and February 1864.[178] Judging from the way in which these daily reports were packaged, it was easy to imagine that I was the first to read these morning reports (scribbled on bits of paper of every description) since the war. Quite naturally, I hoped that reports filed by Dixon concerning the submarine's nightly excursions might be among the faded scraps of paper.

Each time I unfolded a morning report from Battery Marshall (filed by Captain John L. Jones, Company "D" 7th South Carolina Infantry), I quickly scanned the faded hand-writing for any mention of the Hunley. Although Captain Jones occasionally mentioned the passing of a blockade runner, the vast majority of his reports I found to be rather dull - most only reporting the number of shots fired in the past twenty-four hours and adding nothing new from the previous day. There were no reports on the activities of the Hunley. It would appear that Dixon bypassed Captain Jones and reported directly to Confederate military headquarters or, because of the need for secrecy, his nightly patrols were not included in Jones' written reports.

While Jones wrote his morning reports, perhaps in sight of the Hunley, Dixon and his weary crew were just turning in for a few hours of much needed sleep after their long cold night at sea. Turning once again to Alexander's post-war writings we are

informed: "On the last day of January we interviewed the Charleston pilots again, and they gave it as their opinion that the wind would hold in the same quarter for several weeks. We continued to go out as often as the weather permitted; hoping against hope, each time taking greater risks of getting back."[179]

Throughout this chaotic period, evidence would indicate that Dixon's friend and commanding officer, Captain John Cothran, was continually requesting him to return to his post with the 21st. Alabama in Mobile. Turning to a 1900 Montgomery Advisor news article "An Alabama Hero," we are informed of the following. "While contemplating this hazardous enterprise, Lieutenant Dixon received from his old officer, Captain Cothran of Mobile, a letter entreating him to give up the frightful venture saying that he needed Dixon in his command. This gentleman is still living in Mobile, and has Lieutenant Dixon's heroic reply, refusing to retreat from the post of danger he had sought."[180] The "heroic reply" spoken of in this rather distorted account of the Hunley was printed in the Mobile Register a short time later under the headline "Lieutenant Dixon's last letter." To my knowledge this may be the only account written by Dixon regarding the Hunley and the siege of Charleston to have survived into this century. I think the reader will agree that the contents of this letter pretty well sum up Dixon's devotion to duty, and is precisely the sort of letter one would expect from the skipper of the Hunley.

"February 5th, 1864. Captain John F. Cothran. Captain Commanding Ceder Point. Company 'A' Twenty-first Alabama Regiment, Mobile, Alabama. Friend John: Your letter of the 29th came to hand today and contents duly noted. I am glad McCullough has gotten to be a Lieutenant, he has served long enough for it. You stated my presence was very much needed on your little island. I have no doubt it is, but when I will get there is far more than I am able to tell at present, for beyond a doubt I am fastened to Charleston and its approaches until I am able to blow up some of their yankee ships. If I wanted to leave here I could not do it, and I doubt very much if an order from General Maury would have any effect towards bringing me back.

I have been here over three months, have worked very hard, in fact I am working all the time. My headquarters are on Sullivan's Island, and a more uncomfortable place could not be found in the Confederacy. You spoke of being on the front and holding the post of honor. Now, John, make one trip to the besieged city of Charleston and your post of honor and all danger that threatens Mobile will fade away. For the last six weeks I have not been out of the range of the shells and often I am forced to go within very close proximity of the yankee battery. I do not want you and all the company to think that because I am absent from them that mine is any pleasant duty or that I am absent from them because I believe there is any post of honor or fame where there is any danger, I think it must be at Charleston, for if you wish to see war every day and night, this is the place to see it.

Charleston and its defenders will occupy the most conspicuous place in the history of the war, and it shall be as much glory as I shall wish if I can inscribe myself as one of its defenders. My duty here is more arduous than that of any officer of the 21st. Alabama. Simply because I am not present to fulfill the duties of a Lieutenant there are many that have formed the opinion that I am doing nothing; But I say that I have done more already than any of the 21st. Alabama and I stand ready to prove my assertion by the best and highest military authority. What more I will do time alone will tell. My kindest regards to Charley and all enquiring (sic) friends. Hoping to hear from you soon, I remain your friend. George E. Dixon."[181]

With Dixon's thirty-day extended duty quickly coming to an end, we once more find General Jordan requesting an extension for the *Hunley's* skipper from his superiors in Mobile. From the book of telegrams sent from Charleston military headquarters, we read the following entry: "To: Col. Garner, Chief of Staff Mobile. February 5, 1864. Must again ask extension of detail of Lieut. George E. Dixon for 30 days. (sgn) Gen Jordan."[182] From all existing evidence, it could be assumed that the request was again granted from General Maury's headquarters.

By a strange coincidence, it would appear that at precisely the same time that Dixon was writing to his company commander, and having his detached duty in South Carolina extended, orders were being drawn up in Charleston that would come to injure the morale of the *Hunley's* crew and greatly jeopardize the continued efficiency of the submarine.

Drawing from Alexander's Munsey Magazine and his *New Orleans Picayune*, articles we are informed: "We were in readiness when I received an order which at the time was a blow to all my hopes, although only by obeying it did I live to write this narrative. On February 5, 1864, I received orders to report in Charleston to General Jordan, chief of staff, who gave me transportation and orders to report at Mobile, to build a breech-loading, repeating gun (cannon). This was a terrible blow, both to Dixon and myself, after we had gone through so much together. General Jordan told Dixon he would get two men to take my place from the German artillery, but that I was wanted in Mobile.

It was thought best not to tell the crew that I was to leave them. I left Charleston that night and reached Mobile in due course. I received from Dixon two notes shortly after reaching Mobile, one stating that the wind still held in the same quarter, and the other telling the regrets of the crew at my leaving and their feelings towards me; also that he expected to get men from the artillery to take my place. These notes, together with my passes are before me as I write. What mingled reminiscences they bring."[183]

As the reader may have noticed while reading the above narrative, Alexander explicitly states that the number of volunteers to be selected from the artillery after his leaving for Mobile was two. It would seem that the two men in question were to replace Alexander, as well as a second crew member also called away from duty whom Alexander fails to name. In his 1902 Picayune article, this small discrepancy was passed over without clarification: However, a passing line from his 1903 Munsey Magazine article sheds a bit more light on this question. It reads: "All of the crew who had toiled and risked death during those long and weary months were in their places except myself and one other, also ordered to special duty."[184]

The "other" mentioned in this phrase was probably one of the two unnamed associates who had accompanied Dixon and Alexander from Mobile, and been quartered with them in Charleston until the 16th of December. Its highly unlikely that one of the sailors who had served aboard the *Hunley* for over two months would suddenly be called back to the *C.S.S. Indian Chief*. In any case, all of the names of the five men who volunteered from the *Indian Chief* appear on the *Hunley* monument in Charleston. It may be that this mysterious crew member reassigned to "special duty" was none other than our elusive Henry Dillingham, who had been given transportation to and from Mobile along with Dixon on business

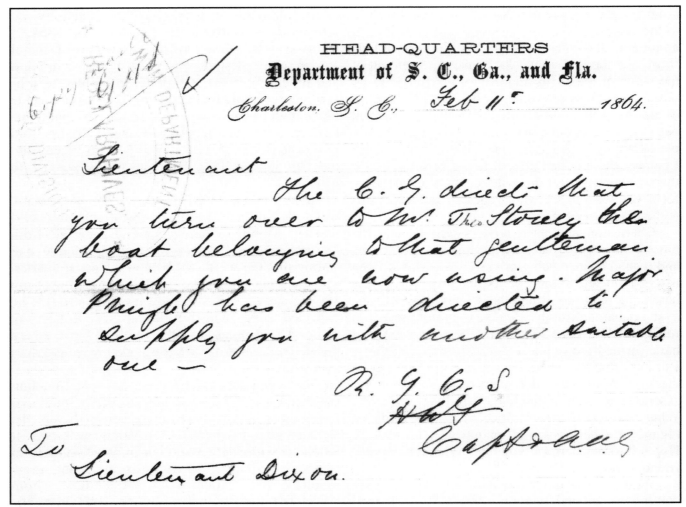

HEAD-QUARTERS
Department of S. C., Ga., and Fla.
Charleston, S. C., Feb 11th 1864.

Lieutenant

The C. G. directs that you turn over to Mr. Theo Stoney the boat belonging to that gentleman which you are now using. Major Pringle has been directed to supply you with another suitable one —

R. G. C. S
Holt
Capt & A. C. S

To
Lieutenant Dixon.

Order from Confederate Military headquarters directing Lt. Dixon to turn over the support vessel he had been using to it's owner Theodore Stoney, Recording Secretary of the Southern Torpedo Company. National Archives

This extremely rare and interesting picture of the "Hunley" is believed to be an actual photograph. The sketch of the man and some other details were apparently added to give the picture more life. This photo is obviously the basis of the painting shown on the title page of this book. Photo by George Cook, December, 1863, as published in *Proceedings*, Naval Institute.

connected with the submarine torpedo boat.[185]

In the course of my research, I discovered that Confederate Agent Henry Dillingham survived the war and was still being pursued by federal authorities after General Lee's surrender at Appomattox. Although I have no proof to back up my theory as to whom this reassigned crew member may have been, I put it forward, none the less, for the readers consideration.

On or about February 7, almost three months to the day after leaving for Charleston with Dixon, Alexander once again entered the noisy Park & Lyons machine shop. Immediately, everyone gathered around the weary engineer to hear the news from Charleston and the current status of their submarine boat. For the next hour the shop remained silent as Alexander told the attentive workmen exciting stories of the *Hunley* and her brave crew who took her to sea night after night under the very keels of the enemy picket boats. He spoke of the terrible siege and desperate fight Charleston was currently facing, and of the bravery shown by her citizens now under the guns of the Union army. As the shop's company hung on every word, Alexander told them of the dedication and courage displayed by the men who now manned the tiny submarine that they had all helped to build, and of the many dangers they had faced together night after night, miles out to sea.

In closing, Alexander would have undoubtedly stated that he was sure that the crew of the *Hunley* would sink an enemy ship very soon, and that the shop's company could all take pride in having built it. As the men dispersed and returned to their work, Alexander unrolled the diagram for the new breach-loading cannon and went about the task for which he had been called back from Charleston to perform.

While William Alexander poured over the drawings of the new breach-loading gun in far away Mobile, Lieutenant Dixon and the crew of the *Hunley* soon secured the services of two volunteers to take the places of Alexander and the other mysterious crew member who had been reassigned to special duty.

From a monument dedicated to the crews of the *Hunley*, located at the foot of Meeting Street in Charleston, we know the names of the last two volunteers. Neither were listed with the sailors from the *Indian Chief*. One of the replacement volunteers was Corporal C.F. Carlson of company "A" South Carolina Light Artillery. Carlson proved

to be the only crew member to have a record of his service aboard the *Hunley* on file at the National Archives.[186] The final volunteer was a man named Miller. Unfortunately, neither Miller's first name nor his initials are listed, and I am at a loss as to who he was or how his name came to appear on the monument. Although surviving Confederate records make no mention of Miller among Dixon's crew, such records or oral tradition apparently existed in 1889 when the United Daughters of the Confederacy erected the memorial.

With the loss of the capable William Alexander, Dixon would have undoubtedly filled his vacant station with the most able crew member still available to him. With the crew of the *Hunley* once more at full strength following the acquisition of the two new volunteers, Dixon once again turned his attentions to the ever-growing enemy fleet lying off shore.

At about the same time that the crew of the *Hunley* was acquainting their two new members with the inner workings of the submarine, their skipper received an order from Charleston military headquarters concerning the boat they had been using as a support vessel. In the course of my investigation of the *Hunley*, I have found this order to be the last official Confederate document to mention Dixon or the submarine boat under his command.

"Headquarters Charleston, S.C. February 11th, 1864, Lieutenant Dixon: The Commanding General directs that you turn over to Mr. Theo Stoney the boat belonging to that gentleman which you are now using. Major Pringle has been directed to supply you with another suitable one."[187]

While checking Stoney in the Confederate civilian files at the National Archives, I learned he was Theodore D. Stoney, recording secretary of the Southern Torpedo Company, and co-designer of the *David* class torpedo boats.

Earlier in this chapter, I put forth the theory that the *Hunley* may have required a support vessel to tow her back to Breach Inlet on those mornings that Dixon had been unable to return to Battery Marshall, and instead run her aground along the coast. If this did indeed happen, it would have been necessary to have a boat capable of towing her to the inlet; other than this, I can see no other reason to have such a vessel. With the *Hunley* being the only offensive weapon in use at the time, it would seem reasonable to assume that military headquarters would have provided Dixon with

These notes, abstracted, from Confederate records after the War, show Corporal Carlson as having enlisted for the duration of the War at McClellanville, South Carolina, on April 1, 1863. His comrades in Company A had yet to learn of his heroic death aboard the "Hunley," when they officially listed him as "Absent without leave" on February 22, 1864. National Archives.

160

*This political cartoon depicting a sinking Confederacy appeared in an early 1864
edition of Frank Leslie's Illustrated Newspaper.*

Political cartoon making fun of the dwindling strength of the army of Jefferson Davis. Frank Leslie's Illustrated Newspaper.

The "Hunley's" successful attack on the "Housatonic" was launched from Breach Inlet, which is shown in this aerial view. Sullivan's Island is located to the left of the inlet and the Isle of Palms (formerly Long Island) is to the right. Air photo by Mark Ragan.

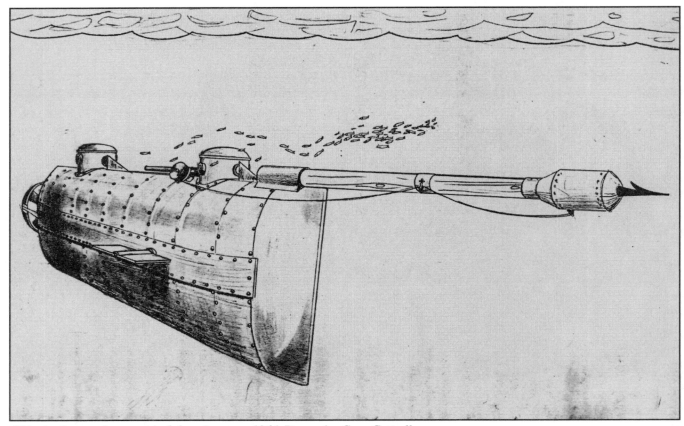

"Hunley" on undersea patrol, late January, 1864. Drawn by Greg Cottrell.

The United States sloop of war "Housatonic" was the first ship in history to be sunk by an enemy submarine.
Illustration from the *Official Records of the Union and Confederate Navies in the War of the Rebellion.*

Civil War photo of the view from battery Marshall on Sullivan's Island.
Reproduced from the Collections of the U.S. Library of Congress.

everything necessary to make the venture a success.

Evidence of this can be seen from an entry in the headquarters' book of endorsements written the previous day. In a short note to a subordinate, we find Beauregard making the following statement concerning the boat then being used by the *Hunley's* crew: "February 10th, 1864. If it is deemed necessary to take this boat from Lt. Dixon, Major Pringle must supply that officer with another as it is essential for the service on which he is employed. By command of General Beauregard."[188]

Judging from the forceful way in which the general worded his communication, there can be little doubt as to whether Pringle was able to supply Dixon with another suitable vessel.

At about the same time that the crew of the *Hunley* was returning the boat they had been using to its owner, the Union fleet was putting into motion a bold new strategy designed to intercept the well camouflaged blockade runners as they made their way down the coast. From the ramparts of Battery Marshall, a swift new sloop-of-war started to be seen at anchor each evening near Rattlesnake Shoal, not three miles past the breakers. The captain of this new vessel, Charles Pickering, was under orders to keep up a full head of steam throughout the night and run down or destroy any blockade runner that attempted to run into Charleston.[189] With her twelve large caliber guns loaded and ready for anything, the 207', 1240 tons, steam sloop-of-war *Housatonic,* [190], gently rocked at anchor within sight of Breach Inlet, unaware that the "diving torpedo" lay in waiting not fifty yards beyond its entrance.

From the sloping sand walls of Battery Marshall, Dixon and his band of underwater raiders leaned against a large Parrot gun and watched the powerful new warship drop her evening anchor within attack range of the *Hunley*. If the cold winter wind would die down, and the large swells flatten out for just one night, the veteran crew of the submarine knew they had her with little more than a two hour run from their dock.

With this menacing new warship lying only about three miles off shore, it would appear that Dixon decided on a swift new plan of attack. Since the ship could be reached within a couple of hours after nightfall, it was arranged that the *Hunley* would attack the vessel on the first calm evening, and once clear of her victim, signal Battery Marshall for a beacon to be exposed at the mouth of

Breach Inlet. The submarine would then make a run for this light before the numerous steam-powered picket boats could converge on the area. From evidence to be presented shortly, it could be assumed that this attack may very well have been the first time that a signal would be used to alert the battery to expose a homing beacon for the *Hunley*.[191]

In the course of my research, I found that the standard means of communication between the various forts and batteries scattered around Charleston harbor after dark was by calcium lights fitted with either a red or blue glass lens. These colored lights could be used individually or in combination depending on the situation. From evidence to be presented shortly, it would seems that Dixon was to take one of these signaling devices aboard his submarine and use it to alert Battery Marshall when he desired a shore beacon to guide him home.

While Dixon finalized his plan of attack, the crew of the *Housatonic* rode at anchor in a heavy sea, night after night guarding Rattlesnake Shoal against any vessels that might attempt to breach the federal blockade. To ensure that no torpedo craft was able to approach their vessel undetected during the night, six well-armed lookouts were posted on deck, one on each cathead, gangway, and quarter. The Officer of the Deck stood on the bridge; with two other officers posted at the forecastle and quarter-deck, each searching the dark horizon with telescopes, hoping to catch a glimpse of an inbound or outbound blockade runner. At the anchor chains, two men stood at the ready to slip the chain and set the ship free at the first sign of trouble. In the hot engine room, sweaty, grease and soot-covered sailors shoveled coal on the fire throughout the night, keeping the pressure within the boiler at a constant twenty-five pounds to ensure that the vessel could steam forward at a moment's notice. On the cold deck above, shivering sailors tried to sleep or played cards around their loaded cannons, ready in an instant to fire on any blockade runners that came within range.[192]

From the ramparts of Battery Marshall, Dixon and his crew could clearly see the twinkling lights of this powerful new warship as she rocked at her station, hoping that she would remain there until the wind and sea died down long enough for them to attack.

We know from contemporary accounts that this winter weather system severely hindered the

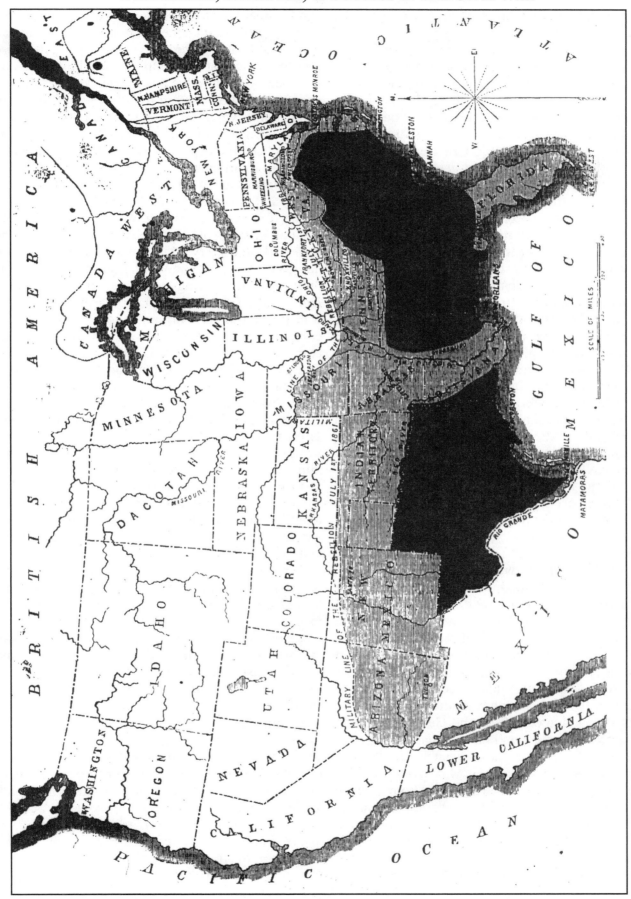

Early 1864 Harper's Weekly map showing how the Confederacy had shrunk since 1861.

Hunley's movements through much of early and mid-February. In fact, the winds were so severe during this period that the *Charleston Daily Courier* reported that several ironclad's were seen to anchor at Light House Inlet (on Morris Island) after dark to escape the rough seas offshore.[193] During this time Dixon and his crew would have monitored the weather very closely, searching for any sign that it might change long enough for an attack to be made on this new menace that lay at anchor just over three miles past the breakers.

Although information is sketchy, it would seem from the following excerpt (taken from a letter received by a northern newspaper from a sailor on blockade duty) that distorted rumors and or scuttlebutt regarding the *Hunley's* accidental sinkings and whereabouts were constantly being circulated through the union fleet; and that it may have been known that the *Hunley's* base of operations had been moved to Breach Inlet. From the following paragraph taken from a February (1864) issue of the New York Times we read.

"The submarine affair, they say, came out of Breach Inlet a week ago, intending to attack the Wabash, but she sunk when on the passage and drowned all hands. She was raised the following night and towed in again. This makes the third time that she has sunk and drowned all hands."

From the above paragraph it could be assumed that distorted accounts of the *Hunley's* duration test at Breach Inlet may have reached the fleet by way of Confederate deserters who were misinformed as to her current status and condition. Unfortunately for history, only the above text appeared in the New York Times article and neither the sender nor source of this fanciful information was revealed.[194]

While Dixon waited for a calm sea, he wrote to his old friend Alexander and informed him as to the current status of the crew and situation at Charleston. From Alexander's post-war writings we are told: "Soon after this I received a note from Lieutenant Dixon, saying that he succeeded in getting two volunteers from the German artillery, that for two days the wind had changed to fair, and he intended to try and get out that night."[195] The note mentioned by Alexander was written on the afternoon of February 17, 1864, just hours before Dixon and the crew of the Confederate submarine *H.L. Hunley* would set out from Breach Inlet and awkwardly usher in the birth of underwater warfare.

As the sun slowly settled behind the distant church steeples of Charleston, Dixon and the crew of the *Hunley* readied their submarine for the attack that would take place later that night. All those present knew that this patrol would be unlike any they had been on in the past. Instead of steering by compass for the phantom lights of a vessel that lay at anchor several miles out to sea, this attempt would be made on a ship that all knew could be approached and torpedoed well before midnight.

From an article that was written over sixty years after the events of February 17, 1864, had taken place, and appeared in the September, 1925, issue of the *Confederate Veteran*, we are informed as to what an 81 years old ex-Confederate, who had been stationed at Battery Marshall remembered of the days activities: "Daniel W. McLaurin is perhaps the only man now living who ever set foot on the *Hunley*, the first successful submarine. During the war he served as Corporal and Sergeant of his company, and in 1864 he was on duty with his command on Sullivan's Island, near Charleston. The port was at the time blockaded by the Federal fleet, and the *U.S.S. Housatonic* was one of the blockading squadron. During the day of February 17, 1864, Corporal McLaurin and another member of his regiment went on board the *Hunley* to adjust some machinery, and of the incident connecting him with it, he says: As I recall, the torpedo was fastened to the end of an iron pipe, about two inches in diameter and twenty or twenty-five feet in length, which could be extended in front and withdrawn at ease by guides in the center of the boat to hold it in place.

Lieutenant Dixon landed and requested that two of my regiment, the 23rd South Carolina Volunteers, go aboard and help them to adjust the machinery, as it was not working satisfactorily. Another man and I went aboard and helped propel the boat for some time while the Lieutenant and others adjusted the machinery and the rods that held the torpedo and got them to working satisfactorily."[196]

From McLaurin's interview it could be assumed that on the afternoon of February 17, 1864, Dixon and several members of his crew were making final adjustments to their torpedo delivery system in the back Bay Behind Battery Marshall. Whether they were experiencing some difficulties with the apparatus as McLaurin remembered, or just fine-tuning the device that afternoon may never be known, for in reading this article one must take into consideration that at the time McLaurin was

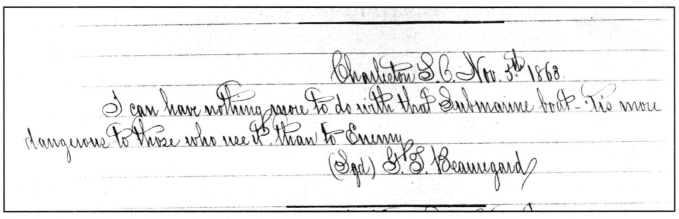

Despite the misgivings he expressed on November 5, 1863, General Beauregard ordered Lt. Dixon to proceed with the vessel to the entrance of the harbor and to "sink and destroy any vessel of the enemy." National Archives.

This picture of the wrecked blockade runner "Celt" was taken in 1865. The wreck of the blockade runner "Stono" (ex-U.S.S. "Isaac Smith") can be seen to the right of the "Celt's" paddle wheels. Both vessels were wrecked on the jetty while trying to avoid capture by ships of the federal blockade. It was hoped that the "Hunley" could force the enemy fleet to retreat further off shore and thus prevent expensive losses like these. Photo courtesy of the U.S. National Archives.

being interviewed for this story, Model "T's" had begun clogging America's roads, and Charles Lindberg was seeking backers for a proposed nonstop flight from New York to Paris. In any event, I feel that history has been well served by McLaurin's observations.

From among a group of Charleston torpedo diagrams captured at the end of the war (and copied by Union torpedo engineer Captain Adalfus Luettwitz, 54th New York Volunteers) comes a detailed blueprint of the Singer Torpedo that was used aboard the *Hunley*. From the angle of the shaft extending from the torpedo, it would appear that the explosive device carried at the end of the spar was to be lowered several feet beneath the surface prior to detonation. This detail is quite compatible with Mr. Mclaurin's recollections, for as cited above Mr. Mclaurin stated that the pipe which carried the device "could be extended in front and withdrawn at ease".

From McLaurin's description it would appear that the "machinery and the rods that held the torpedo" were in fact mechanisms designed to lower the explosive device beneath the *Hunley's* bow. This torpedo configuration was standard on the *David* class torpedo boats, and strong evidence exists suggesting that the designers of the *David's* torpedo configuration took part in re-designing the *Hunley's* revised spar apparatus as well. Evidence of this cooperation can be found in a letter sent to Captain Francis Lee (designer of the *David's* spar mounted torpedo system) from the Confederate Engineering Department in early March of 1864, for the text found within the communication in question glowingly praised Captain Lee for his contribution toward designing the torpedo delivery system on the submarine boat. [197]

Further evidence pointing to the fact that the *Hunley* adopted a *David* style torpedo configuration can be seen in a *Hunley* diagram drawn for Simon Lake by Charles Hasker during his visit in the summer of 1897. The diagram in question clearly show the subs diving planes in the up position (so as to keep the forward viewport above the surface while trimmed at natural buoyancy), with the spar of the *Hunley* angled down beneath the bow of the vessel. Since the powder filled explosive device was positively buoyant (and would therefore have to be forcibly lowered beneath the surface), no secondary means, other than the sleeve shown in the captured diagrams, would have been necessary for securing

the torpedo to the spar.

Unfortunately the barbed steel lance head that presumably attached the device to a ships wooden hull is not shown in the captured plans, and it could be assumed that the diagram for this spear head was either missing or considered too rudimentary for duplication in Captain Luettwitz's (May 12, 1865) report to General Gillmore on Charleston torpedoes.[198]

As the late afternoon slowly turned to twilight, Dixon and the crew of the *Hunley* continued to prepare their little diving machine for her dangerous rendezvous with the enemy sloop. While the submarine gently rocked in her slip, Dixon and several of his men walked to the mouth of Breach Inlet and took a final compass heading on the blockader they would be attacking later that evening. Although the weather had broken, and the sea was relatively smooth, Dixon knew that he would be unable to see the ship from surface level (when they came up for air) until they were quite close to the vessel. Another hindrance to the mission would be the expected bright moonlight. From previous evenings it was known that the moon that night would be very bright. If the *Hunley* was to approach the enemy ship in the final seconds of the attack undetected, a cloud cover would be necessary to blot out the light that could expose them. In spite of the the almost full moon, Dixon decided that they had waited long enough: the attack was on.

While the crew of the *Hunley* patiently waited for the sun to disappear over the marshes behind Sullivan's Island, Captain Pickering prepared his ship for the first calm night at their new station. From the Court of Inquiry held nine days after the attack on his vessel (a document from which I will quote frequently from this point forward), we are informed as to the captain's orders for the night of the 17th.

"The orders to the Executive Officer and the Officer of the Deck were to keep a vigilant lookout, glasses in constant use; there were three glasses in use by the Officer of the Deck, Officer of the Forecastle and Quarter Master, and six lookouts besides; and the moment he saw anything suspicious to slip the chain, sound the gong, without waiting for orders, and send for me. To keep the engines reversed and ready for going astern, as I had on a previous occasion got my slip rope foul of the propeller by going ahead.

I had the Pivot guns pivoted in broadside, the

Rear Admiral John A. Dahlgren (Commanding the South Atlantic Blockading Squadron), first learned of the "Hunley's" existence from Confederate deserters. Referred to in dispatches as the "Diver," or "Fish Boat," Dahlgren issued orders to the fleet to be on the lookout for the "infernal machine." In this picture, Dahlgren poses by one of the big guns that bore his name. The shattered remains of Fort Sumter can be seen over his shoulder. Courtesy of the U.S. Library of Congress.

(EXTRACT.)

HEAD QUARTERS, 1st MILITARY DISTRICT

Department of South Carolina, Georgia and *F*

Mt Pleasant, Charleston, Febuy 15 18.4

SPECIAL ORDERS,
No. 56

X   X   X

X The following Watchwords And Replies will be used on the dates mentioned below.

	Watchwords	Replies
Febuy 15th	Moon	Light
" 16th	White	Squall
" 17th	Green	Briar
" 18th	Yellow	Plush
" 19th	Stand	Advance
" 20th	Duty	Death
" 21st	West	End

X   X   X

By Command of
Brig Genl Ripley
Wm Ware
adjutant

Charleston Harbor watch words for the week of February 15-21, 1864. The pass word for the night of February 17th was Green-Briar. National Archives.

100 pounder on the starboard side, and the eleven inch gun on the port side; the battery all cast loose and loaded, and a round of cartridges kept in the arm chest so that two broadsides could be fired before the reception of powder from the magazine. Two shells, two canister and two grape were kept by each gun. The Quarter Gunner was stationed by the match, with the gong. Watch and lookouts armed as at Quarters. Three rockets were kept in the stands ready for the necessary signal. Two men were stationed at the slip rope, and others at the chain stopper and shackle on the spar deck. The chain was prepared for slipping by reversing the shackle, bow aft instead of forward. The pin which confined the bolt removed and a wooden pin substituted, and the shackle placed upon chain shoes for knocking the bolt out; so that all that was necessary to slip the chain was to strike the bolt with the sledge once, which broke the wooden pin, and drove the bolt across the deck, leaving the forward end of the chain clear of the shackle. I had all the necessary signals at hand, ready for an emergency. The order was to keep up 25 pounds of steam at night always, and have every thing ready for going astern instantly."[199] As the cooks in the galley of the *Housatonic* prepared to dish out the evening meal, Dixon, less than three miles away, checked the spindle and reel on the torpedo detonation system by the light of an oil lamp. All the soldiers at Battery Marshall knew that the crew of the *Hunley*, whom they had gotten to know over the past month, were going out that night and attempt to destroy the new blockader at anchor on the horizon. The dock from which the submarine was to depart would have been well lit with oil lanterns as curious onlookers watched Dixon make final adjustments to the torpedo at the end of the long spar. The men who had risked their lives so many nights in the past now stood together, rubbing their hands to keep warm while debating how long it might take to reach their target.

While the anxious crew of the *Hunley* stamped their feet and talked among themselves, Dixon rolled his sweethearts mangled good luck piece between his fingers and stared at the moon rising over the Atlantic. At the Battle of Shiloh in 1862, the good luck gold piece had taken the brunt of a bullet, and perhaps saved his now weakened leg from the surgeon's saw. Maybe it would bring him luck once again tonight. As he watched the moon rise over the calm ocean, he found to his dismay that it was even brighter than it had been on the

previous evening, and no cloud cover in sight. Since he knew that this new blockading sloop could be moved to a another station at any time, it was decided to risk being observed in the moonlight and proceed with the attack as planned.

From a relatively obscure booklet titled Reminiscences Charleston published just two years after the attack on the *Housatonic* (now on microfilm in the Library of Congress), we are informed as to the signal arrangement agreed upon to be given by Dixon after the attack: "The day of the night the perilous undertaking was accomplished, the little war vessel was taken to Breach Inlet. The officer in command (Dixon) told Lieutenant-Colonel Dantzler (Commander of Battery Marshall) when they bid each other good-by, that if he came off safe he would show two blue lights.[200]

As we shall see shortly, these blue lights agreed upon as the signal to light the shore beacon at Breach Inlet have become one of the most important keys to unraveling the mystery of the *Hunley*.

At about the same time that Dixon and Dantzler were having their last minute conversation at Breach Inlet, *Housatonic's* executive officer F.J. Higginson was preparing to go on deck to start his evening watch. From testimony given by him nine days later, we are informed as to the weather and location of the *Housatonic* on the night of February 17, 1864: "The weather was clear and pleasant - moonlight, not very bright, the sea was smooth; wind about North West force 2. It was low water, and there was about 28 feet of water at her anchorage. Fort Sumter bore about West North West six miles distance. The Battery on Breach Inlet, Sullivan's Island, was the nearest land, about two and a half miles distant."[201]

At about 7 o'clock, well over an hour after the sun had disappeared over the winter horizon, Dixon squeezed through the forward hatch of the *Hunley* and lit the candle. As the dark cold interior became illuminated from the tiny flame, Dixon's men climbed down through the narrow hatches and took their places at the crankshaft. In the faint shadowy light of the flickering candle, Dixon could make out the familiar faces of his uneasy crew as they looked to him for the order to move forward. With a nod of his head the heavy iron propeller shaft slowly started to turn in its metal braces. As the *Hunley* glided away from the crowded dock, Dixon turned her bow toward the faint lights of the enemy sloop-of-war. With a gentle turn of the rudder, the *Hunley*

Destruction of the U.S.S. "Housatonic" as sketched by a federal sailor. Courtesy of the U.S. Library of Congress.

This depiction of the destruction of the U.S.S. "Housatonic" appeared in a book published in 1899. It was probably based on the above sketch, but appears to be a more accurate portrayal of the vessel's masts, spars and rigging.
Used courtesy of Thomas E. Nease, Edisto Island Historic and Preservation Society.

maneuvered toward the mouth of Breach Inlet to embark on a mission that made history.

The exact events that transpired aboard the submarine after leaving her dock that evening can only be guessed at. As the *Hunley* put out to sea, Dixon probably paused shortly after clearing the mouth of Breach Inlet to ballast his vessel to neutral buoyancy. Once neutral, he would have continued his approach on the *Housatonic* from about six feet beneath the surface, occasionally coming up for air and observations. Within the damp submarine the confident crew of the *Hunley* continued to turn the crankshaft, while Dixon monitored the compass in the flickering candle light. If luck was with them, and they kept on course, they would be nearing their quarry within a couple of hours.

While candle wax dripped onto the floor of the submerged *Hunley*, Officer of the Deck John Crosby stood on the bridge of the *Housatonic*, scanning the calm horizon for any sign of a blockade runner. At the guns of the powerful vessel, sailors lounged and talked amongst themselves as the sloop-of-war gently rocked at anchor. Below decks, Pickering was seated at a desk in his cabin, reviewing and updating a book of charts. Not far from his quarters, Assistant Engineer Holihan monitored the steam gauge in the *Housatonic's* engine room, making sure that the pressure never fell below 25 pounds per square inch. We know from the testimony given at the Board of Inquiry, that the events just described are based in fact. Although we will never know what exactly transpired aboard the *Hunley* on the evening of February 17, 1864, we will forever know, in great detail, the individual experiences regarding the attack, from testimony given by various members of the *Housatonic's* crew on February 26, 1864.

We are very fortunate that this unique document has come down to us, for within it's faded handwritten pages, we are informed in vivid detail as to the events that took place during history's first successful submarine attack. From this point in our story, I will be able to share with the reader the exact words spoken by the *Housatonic's* officers and men, regarding their personnel observations.

While the deck crew assigned to the XI-inch Dahlgren smoothbore[202] loaded the huge cannon with grape shot,[203] Dixon and the crew of the *Hunley* were closing in on their victim from several feet below the surface. After over an hour of hard cranking, Dixon knew they must be getting close. As his anxious crew breathed in their ever-dwindling oxygen supply, it was decided to surface once again for observations and fresh air. As Dixon pulled back on the heavy diving planes, he put his eye to the forward view port. Within seconds, the forward hatch was above the surface creating a wake of white water as it cut through the small waves. Dixon quickly looked through each of the tiny windows trying to catch a glimpse of any picket boats that might be lurking nearby. With none in sight he shouted to his second officer to open the rear hatch for the much needed air. As a gush of sweet air flowed through the dark hull, Dixon noticed the twinkling lights of the *Housatonic* several hundred yards dead ahead; for once the compass had not let them down. After several anxious moments of running exposed on the surface, Dixon once again ordered the rear hatch sealed. With a powerful push on the diving lever, the submarine once more vanished beneath the waves.

As Dixon leveled off the diving machine, he informed his crew that tonight would be the night that they had all been waiting for. With this encouraging news, the crew of the *Hunley* let out a cheer as they cranked the shaft with renewed vigor. As the cheering died down, Dixon once again knelt down next to the dimly lit compass. With a firm grip on the rudder's wheel, he continued to guide the submarine towards her unsuspecting victim.

While Dixon struggled to keep the *Hunley* on course, Crosby, paced the deck of the big ship as he continued to search the horizon for any sign of an approaching vessel. From his testimony given on February 26, just nine days after the historic attack, we are told in great detail what that officer remembered of the encounter: "I took the deck at 8 P.M. on the night of February 17th. About 8:45 P.M. I saw something on the water, which at first looked to me like a porpoise, coming to the surface to blow."[204]

Could this officer have actually seen the *Hunley* surfacing for her final observation? Turning once again to William Alexander's 1902 Picayune article, we read "Dixon, who had been waiting so long for a change of wind, took the risk of the moon light and went out. The lookout on the ship saw him when he came to the surface for his final observation before striking her."[205] It would appear from Alexander's post-war writings that he considered the moonlight that evening to have been the main reason for the *Hunley's* premature discovery. Continuing now with Crosby's

Although ironclad gunboats were used throughout the United States Blockading Squadron, it also depended on her iron men and wooden ships. Navy Historical Center

The shock wave created when the torpedo exploded may have loosened rivets, opened seams, or cracked one of the submarine's glass viewing ports. Since the "Hunley" attacked on the surface, one of her hatches may have been purposely left open as an emergency escape route, or may have been improperly sealed as she tried to dive to escape detection. Any one of these could have been the actual cause of the loss of the "Hunley" and her men. Close-up photo by Mark Ragan of the forward hatch and snorkel assembly on the life-size replica of the *Hunley* on display in front of the Charleston Museum.

testimony, we read:

"It was about 75 to 100 yards from us on our starboard beam. The ship heading northwest by west 1/2 west at the time, the wind two or three points on the starboard bow. At that moment I called the Quartermaster's attention to it asking him if he saw any thing; he looked at it through his glass, and said he saw nothing but a tide ripple on the water. Looking again within an instant I saw it was coming towards the ship very fast. I gave orders to beat to quarters slip the chain and back the engine, the orders being executed immediately."

Crosby's testimony suggests that Dixon may have come to the surface for a final observation, and once seeing how close he was to the vessel's hull, quickly decided to make the final run. As the forward view port rose above the surface, Dixon's eye caught the massive hull of his target looming before him in the moonlight. In a hushed voice, he would have informed his crew that their target was less than one hundred yards in front of them and that he was going to attack her immediately. With whispers of approval the crew of the *Hunley* spun the crankshaft as fast as they could while their skipper peered through the tiny glass view port only inches above the surface.

As Dixon steered the submarine toward it's target, Executive Officer Higginson ran to the rail to see what all the commotion was about. From part of his testimony, we are informed as to what he saw coming towards him on the moonlit surface: "It had the appearance of a plank sharp at both ends; it was entirely on awash with the water, and there was a glimmer of light through the top of it, as though through a dead light." At about the same time that Higginson first caught sight of the candlelight illuminating the water through the *Hunley's* forward view ports, lookouts on the starboard side started to fire their muskets at the mysterious craft that was quickly approaching them.

With bullets ricocheting off the *Hunley's* iron hull, Dixon continued to hold the wheel firmly on course, oblivious to the lead striking the water all around him. Within moments he could expect the familiar jolt that accompanied the ramming of the torpedo's barbed metal head into the timbers beneath the water line. In the final seconds before impacting the *Housatonic's* hull, my imagination clearly sees Dixon letting out a high-pitched rebel yell, much as he had done many times while on the attack with the 21st Alabama. Immediately, his eager crew would have joined their skipper in

yelping out the shrill Confederate battle cry.

As high-pitched shouts echoed from within the *Hunley's* metal hull, Captain Pickering was just coming on deck to find out why the ship's company had been called to quarters. From his testimony given at the Board of Inquiry, we read the following: "I sprang from the table under the impression that a blockade runner was about. On reaching the deck I gave the order to slip, and heard for the first time it was a torpedo, I think from the Officer of the Deck. I repeated the order to slip, and gave the order to go astern, and to open fire. I turned instantly, took my double barreled gun loaded with buck shot, from Mr. Muzzey, my aide and clerk, and jumped up on the horse block on the starboard quarter which the first Lieutenant had just left having fired a musket at the torpedo.

I hastily examined the torpedo; it was shaped like a large whale boat, about two feet, more or less, under water; its position was at right angles to the ship, bow on, and the bow within two or three feet of the ships side, about abreast of the mizzen mast, and I supposed it was then fixing the torpedo on. I saw two projections or knobs about one third of the way from the bows. I fired at these, jumped down from the horse block, and ran to the port side of the Quarter Deck as far as the mizzen mast, singing out 'Go astern faster.'"

At about the same time that Pickering was emptying his double barreled shot gun into the *Hunley's* forward conning tower, Dixon would have been shouting his orders to back off or reverse propeller. While frantic sailors leaned over the rail firing muskets and pistols at the deadly contraption, Higginson stood on the bridge watching the action. From his sworn testimony we are informed: "I went on deck immediately, found the Officer of the Deck on the bridge, and asked him the cause of the alarm; he pointed about the starboard beam on the water and said 'there it is.' I then saw something resembling a plank moving towards the ship at a rate of 3 or 4 knots; it came close along side, a little forward of the mizzen mast on the starboard side. It then stopped, and appeared to move off slowly. I then went down from the bridge and took the rifle from the lookout on the horse block on the starboard quarter, and fired it at this object."

While chaos reigned on the decks above, Assistant Engineer Mayer was in the engine room, desperately trying to engage the huge propeller and move the powerful warship astern. From his testimony, we read: "Three bells were struck a few

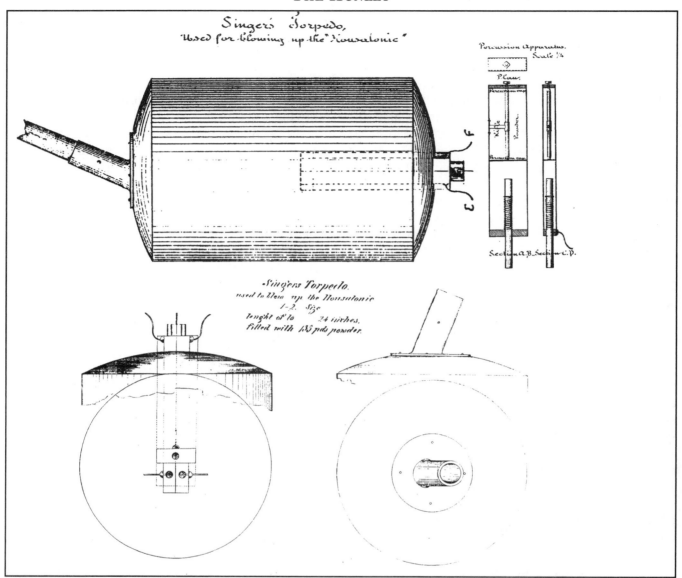

Captured diagram of the Singer torpedo used by the "Hunley" on February 17, 1864. National Archives.

Wartime engraving of the sinking of the "Housatonic." From *Frank Leslie's Illustrated Newspaper*, March 1864.

seconds after I got there, the engine was immediately backed, and had made three or four revolutions when I heard the explosion, accompanied by a sound of rushing water and crashing timbers and metal. Immediately the engine went with great velocity as if the propeller had broken off. I then throttled her down, but with little effect. I then jumped up the hatch, saw the ship was sinking and gave orders for all hands to go on deck."

At about the same time that the three bells were being struck to inform the engine room to go astern, Ensign Charles Craven was springing from his bunk and rushing on deck. In his own words we are informed as to what he remembered of his final moments aboard the *Housatonic*: "I heard the Officer of the Deck give the order 'Call all hands to Quarters.' I went on deck and saw something in the water on the starboard side of the ship, about 30 feet off, and the captain and the executive officer were firing at it. I fired two shots at her with my revolver as she was standing towards the ship as soon as I saw her, and a third shot when she was almost under the counter, having to lean over the port to fire it.

I then went to my division, which is the second, and consists of four broadside 32 pounder guns in the waist, and tried with the Captain of number six gun to train it on this object, as she was backing from the ship, and about 40 of 50 feet off then. I had nearly succeeded, and was almost about to pull the lock string when the explosion took place. I was jarred and thrown back on the topsail sheet bolts, which caused me to pull the lock string, and the hammer fell on the primer but without sufficient force to explode it. I replaced the primer and was trying to catch sight of the object in order to train the gun again upon it, when I found the water was ankle deep on deck by the main mast. I then went and assisted in clearing away the second launch."

In the raw excitement and confusion of the attack, one can only imagine the frenzied scene taking place within the *Hunley's* dimly lit hull, while sailors from the *Housatonic* desperately tried to destroy the diving machine with small arms fire. As bullets slammed into the exposed hatches and topsides of the submarine, all on board must have known that they were in a life or death struggle. If the powerful ship were not destroyed then and there, they knew that, although partially submerged, their vessel would still be an easy target for the large caliber guns that would be brought to

bear on them as they backed away. Even a viewing port pierced or cracked by a bullet or an exploding shell could spell their doom, as, if detected, it would force them to remain on the surface where they would be vulnerable to attack or capture. If a cracked port went undetected and the submarine submerged the result could be just as catastrophic.

From testimony given before the Board of Inquiry, it would appear that the *Hunley* was much closer to the *Housatonic's* hull when the explosion occurred than Dixon would have wanted. It's highly unlikely that ninety pounds of gun powder had ever been detonated so near the submarine's hull at any time in the past. With this fact in mind, one can only wonder at the magnitude of the powerful concussion felt by the crew of the submarine, as their tiny vessel was enveloped in the exploding torpedoes deadly shock wave.

As the *Hunley* pitched and shuttered in the reverberating waves caused by the powerful blast, sailors who had been below decks desperately struggled in the cold rising water to reach an open hatch. With sea water now pouring through the gaping hole made by the exploding torpedo, the hull of the doomed *Housatonic* violently rolled to port as water rose beneath her decks. In a desperate attempt to escape the rising water, sailors scrambled into long boats and the rigging that remained above the surface. Turning once again to Ensign Craven's testimony we are informed:

"Feeling the water around my feet, I started forward and found the ship was sinking very rapidly aft. Almost immediately she gave a lurch to port and settled on the bottom. Afterwards in looking about aft - for the body of Mr. Hazeltine; I saw that the starboard side of the Quarter Deck, aft the mizzen mast - furniture of the Ward Room and cabin floating within, so that I supposed the whole starboard side of the ship aft the mizzen mast was blown off. I heard a report like the distant firing of a howitzer. The ship went down by the stern, and about three or four minutes after the stern was submerged, the whole ship was submerged."

Adding to this testimony, Acting Master Joseph Congdon informs us of the following: "I drew my revolver, but before I could fire, the explosion took place. I immediately went forward and ordered the launches to be cleared away, supposing the captain and executive officer had both been killed by the explosion. The ship was sinking so rapidly, it seemed impossible to get the launches cleared away, so I drove the men up the rigging to save themselves.

After I got into the rigging I saw two of the boats had been cleared away, and were picking up men who were overboard. As soon as I saw all were picked up, I sent one of the boats to the *Canandaigua* for assistance."

Turning now to the log of the *Canandaigua* we read the following entry penned by the ship's captain, Joseph Green. "February 17th, 1864. At 9:20 P.M. discovered a boat pulling towards us. Hailed her and found her to be from the *Housatonic*. She reported the *Housatonic* sunk by a torpedo. Immediately slipped our chain and started for the scene of danger, with the *Housatonic's* boat in tow. At same time sent up three rockets and burned Coston signals number 82. At 9:30 P.M. picked up another boat from the *Housatonic*, with Captain Pickering on board. At 9:35 arrived at the *Housatonic* and found her sunk. Lowered all boats, sent them alongside, and rescued the officers and crew, clinging to the rigging."[206]

In those desperate minutes following the terrific underwater blast, one can only imagine the events unfolding on board the submarine. If the candle's flame had managed to survive the powerful concussion, what was the situation it now illuminated once the deadly shock wave had passed? Since Ensign Craven testified that he was attempting to bring one of the deck guns to bear on the object as it was backing away from the ship, we can assume that the *Hunley* was still maneuvering prior to the explosion. From the testimony given by over half a dozen eye witnesses, it was reported that the *Hunley* was met with a fierce barrage of small arms fire while approaching the sloop-of-war. Most of these bullets probably ricocheted off her iron skin with no damage, but what of the many loaded deck guns standing at the ready to destroy any vessel that came within range.

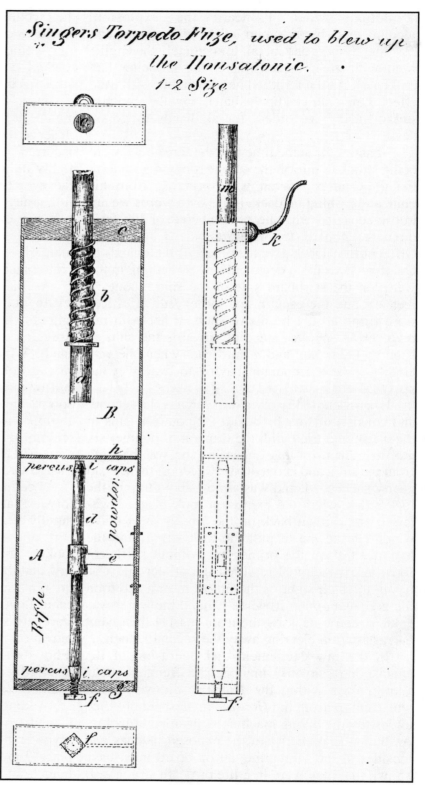

This Captured diagram shows how the spring loaded detonator on the *"Hunley's"* torpedo was fired.
General Gilmore's Private Papers, National Archives.

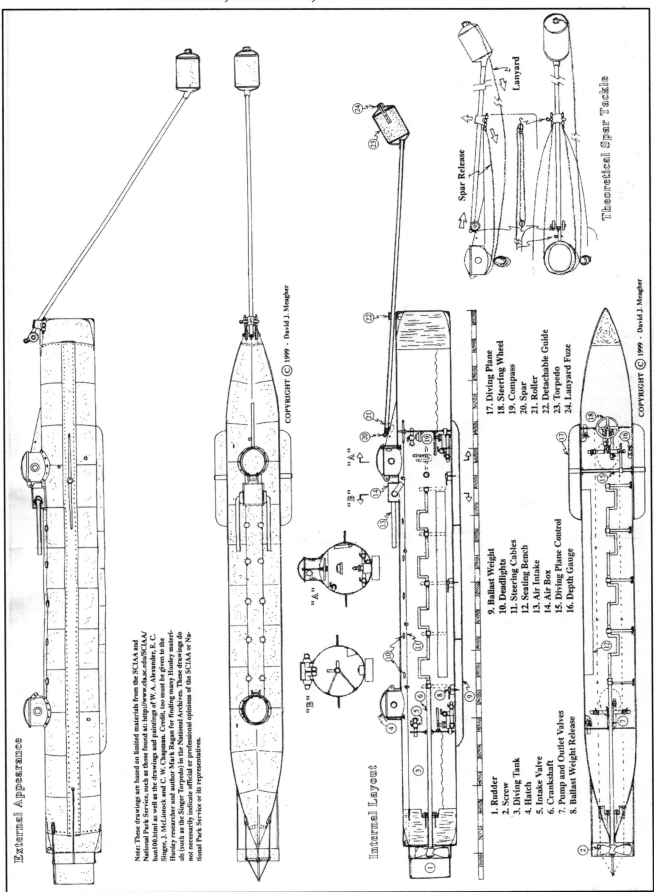

External Appearance

Note: These drawings are based on limited materials from the SCIAA and National Park Service, such as those found at: http://www.cla.sc.edu/SCIAA/hun100.html as well as the drawings and paintings of W. A. Alexander, E. C. Singer, J. McLintock and C. W. Chapman. Credit, too must be given to the Hunley researcher and author Mark Ragan for finding many Hunley materials (such as the Singer Torpedo) in the National Archives. These drawings do not necessarily indicate official or professional opinions of the SCIAA or National Park Service or its representatives.

COPYRIGHT © 1999 · David J. Meagher

Internal Layout

1. Rudder
2. Screw
3. Diving Tank
4. Hatch
5. Intake Valve
6. Crankshaft
7. Pump and Outlet Valves
8. Ballast Weight Release
9. Ballast Weight
10. Deadlights
11. Steering Cables
12. Seating Bench
13. Air Intake
14. Air Box
15. Diving Plane Control
16. Depth Gauge
17. Diving Plane
18. Steering Wheel
19. Compass
20. Spar
21. Roller
22. Detachable Guide
23. Torpedo
24. Lanyard Fuze

Spar Release

Lanyard

Theoretical Spar Tackle

COPYRIGHT © 1999 · David J. Meagher

This diagram shows the "Hunley's" torpedo configuration as drawn by David J. Meagher. Used courtesy of the artist.

CORRESPONDENCE.

THE LOSS OF THE HOUSATONIC.

To the Editor of the Army and Navy Journal:

SIR:—As a history of the recent disaster of the U. S. steamer *Housatonic* may be of interest to many of your readers, I will attempt a brief statement of facts:

On the evening of February 17th, the *Housatonic* was anchored outside the bar, two and a half miles from Breach Inlet battery, and five miles and three-fifths from the ruins of Sumter—her usual station on the blockade. There was but little wind or sea, the sky was cloudless and the moon shining brightly. A slight mist rested on the water, not sufficient, however, to prevent our discerning other vessels on the blockade two or three miles away. The usual lookouts were stationed on the forecastle, in the gangway and on the quarter-deck.

At about 8.45 of the first watch, the officer of the deck discovered, while looking in the direction of Breach Inlet battery, a slight disturbance of the water, like that produced by a porpoise. At that time it appeared to be about one hundred yards distant and a-beam. The quartermaster examined it with his glass and pronounced it a school of fish. As it was evidently nearing the ship, orders were at once given to slip the chain, beat to quarters, and call the captain. Just after issuing these orders, the master's mate from the forecastle reported the suspicious appearance to the officer in charge. The officers and men were promptly on deck, but by this time the submarine machine was so near us that its form and the phosphorescent lights produced by its motion through the water were plainly visible. At the call to quarters it had stopped, or nearly so, and then moved towards the stern of the vessel, probably to avoid our broadside guns. When the captain reached the deck, it was on the starboard quarter, and so near us that all attempts to train a gun on it were futile. Several shots were fired into it from revolvers and rifles; it also received two charges of buckshot from the captain's gun.

The chain had been slipped and the engines had just begun to move when the crash came, throwing timbers and splinters into the air, and apparently blowing off the entire stern of the vessel. This was immediately followed by a fearful rushing of water, the rolling out of a dense, black smoke from the stack and the settling of the vessel.

Orders were at once given to clear away the boats, and the men sprang to the work with a will. But we were filling too rapidly. The ship gave a lurch to port, and all the boats on that side were swamped. Many men and some officers jumped overboard and clung to such portions of the wreck as came within reach, while others sought safety in the rigging and tops. Fortunately we were in but twenty-eight feet of water, and two of the boats on the starboard side were lowered. Most of those who had jumped overboard were either picked up or swam back to the wreck. The two boats then pulled for the *Canandaigua*, one and a half miles distant. Assistance was promptly rendered by that vessel to those remaining on the wreck.

At muster the next morning, five of our number were found missing.

E. C. HASSELTINE, ensign, was attempting to clear a boat on the port-side when it was swamped. He seized the backboard and jumped into the sea, and was seen to go down, but it was impossible to render him any assistance. He was a promising young officer, beloved by all of us.

C. O. MUZZEY, captain's clerk, is supposed to have been in the cabin, and was probably killed by the explosion of the torpedo. One of the lookouts on the quarter-deck was never heard of.

A quartermaster jumped overboard and was drowned. A fireman went below for his money, when the ship was sinking, and never came back. The captain was thrown several feet into the air by the force of the explosion, and was painfully but not dangerously bruised and cut.

It was the opinion of all who saw the strange craft, that it was very nearly or entirely under water, that there was no smoke-stack, that it was from twenty to thirty feet in length.

Story of the sinking of the "Housatonic" that appeared in the March 5, 1864 edition of Army and Navy Journal.

Turning once again to Crosby's testimony, we read the question-and-answer as to why the *Hunley* was not blown out of the water by one of these large cannons.

"Question by the Court - Could a gun or guns have been brought to bear on the object at any time after its discovery? and were any fired at it? if nay, state the reasons there were not. Answer - No guns could have been brought to bear on the object because there was no time to train one in consequence of its moving so rapidly towards the ship; therefore no gun was fired." In regards to the explosion that destroyed the *Housatonic*, Crosby stated the following: "The explosion started me off my feet, as if the ship had struck hard on the bottom. I saw fragments of the wreck going up into the air. I saw no column of water thrown up, no smoke and no flame. There was no sharp report, but it sounded like a collision with another ship."

From Crosby's testimony, it appears that the torpedo had been detonated well below the *Housatonic's* water line. This would account for the fact that no terrific explosion was heard. With the blast taking place several feet beneath the surface of the water, the force of the concussion would have been almost entirely directed against the *Housatonic's* hull (path of least resistance). Unfortunately for the crew of the *Hunley*, this same shock wave would have been much more powerful having been detonated underwater instead of at the surface.

The ferocity of the unexpectedly close explosion may have severely crippled the submarine; bolts and rivets may have been loosened, or shafts that penetrated the hull could have been jarred or bent in their stuffing boxes. One must remember when reading this account that virtually nothing was known during the Victorian period regarding underwater acoustics, sound reverberation, or shock waves. The crew of the *Hunley* could only hope that their trip line allowed them to get far enough away from their victim when the explosive was detonated so as not to injure their vessel in the blast.

From the testimony given by numerous survivors of the attack, it would appear that the submarine was still relatively close to the *Housatonic* when the torpedo exploded. Perhaps the reel holding the line was struck by one of the many bullets fired at the submarine, thereby causing the reel to jam or otherwise malfunction. In any event, it becomes obvious that the *Hunley* was much closer to the gunboat at the time of the explosion than Dixon would have wanted. If his craft was damaged, Dixon could have done little except try to limp away under the cover of darkness, and, when safe, signal Battery Marshall to expose a shore beacon by which to guide his crippled vessel home.

Turning once again to the Board of Inquiry, we are informed as to a fascinating observation made by seaman Robert Flemming, the lookout posted at the starboard cathead. Flemming states that after the *Housatonic* sank, he climbed into the rigging that remained above the water. In his testimony, he informs us of the following. "When the *Canandaigua* got astern, and was lying athwart, of the *Housatonic*, about four ship lengths off, while I was in the fore rigging, I saw a blue light on the water just ahead of the *Canandaigua*, and on the starboard quarter of the *Housatonic*. "Could Flemming have actually seen the signal from the *Hunley* to Battery Marshall? Unfortunately the court's following question moved to another topic.

From a soon-to-be-cited report filed just 48 hours after the attack, it becomes clear that Flemming may very well have seen Dixon's signal; for Lt. Colonel Dantzler of Battery Marshall clearly states that the agreed signal from the *Hunley* was "observed and answered" that evening.[207] Judging from the testimony given by the officers and men of the *Housatonic*, and the fact that the agreed signal to light the shore beacon was observed from Battery Marshall, surviving documentation would indicate that the *Hunley* had survived the attack and met with some misfortune while returning to her docks at Breach Inlet. Whatever the cause of this accident might have been may forever remain a mystery to us, for of all the legends and rumors that have grown up surrounding the events that took place on the night of February 17, 1864, only one detail is known for sure; after successfully sinking the United States Sloop-of-War *Housatonic*, Lieutenant George E. Dixon and the crew of the Confederate States Submarine *H.L. Hunley* vanished without a trace and were never heard from again.

———————————

A blue light is observed on the horizon by an officer at Battery Marshall. Author's collection.

THE MERCURY

BY R. B. RHETT, JR.

OFFICE NO. 424 KING-STREET, CHARLESTON.

THE DAILY MERCURY, fifteen cents per copy, $15 for six months.
THE TRI-WEEKLY MERCURY, issued on Tuesdays, Thursdays and Saturdays, fifteen cents per copy, $8 for six months.
ADVERTISEMENTS, Three Dollars per square of 13 lines.

MONDAY, FEBRUARY 29, 1864.

SIEGE MATTERS—TWO HUNDRED AND THIRTY FIFTH DAY.

The news this morning from our immediate vicinity is quite as cheering as that which is echoed along the wires from the far off battle fields of Georgia and the Southwest.

An official despatch was received from Colonel ELLIOTT at Fort Sumter, on Saturday, conveying the gratifying news that one of our picket boats, commanded by boatswain SMITH, had captured a Yankee picket boat containing one officer and five men. The prisoners have arrived in the city. Their accounts of the success of the pioneer of our fleet of torpedo boats are really exhilirating. They state that the vessel sunk off the harbor on the night of the 16th, and reported lost in a gale, was the U. S. steamer *Housatonic*, carrying 12 guns and three hundred men, and that she was blown up by our torpedo boat.

This fine and powerful vessel was sunk in *three minutes*. The whole stern of the steamer was blown off by the explosion. All of the crew of the *Housatonic* are said to have been saved, except five—two officers and three men—who are missing and supposed to be drowned. As a practical and important result of this splendid achievement, the prisoners state that all the wooden vessels of the blockading squadron now go far out to sea every night, being afraid of the risk of riding at anchor in any portion of the outer harbor.

The torpedo boat that has accomplished this glorious exploit was under the command of Lieut. DIXON. We are glad to be able to assure our readers that the boat and crew are now safe.

Since our last report the shelling of the city has been maintained by the enemy with undiminished vigor. Two hundred and six shells had been thrown—one hundred and six on Saturday and one hundred on Sunday. At midnight the bombardment was still going on very briskly, one shell being thrown every five minutes.

The report from Fort Sumter is, "All quiet!"

DEATH OF CONDUCTOR PASSAILAIGUE.—The many friends of Mr. LOUIS J. PASSAILAIGUE, the well known and efficient Conductor on the South Carolina Railroad, will be shocked to learn by the announcement in another column that he is no more. He died at eleven o'clock on Saturday night, of Congestive Chills, after twelve days' illness. The deceased has been connected with the South Carolina Railroad, we believe, since his boyhood, and the energy, steadiness and urbanity with which, for several years past, he has filled the position of Conductor had won him general popularity. Mr. PASSAILAIGUE was in his thirty-third year. He leaves a wife and six children.

THE ALARM OF FIRE last evening at ten o'clock was caused by the partial burning of a small wooden building in Magazine street, opposite the Jail.

This story of the sinking of the "Hunley" was published in the Charleston "Mercury" of February 29, 1864. The day before Augustine Smythe, incorrectly believing local rumors, had written his "Little Sister" to tell her that the torpedo boat had succeeded in its mission and had safely run into the port of Georgetown. Article reproduced from the Charleston *Mercury*, February 29, 1864. Letter courtesy of the South Carolina Historical Society.

CHAPTER FIVE
Success & Sacrifice off Sullivan's Island

"As soon as its fate shall have been ascertained, pay a proper tribute to the gallantry and patriotism of its crew and officers." – General G.T. Beauregard, CSA, (Charleston, SC, February 20th, 1864)

Throughout the long, cold night of February 17, shivering guards walked the ramparts of Battery Marshall, waiting in vain for the return of the *Hunley* and her daring crew. In McLaurin's interview in the *Confederate Veteran*, we are informed that soldiers quartered at the end of Sullivan's Island watched the twinkling lights of the enemy's fleet that evening, anxiously waiting for some sign of the expected attack. McLaurin, while recalling that cold winter night so long ago, stated:

"About sundown the crew went aboard (the submarine) and put out to sea through the inlet between Sullivan's Island and Long Island, now called Isle of Palms, to search for their prey, the blockading fleet. The sinking of the *Housatonic* soon followed. We could see the commotion created by the frantic signaling from the various vessels of the blockade fleet."[208]

Although McLaurin states that "frantic signaling" between the enemy ships was observed that night from the beach, surviving documents point to the fact that the actual sinking of the *Housatonic* was not known at Confederate military headquarters until three or four days later. To trace the events leading up to the discovery of the *Housatonic's* destruction in Charleston, we must first read the report filed by Battery Marshall's commanding officer Lieutenant Colonel O.M. Dantzler.

"Head Quarters, Battery Marshall, Sullivan's Island. Feb. 19th, 1864. Lieutenant: I have the honor to report that the torpedo boat stationed at this post went out on the night of the 17th instant (Wednesday) and has not yet returned. The signals agreed upon to be given in case the boat wished a light to be exposed at this post as a guide for its return were observed and answered. An earlier report would have been made of this matter, but the Officer of the Day for yesterday was under the impression that the boat had returned, and so informed me. As soon as I became apprised of the fact, I sent a telegram to Captain Nance assistant adjutant-general, notifying him of it. Very respectfully Col. Dantzler."[209]

Judging from this report, it would appear that the *Hunley* had indeed survived the attack on the *Housatonic*, and had remained maneuverable long enough after the sinking to send a signal to the battery for a light to be exposed at Breach Inlet. Whatever the condition of the little vessel and the men inside her may have been at that time, I shall leave to the reader's imagination. Since no reference to the sinking of a ship was mentioned in Dantzler's report, it could be assumed that the weather conditions for the 18th and 19th were too hazy for the *Housatonic's* masts remaining above the surface to be observed from his post, or they saw them and incorrectly assumed that the *Housatonic* had simply moved just over the horizon, where her masts would still be visible but not her hull.

On the 18th, while Dantzler and the men under his command were wondering as to the whereabouts of Dixon and the overdue submarine torpedo boat, Captain Joseph Green of the *Canandaigua* was hastily writing the following report to Commodore Rowan. "*U.S.S. Canandaigua*, off Charleston, S.C., February 18, 1864. Sir: I have respectfully to report that a boat belonging to the *Housatonic* reached this ship last night at about 9:20, giving me information that vessel had been sunk at 8:45 p.m. by a rebel torpedo craft.

I immediately slipped our cable and started for her anchorage, and on arriving near it, at 9:35, discovered her sunk with her hammock netting under water; dispatched all boats and rescued from the wreck 21 officers and 129 men.

Captain Pickering was very much, but not dangerously, bruised and one man is slightly bruised. I have transferred to the *Wabash*, 8 of her officers and 49 men, on the account of the limited accommodations on board of this vessel. Very respectfully, your obedient servant, J.F. Green, Captain."[210]

The badly injured Pickering delegated to his executive officer the responsibility of reporting the disaster to Dahlgren, who was then at Port Royal, South Carolina. Executive Officer Higginson submitted the following report:

"*U.S.S. Canandaigua*, off Charleston, S.C., February 18, 1864. Sir: I have the honor to make the following report of the sinking of the *U.S.S.*

Housatonic, by a rebel torpedo off Charleston, S.C. on the evening of the 17th instant:

About 8:45 p.m. the officer of the deck, Acting Master J.K. Crosby, discovered something in the water about 100 yards from and moving toward the ship. It had the appearance of a plank moving on the water. It came directly toward the ship, the time from when it was first seen till it was close alongside being about two minutes.

During this time the chain was slipped, engine backed, and all hands called to quarters. The torpedo struck the ship forward of the mizzenmast, on the starboard side, in a line with the magazine. Having the after pivot gun pivoted to port we were unable to bring a gun to bear upon her.

About one minute after she was close alongside the explosion took place, the ship sinking to stern first and heeling to port as she sank. Most of the crew saved themselves by going into the rigging, while a boat was dispatched to the *Canandaigua*. This vessel came gallantly to our assistance and succeeded in rescuing all but the following named officers and men, viz, Ensign E.C. Hazeltine, Captain's Clerk C.O. Muzzey, Quartermaster John Williams, Landsman Theodore Parker, Second-Class Fireman John Walsh.

The above officers and men are missing and are supposed to have been drowned. Captain Pickering was seriously bruised by the explosion and is at present unable to make a report of the disaster."[211]

While Captain Pickering and the men of the *Housatonic* tried to sort out the details of the attack that had killed five of their fellow crew men and destroyed their vessel, General Ripley's headquarters at Mount Pleasant was just receiving Col. Dantzler's report on the overdue Hunley. After reading this report, General Ripley forwarded the document along with the following summary to General Jordan of Beauregard's staff.

"Head Quarters, Mount Pleasant, February 19th, 1864. General: Lieut. Col. Dantzler Commanding at Battery Marshall, reports that on the night of the 17th, the Torpedo Boat went out from Breach Inlet and has not returned. The signals agreed upon in case she wished to return were observed and answered from that post. Unless she has gone to Charleston, the boat has probably been lost or captured. I have no reason to believe that the crew would have deserted to the enemy. They were not however under my directions, and I fear that it is more likely that she has gone down judging from past experience of the machine."[212]

While going through the daily reports from Sullivan's Island (discussed in the last chapter), I was disappointed to discover that on about the first of February 1864, morning reports ceased being filed by each encampment, and instead one report covering the activities that had taken place in a ten day period were condensed into a single report. In the report filed for the period of February 10-20, Colonel Keitt (commanding Sullivan's Island, having taken the place of General Clingman) noted the following. "February 19: 94 shots fired by enemy at the city. February 20: 106 shots fired at city, Lt Col. Dantzler reports supposed loss of torpedo boat off Battery Marshall of which a special report was made."[213]

Judging from the large number of shells being hurled at the city during this period, it would seem that the activities taking place on the island had become somewhat chaotic, and the fact that the *Hunley* was overdue seems to have been regarded as trifling when measured against the actions taking place elsewhere. On the same day that this report was being filed with Confederate military head quarters, the mystery of the *Hunley's* strange disappearance was at last starting to unravel at Battery Marshall.

From the ramparts of the fortification, three masts could be seen protruding from beneath the water two or three miles off shore. Several federal tugs and barges were observed around the sunken vessel, and it was quickly assumed that the ship must have been a victim of the missing Hunley. Within an hour after the sighting, Col. Dantzler sent word of the discovery to General Ripley at Mount Pleasant, and later that day, the following report was on General Jordan's desk.

"Mount Pleasant, February 20th, 1864, Brig. General Jordan, Chief of Staff: Lt. Col. Dantzler reports a gunboat sunk off Battery Marshall, smoke stack and rigging visible, a tug boat and barge are around her, supposed to be the 'Flambeau.' Another has not been seen since Wednesday night and it may be that she was blown up by the missing torpedo boat."[214]

From a report filed that same day by Captain Green of the *Canandaigua*, we are informed as to the condition of the *Housatonic*, as seen by him that afternoon while Confederate soldiers at Battery Marshall watched from shore. "*U.S.S. Canandaigua*, February 20, 1864, Sir: I have examined the wreck of the *Housatonic* this morning and find her spar deck about 15 feet below the

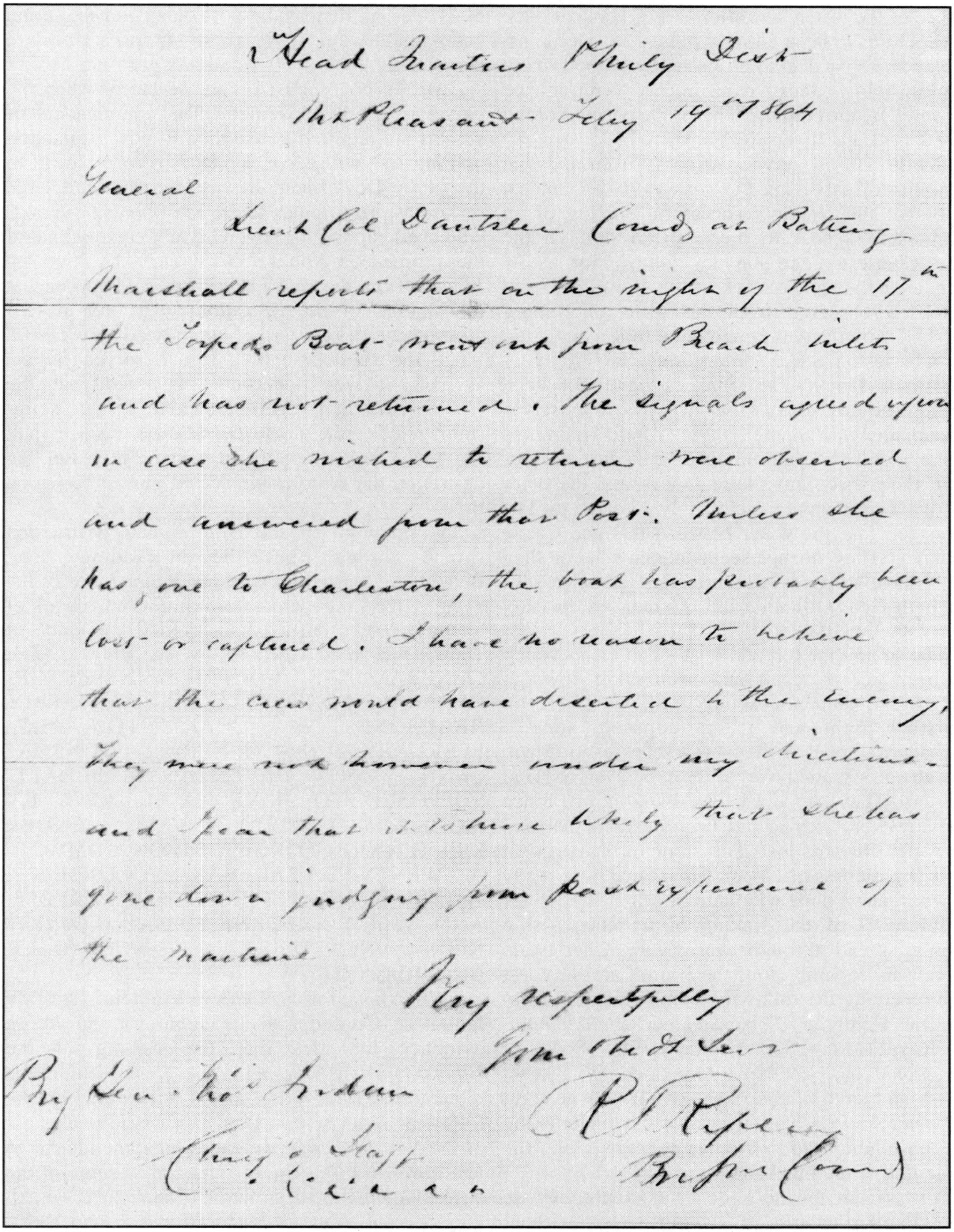

Head Quarters 1st Mily Dist

Mt Pleasant Feby 19th 1864

General

Lieut Col Dantzler Comdg at Battery
Marshall reports that on the night of the 17th
the Torpedo Boat went out from Breach Inlet
and has not returned. The signals agreed upon
in case she wished to return were observed
and answered from this Post. Unless she
has gone to Charleston, the boat has probably been
lost or captured. I have no reason to believe
that the crew would have deserted to the enemy,
They were not however under my directions.
and I fear that it is more likely that she has
gone down judging from past experience of
the machine

Very Respectfully
Your Obedt Servt
P T Ripley
Brigr Genl Comdg

Brig Gen Thos Jordan
Chiefs Staff
Charleston

General Ripley's letter of February 19, 1864, to General Jordan, stating that the "Hunley" had not returned and was feared lost with all hands. Courtesy of the U.S. National Archives.

surface of the water. The after part of her spar deck appears to have been entirely blown off. Her guns, etc., on the spar deck, and probably a good many articles below deck, can, in my opinion, be recovered by the employment for the purpose of the derrick boat and divers."215

While Union naval officers discussed the feasibility of salvaging the *Housatonic's* cannons, rumors of the *Hunley's* successful sinking of an enemy ship appear to have spread through the weary Charleston garrison like wild fire, for just 24 hours after the smoke stack of the *Housatonic* had first been observed from the walls of Battery Marshall, Smythe was penning the following letter.

"Charleston, S.C. February 21st, 1864. My very dear Aunt Janey: The Yankees have not been shelling the city today - but occupied themselves occasionally with Sumter, but not often. Their guns must evidently be wearing out. For the last week or so all their shells have fallen short, and the other day of 100 thrown at the city, only 12 came in. The others fell into the water between this and Castle Pinckney. They do not seem to know it, or they would have stopped. A deserter just come in says that both Gen. Gillmore and his men are heartily sick of shelling the city.

The submarine torpedo boat - The Fish - which has been put in repair and been lying down at Sullivan's Island for some time, went out on Thursday night and it is supposed, sunk a blockader, as one of them was seen to go down. This attack was unknown at the time even at Head Quarters. They supposed it was the storm. Since then however, nothing has been heard of her and she is put down as lost. The common name given her is 'murdering machine'. The *David's* are ready for work, and I hope will soon be put at it."

As news of the sinking of an enemy ship quickly spread through war weary Charleston, federal ship captains along the South Carolina coast were receiving the following communication from Admiral Dahlgren. "Flag-Steamer *Philadelphia*, Port Royal Harbor, S.C., February 19th, 1864. The *Housatonic* has just been torpedoed by a rebel *David*, and sunk almost instantly. It was at night and water smooth. The success of this undertaking will, no doubt, lead to similar attempts along the whole line of the blockade.

If vessels on the blockade are at anchor they are not safe, particularly in smooth water, without outriggers and hawsers stretched around with rope netting dropped into the water. Vessels on inside

blockade had better take post outside at night and keep underway, until these preparations are completed.

All the boats must be on the patrol when the vessel is not in movement. The commanders of vessels are required to use their utmost vigilance - nothing less will serve. I intend to recommend to the Navy Department the assignment of a large reward as prize money to crews of boats or vessels who shall capture, or beyond doubt destroy, one of these torpedoes. Admiral Dahlgren."216

Judging from the above order, it would appear that the sinking of the *Housatonic* was not at first attributed to a submarine, but instead to a *David*. Since the submarine had been observed on the surface, it was apparently assumed that the *Housatonic* had been attacked by a semi-submersible craft of the *David* class. As we shall see, this misinterpretation of the type of vessel that destroyed the *Housatonic* would persist for some time.

While word of the *Housatonic's* destruction spread through out the blockading fleet, Beauregard wasted no time in sending word of the event to the Confederate Capitol. From his book of telegrams sent during January and February of 1864, we read the following entry. "TO: GENERAL S. COOPER, INSPECTOR-GENERAL, CONFEDERATE STATES ARMY, RICHMOND, VA. CHARLESTON, S.C., FEBRUARY 21, 1864, GENERAL: A GUNBOAT SUNK OFF BATTERY MARSHALL. SUPPOSED TO HAVE BEEN DONE BY MOBILE TORPEDO BOAT UNDER LIEUTENANT GEORGE E. DIXON, COMPANY A. TWENTY-FIRST ALABAMA VOLUNTEERS, WHICH WENT OUT FOR THAT PURPOSE, AND WHICH I REGRET TO SAY HAS NOT BEEN HEARD OF SINCE. G.T. BEAUREGARD."217

While hope for the *Hunley's* safe return steadily faded at Confederate headquarters, surviving evidence indicates that the sinking of the *Housatonic* was causing great alarm within the blockading fleet lying off Charleston. In the following letter sent to Dahlgren from the Captain of the *New Ironsides*, we can form some idea as to just how wary the Union fleet had become in the days following the destruction of their sister vessel. "*U.S.S. New Ironsides*, Off Morris Island, S.C., February 23, 1864. Sir: since the *Housatonic* was sunk, the only picket boat that has reported for duty

Post war photograph of Confederate General R. S. Ripley. In this letter, Ripley passed on the news of "a gunboat sunk off Battery Marshall, smoke stack rigging visible" and speculated that she had been "blown up by the missing torpedo boat."
Photo reproduced from the collections of the Library of Congress, letter courtesy of the U.S. National Archives.

is that of the 'Supply.'"[218]

As the sun slowly disappeared over the western horizon each evening, nervous Union sailors must have stayed on deck as much as possible, straining their eyes in the darkness trying to catch a glimpse of the expected torpedo boat. If the vessel that had destroyed the *Housatonic* had been observed approaching the ship and was not stopped, what action they thought could be taken against the diving torpedo boat they had heard rumors of? Since nothing was known regarding the present status or location of the enemy vessel, those first few nights after the sinking must have been marked by many a sleepless Union sailor.

Turning once again to the post-war writings of Alexander, we are informed as to what he remembered of his first receiving news of the sinking, and of his original theory as to why the submarine and her crew had not returned. From his 1902 *New Orleans Picayune* article we read: "Next came the news that on February 17th the submarine torpedo boat 'Hunley' had sunk the United States sloop-of-war *Housatonic* outside the bar off Charleston, S.C. As I read, I cried out with disappointment that I was not there. Soon I noted that there was no mention of the whereabouts of the torpedo boat. I wired General Jordan daily for several days, but each time came the answer, 'No news of the torpedo boat.' After much thought, I concluded that Dixon had been unable to work his way back against wind and tide, and been carried out to sea."[219]

While Alexander daily telegraphed Jordan for information regarding the fate of his missing comrades, rumors of the submarine's survival and current whereabouts appear to have started circulating around the city. Just where these rumors regarding the *Hunley's* survival may have originated might never be known. However, judging from the evidence I shall put forward shortly, it would appear that intentional rumors were broadcast around the city, informing the Charleston garrison and citizenry that the *Hunley* had survived her attack on the enemy warship, and had gone to Georgetown (about forty miles up the coast) after destroying the vessel.[220]

On the night of February 26, a Union picket boat accidentally strayed too close to Fort Sumter and was captured by a craft belonging to the *C.S.S. Indian Chief*. Upon interrogating the crew of this vessel, it was discovered that the name of the United States warship sunk six days before was the

Housatonic and that five crewmen had been killed in the attack. As soon as news and confirmation of the sinking had been received at military headquarters, Beauregard hastily sent the following telegram to the Inspector General in Richmond: "CHARLESTON, S.C., FEBRUARY 27, 1864. GENERAL S. COOPER: PRISONERS REPORT THAT IT WAS THE U.S. SHIP OF WAR *HOUSATONIC*, 12 GUNS, WHICH WAS SUNK ON NIGHT 17TH INSTANT BY THE SUBMARINE TORPEDO BOAT, LIEUTENANT DIXON, OF ALABAMA, COMMANDING. THERE IS LITTLE HOPE OF SAFETY OF THAT BRAVE MAN AND HIS ASSOCIATES, HOWEVER, AS THEY WERE NOT CAPTURED. G. T. BEAUREGARD."[221]

News of the sinking of the *Housatonic* must have spread through Charleston very quickly, for the day before the story of the ship's destruction was printed in the Charleston papers, we find Smythe writing the following letter to his sister:

"February 28th, 1864. My dear little sister: There is a good piece of news here. The submarine torpedo boat was not lost, but had to go into Georgetown on account of the head wind, and she is there safe. She sunk the *Housatonic*, a splendid sloop of war, built since the war. Is this not fine? We captured on Friday night a Yankee picket boat, with an officer and six men, all fully armed. Our boat ran up to her, and though there was another large Yankee barge in sight, she had to surrender. This makes several boats we have taken from the Yankees.

The enemy are busy shelling the city and have been steadily at it now for three or four days, throwing one about every ten minutes. Very little damage now, compared to what was expected of them. They do set a few fires now and then, but these are quickly extinguished by our engines. One shell struck the hardware store the other day, bursting into the upper garret, and doing considerable damage. Give my love to all at home. Gus."[222]

With the city being constantly shelled by the enemy army, the news of the sinking of an enemy ship would have been reason for great rejoicing, and the fact that the submarine torpedo boat had not returned after the attack would have been suppressed for both morale and security reasons. With refugees and deserters constantly trickling from the city, it was probably decided at Confederate military headquarters to keep the facts of the *Hunley's* loss a secret so that the truth would not be discovered by the enemy. As long as the blockaders didn't know the submarine was lost they would be forced to waste time protecting themselves against a second attack that would never come.

On the day after Smythe had sent the letter to his sister informing her of the sinking, both the *Charleston Mercury* and the Daily Courier printed detailed reports of the *Housatonic's* destruction. While the Courier failed to mention the current status of the torpedo boat, the Mercury informed its readers of the following: "The torpedo boat that has accomplished this glorious exploit was under the command of Lieut. Dixon. We are glad to be able to assure our readers that the boat and crew are now safe." Since I have included a copy of the Mercury article, just as it appeared to the citizens of Charleston, I shall quote to the reader what the Daily Courier had to say of the event.

"February 29, 1864. On Friday night about half past nine o'clock one of our naval picket boats, under command of Boatswain J. M. Smith, captured a Yankee picket boat off Fort Sumter containing one commissioned officer and five men. A large barge, which was in company with the captured boat, managed to escape. The officer taken prisoner is Midshipman William H. Kitching, acting master's mate of the United States blockading steamer *Nipsic*. The rest of the prisoners are landsmen.

By the prisoners we learn that the blockader sunk by our torpedo boat on the night of the 16th instant was the United States steam sloop of war *Housatonic*, carrying twelve guns and a crew of three hundred men. They state that the torpedo boat, cigar shape, was first seen approaching by the watch on board the *Housatonic*. The alarm was given, and immediately all hands beat to quarters. A rapid musket fire was opened upon the boat, but without effect. Being unable to depress their guns, the order was given to slip the cable. In doing this, the *Housatonic* backed some distance and came in collision with the cigar boat. The torpedo exploded almost immediately, carrying away the whole stern of the vessel.

The steamer sunk in three minutes time, the officers and crew barely escaping to the rigging. Everything else on board - guns, stores, ammunition, etc., together with the small boats went down with her. The explosion made no noise and the affair was not known among the fleet until daybreak, when the crew was discovered and released from their uneasy positions. They had remained there all night. Two officers and three men are reported missing and supposed to be drowned.

The loss of the *Housatonic* caused great consternation in the fleet. All the wooden vessels are ordered to keep up steam and go out to sea every night, not being allowed to anchor inside. The picket boats have been doubled and the force in each boat increased.

This glorious success of our little torpedo boat, under the command of Lieutenant Dixon, of Mobile, has raised the hopes of our people, and the most sanguine expectations are now entertained of our being able to raise the siege in a way little dreamed of by the enemy.

Since our last report two hundred and six shells have been fired at the city up to five o'clock Sunday evening. The shelling of the city continued up to the hour of closing our report."[223]

During the course of my researching the history of the *Hunley* in Mobile, Alabama, I happened on an interesting letter in the city's library written by the head of the British Consulate in Charleston to his supervisors at the British Admiralty in London. From the following letter describing the attack on the *Housatonic*, it would appear that members of the English community in the city had heard the same rumors regarding the *Hunley's* survival as Smythe:

"British Consulate, Charleston, February 29, 1864. My Lord: I have the honor to report to your Lordship that on the night of the 17th instant, a torpedo boat was sent from this Harbor and encountered and destroyed the United States Steamer *Housatonic*, stationed off the bar on Blockading Service. The *Housatonic* was a large three masted propeller carrying twelve guns, and a crew of three hundred men.

From the crew of a small boat captured on the 27th instant, it is ascertained that the stern of the *Housatonic* was blown away, and the ship sunk in a few minutes; but, having been stationed in shallow water, her crew with the exception of five were enabled to save themselves by climbing the rigging and clinging to it until taken off by the boats from the United States Fleet, the next morning.

The torpedo boat proceeded to another port without sustaining any injury from the shock. As a result of this expedition, I have the honor to report the Blockading vessels are no longer stationary by

U.S.S. New Ironsides
Off Morris Island S.C.
February 23: 1864

Sir;—

Since the "Housatonic"
was Sunk, the only Picket boat
that has reported for duty is
that of the "Supply."

Very Respectfully
Your Obdt Servt

S.C. Rowan
Capt Comdg

Rear Admiral
Jnor't Dahlgren
Comdg S.A. B Squadron

As evidenced by this report, the sinking of the U.S.S. "Housatonic" temporarily interrupted the routine of the blockade. Letter courtesy of the U.S. National Archives.

night, and it is not unreasonable to suppose that the Blockade of the whole coast will very speedily be raised."[224]

While rumors of the *Hunley* having gone up the coast to Georgetown spread throughout Charleston, Captain Pickering and the officers of the *Housatonic* were being questioned in a Board of Inquiry (from which I quoted extensively in the last chapter) to determine the cause of the tragic sinking that had cost the fleet a sloop-of-war and five officers and men. After questioning all those who had witnessed the attack, the following conclusions were made by the naval officers who heard the case:

"First, That the *U.S.S. Housatonic* was blown up and sunk by a rebel torpedo craft on the night of February 17 last, about 9 o'clock p.m., while lying at an anchor in 27 feet of water off Charleston S.C., bearing E.S.E, and distant from Fort Sumter about 5 1/2 miles. The weather at the time of the occurrence was clear, the night bright and moonlight, wind moderate from the northward and westward, sea smooth and tide half ebb, the ship's head about W. N. W.

Second. That between 8:45 and 9 o'clock p.m. on said night an object in the water was discovered almost simultaneously by the officer of the deck and the lookout stationed at the starboard cathead, on the starboard bow of the ship, about 75 or 100 yards distant, having the appearance of a log. That on further and closer observation it presented a suspicious appearance, moving apparently with a speed of 3 or 4 knots in the direction of the starboard quarter of the ship, exhibiting two protuberances above and making a slight ripple in the water.

Third. That the strange object approached the ship with a rapidity precluding a gun of the battery being brought to bear upon it, and finally came in contact with the ship on her starboard quarter.

Fourth. That about one and a half minutes after the first discovery of the strange object the crew were called to quarters, the cable slipped, and the engine backed.

Fifth. That an explosion occurred about three minutes after the first discovery of the object, which blew up the after part of the ship, causing her to sink immediately after to the bottom, with her spar deck submerged.

Sixth. That several shots from small arms were fired at the object while it was alongside or near the ship before the explosion occurred.

Seventh. That the watch on deck, ship, and ship's battery were in all respects prepared for a sudden offensive or defensive movement; that lookouts were properly stationed and vigilance observed, and that officers and crew promptly assembled at their quarters.

Eighth. That order was preserved on board, and orders promptly obeyed by officers and crew up the time of the sinking of the ship. In view of the above facts the court have to express the opinion that no further military proceedings are necessary. J.F. Green, Captain and President."[225]

Shortly after Pickering and the officers of the *Housatonic* had closed the book on the sinking of their vessel, federal intelligence officers seem to have formed an interesting theory concerning the fate of the torpedo craft that sunk their blockader off Charleston. Since the sinking of the *Housatonic* was not reported in the Charleston papers until the 29th of February (12 days after the attack), it was apparently decided by military intelligence officers, (who regularly read all the Confederate news papers they could obtain), that the torpedo boat must have been lost in the attack, for if she had returned to port, news of the sinking would have been reported much earlier.

Shortly after coming to this conclusion, the following telegram was sent to the Navy Department in Washington. "BALTIMORE, MARCH 2, 1864., SECRETARY OF THE NAVY: THE TORPEDO BOAT *DAVID*, THAT SUNK THE *HOUSATONIC*, UNDOUBTEDLY SUNK AT THE TIME OF THE CONCUSSION, WITH ALL

Hd. Qr. &c
Ma 10ᵗʰ 1864.

Sir

I am directed by the Comᵈᵍ General to inform you that it was the Torpedo boat "H. L. Hunley" that destroyed the Federal man of War "Housatonic" and that Lieut Dixon commanded the expedition; but I regret to ~~It is with profound the greatest regret that~~ say that nothing since has been heard either of Lieut Dixon or the Torpedo boat, it is therefore feared that that gallant officer and his brave companions have perished ~~in the patriotic~~

R. G. C. S

To
H. J. Lesoy Eqʳ
Marietta Ga.

H. W. L
Capt & a. a. c,

"It was the torpedo boat 'H.L. Hunley' that destroyed the Federal man of war 'Housatonic' • • • but I regret to say that nothing has been heard either of Lieut. Dixon or the Torpedo boat, it is therefore feared that gallant officer and his brave companions have perished. Letter courtesy of the U.S. National Archives.

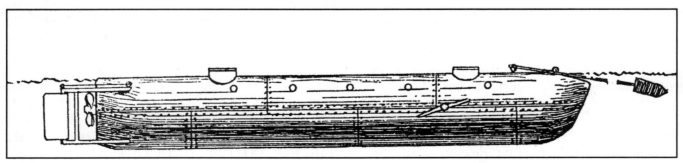

Charles Hasker's 1897 diagram of the Hunley depicts how the torpedo was configured. McLure's magazine, January, 1899.

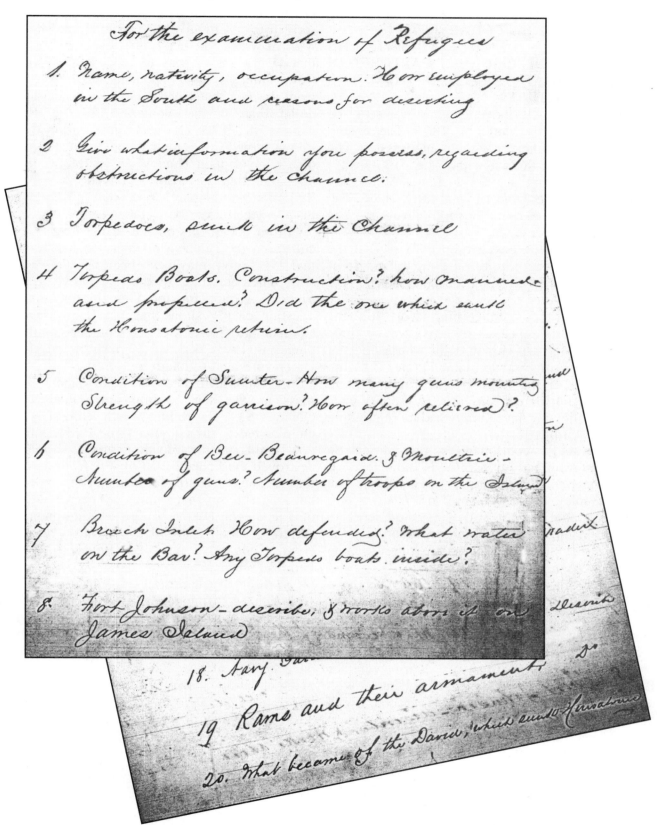

For the examination of Refugees

1. Name, nativity, occupation. How employed in the South and reasons for deserting

2. Give what information you possess, regarding obstructions in the Channel.

3. Torpedoes, sunk in the Channel

4. Torpedo Boats. Construction? how manned and propelled? Did the one which sunk the Housatonic return.

5. Condition of Sumter—How many guns mounting and Strength of garrison? How often relieved?

6. Condition of Bee—Beauregard. & Moultrie—Number of guns? Number of troops on the Island?

7. Breach Inlet How defended? What water on the Bar? Any Torpedo boats inside?

8. Fort Johnson—describe, & works above it on James Island

18. Navy...

19. Rams and their armaments

20. What became of the David, which sunk Housatonic

All "refugees" and prisoners of war taken by the blockade fleet at Charleston were carefully queried. One of the important questions was "Did the (torpedo boat) which sank the 'Housatonic' return?"
Courtesy of the U.S. National Archives.

HANDS. HOW THE *HOUSATONIC* WAS SUNK WAS NOT KNOWN AT CHARLESTON UNTIL THE 27TH, WHEN THE PRISONERS, CAPTURED IN A PICKET BOAT, DIVULGED THEM THE FACTS. C. C. FULTON."[226]

The day after the above telegram was sent, the Mercury reported. "March 3, 1864. The enemy continues to shell the city without intermission. The number of shells thrown within the past twenty-four hours, closing at 5 o'clock on Wednesday evening, was one hundred and forty eight. The results are about as usual. Several narrow escapes were made yesterday.

The enemy were engaged on the wreck of the *Housatonic*, endeavoring to raise the armament of the sunken vessel. No change has taken place in the position of the fleet."[227]

Brief references concerning work on the *Housatonic* also appeared in next two or three issues of the Mercury. However, the whereabouts of the missing *Hunley* was left unmentioned. Judging from reports of the large number of exploding shells being hurled into the heart of the city each day, the public may have simply had more pressing things on their mind.

While shells continued to rain down on Charleston from far off Morris Island, Henry J. Leovy, a pre-war friend and associate of the late Horace Hunley, heard rumors of the *Housatonic's* destruction and sent the following short letter to General Beauregard, requesting confirmation of the story and current status of the submarine which he claimed to be part owner.

"March 5th, 1864. Sir: Vague dispatches have reached me with reference to the destruction of the *Housatonic*, and as I am one of the owners of the Torpedo Boat *H.L. Hunley* and also the executor of the late Captain Hunley, who sacrificed his life. I am exceedingly anxious to learn whether Lieutenant Dixon accomplished his gallant act with our boat or not, and whether he has escaped. It will be a source of infinite pride to me to learn this...Respectfully Henry Leovy." [228]

Judging from the contents of the above communication it would appear that the mysterious Mr. Leovy had more than a casual relationship with the Singer Submarine Corps. From as early as the inception of the Privateering submarine vessel *Pioneer*, it would seem that Henry Leovy had been in the shadows, or fringes, of these undersea projects, for his name appears along side that of

Horace Hunley on the Pioneer's letter of Marque (privateering Commission). From Horace Hunley's will (of which Mr. Leovy was executor) we know that Henry Leovy was to receive $5000 dollars from Hunley's estate upon his death.[229] Judging from the fact that Horace Hunley owned a $5000 dollar share of the submarine boat, it could be assumed from the above communication that Mr. Leovy turned down the cash and instead opted to take over Captain Hunley's share of the torpedo boat. (Mr. Leovy is also mentioned in the Gardner Smith letter to Hunley's sister that informed her of his accidental death on October 15th.)

From documents on file in the Louis Genella collection (at Tulane University) comes evidence that Mr. Leovy may have been too pre-occupied with other activities to take an active roll with Singer's group; for the Genella documents in question clearly show that Mr. Leovy headed a Confederate Secret Service counter intelligence bureau that was assigned the task of ferreting out Union spies and southern traitors.

In response to Leovy's inquiry, the following message was sent to him immediately. "Head Quarters S.C., Ga. & Fla. March 10th, 1864. Sir: I am directed by the commanding General to inform you that it was the torpedo boat *H.L. Hunley* that destroyed the Federal man of war *Housatonic* and that Lieutenant Dixon commanded the expedition; but I regret to say that nothing has been heard either of Lieutenant Dixon or the torpedo boat, it is therefore feared that gallant officer and his brave companions have perished. Respectfully H.W. Feilden."[230]

With all of Charleston's hospitals overflowing with sick and wounded, mixed with the fact that over one hundred shells a day were being indiscriminately hurled into the heart of the city, it would appear that with so many being killed each day, the fate of nine missing men was not given much attention, and soon disappeared from the list of priorities at Charleston military headquarters.

As the bombardment of the city continued night and day, many within its battered fortifications decided that they had enough and deserted to the federal forces firmly entrenched on Morris Island. With a steady trickling of refugees, runaway slaves and deserters coming into the Union lines each week, a list of questions to be asked each new-comer was drawn up at headquarters. From the list of twenty questions to be asked each deserter for the months of March and April, 1864, we find that

No 1.—

The American Diver was built at Mobile and was brought on two flatform cars from Mobile to Charleston, Saw her in all stages of construction at Mobile Sometimes worked near her in the Same Shop – thinks She is about 35 feet long, height about same as David (5½ ft) has propeller at the end, She is not driven by steam, but her propeller is turned by hand,— Has two man heads on the upper Side, about 12 to 14 feet apart. The entrance into her is through these man heads; the heads being turned back, they are all used to look out of. (Will give a sketch and description of her) She has had bad accidents hitherto – but was owing to those in her, not understanding her, thinks that She can be worked perfectly safe by persons who understand her, can be driven 5 knots an hour without exertion to the men working her, manheads are about 16 in high, and are just above water when trimmed. Believes was brought here about 1st Sept. has seen her working in the water afloat, passed her in the gig— she being the last time before his arrival

This testimony from a Confederate deserter, who had worked in the Parks & Lyons machine shop in Mobile and later served aboard the C.S.S. "Indian Chief" in Charleston Harbor, refers to the "Hunley" as the "American Diver," but he may be confusing the historic submarine with her immediate predecessor, not realizing that more than one similarly sized submarine had been built in the Alabama machine shop. Document courtesy U.S. National Archives.

Has drowned 3 crews, one at Mobile and 2 here, 17 men in all, when She went down the last time, was on the bottom 2 weeks before she was raised; — Saw her when she was raised the last time. They then hoisted her out of the iron, refitted her, and got another crew, — Saw her after that submerged, Saw her go under the "Indian Chief", an then Saw her go back under again, she made about ½ mile in the dives; Saw her dive under the Charleston — went under about 250 feet from her, and came up about 300 feet beyond her — was about twenty minutes under the water, when She went under the "Indian Chief" — her keel is of cast iron in sections, which can be cast loose when She wishes to rise to the surface of the water — believes she is at Mount Pleasant — One of her crew who belongs to his vessel, came back for his clothes, and said she was going down there as a Station, where they would watch her time for operation. —

This January 7, 1864, account by a Confederate deserter, states that the "Hunley" had already drowned three crews, one at Mobile and two at Charleston. The alleged sinking in Mobile is not supported by other evidence and was probably mere rumor. Document courtesy of the U.S. National Archives.

the fourth and twentieth ask information regarding the fate of the *Hunley*. After asking why the individual deserted and the current situation in Charleston, the fourth and last inquiries on the list read as follows. "4.) Torpedo boats. Construction? How manned and propelled? Did the one that sunk the *Housatonic* return? 20.) What became of the *David* that sunk the *Housatonic?*" [231]

While going through the summaries of deserters testimonies for this period at the National Archives, I was surprised to find a report filed on a Confederate deserter named John Clongh who evidently had heard the same rumors as Smythe; for in this summary of his testimony dated March 16, 1864, we read the following. "Name: John Clongh, Born: Ireland. Came to South Carolina in 1850, in Charleston five years. Worked on breastworks in forts of the rear, never worked on Sumter. Did not know in Charleston that the *Housatonic* was sunk until boats crew of *Nipsic* reported it. He has no knowledge of arrival back of torpedo boat. Report was that it went in at Georgetown."[232]

The above evidence suggests that the Charleston garrison had been hoodwinked by rumors claiming that the *Hunley* survived her attack on the *Housatonic* and had lived to fight another day from forty miles up the coast. With so many shells exploding in the city daily, this rumor was probably taken cheerfully at face value and widely circulated by the hopeful citizens of unyielding Charleston.

The last word on the sinking of the *Housatonic* appeared in the March 14, 1864, morning edition of the *Charleston Mercury*. A sailor attached to the *Housatonic* had written a letter describing the attack. The letter was printed in the Boston Herald and subsequently read by Confederate agents who apparently forwarded the story to Charleston. (This is a good example of how enemy newspapers were constantly being read and quoted by both sides.) In the following narrative, we read what one Union sailor wrote of the attack and sinking of his vessel while on blockade duty off Charleston:

"The destruction of the *Housatonic* off Charleston - A letter in the Boston 'Herald,' from off Charleston, gives an account of the blowing up of the corvette *Housatonic* by a Confederate torpedo steamer. The event took place about 9 o'clock on one of the coldest nights of the Winter. The letter says:

A long object just on the edge of the water, was discovered astern of the ship. In an instant the cable was slipped, the alarm sounded, and all hands beat to quarters, but before the ship had made any headway the torpedo exploded under her starboard quarter, making a most frightful report. The propeller was broken off, the stern was torn to pieces, and the ship sunk rapidly in less than eight minutes from the time that the torpedo machine was first seen. The vessel sunk in six fathoms of water. As she began to sink the most frightful scenes were witnessed. Men with nothing but their shirts on were seen struggling in the water, officers were trying to get the boats loose, while others were mounting the rigging. Three boats were finally unlashed, and these were sent to rescue those in the water. the gig at once started for the *Canandaigua*, carrying Captain Pickering who was badly injured, but is now doing well.

As soon as Capt. Greene, of the *Canandaigua*, got the news, he at once hoisted signals of distress and came to our assistance, and in three hours after the attack on the *Housatonic* all hands that were saved were safely transferred to that ship, where they received every attention. Subsequently a portion of the survivors were transferred to the *Wabash*.

The *Housatonic* is a total loss, all hands lost all they possessed - money, clothes, etc. In fact many of them, including some of the officers, went on board of the *Canandaigua* in a naked state. A sad accident of the disaster is the loss of Ensign Hazeltine, of Concord, New Hampshire; Mr. Muzzey, Captains Clerk; John Williams, Quartermaster, and John Welsh, coal heaver of Boston, were drowned. The latter had got safely on the deck, but ventured back to save $300, which he had in his bag on the berth deck. Poor fellow, he never returned. Theo. Parker, who was on the lookout directly over where the ship was struck, was blown into the air, and instantly killed. Captain Pickering was slightly injured by the explosion. John Goff, the Captain's steward, was somewhat injured. these were all the casualties. The officers and men of the ship displayed the greatest coolness during the trying scene, and thereby saved many lives. The *Housatonic* has been the especial spite of the rebels. Three times they have tried to destroy her, and now they have succeeded.

It is feared that many other of the vessels on the blockade will follow the fate of the *Housatonic*. It is well known that the rebels have six or eight more of these infernal machines ready to pounce upon the fleet. The masts of the *Housatonic* are all that

Despatch No. 69.

Flag Steamer Philadelphia.
Port Royal Harbor S.C.
February 19th 1864

Honorable Gideon Welles.
Secretary of the Navy
Washington D.C.

Sir:—

I much regret to inform the Department, that the U.S. Steam Sloop Housatonic, on the blockade off Charleston S.C., was torpedoed by a Rebel "David", and sunk on the night of the 17th February, about nine o'clock.

From the time the "David" was seen, until the vessel was on the bottom, a very brief period must have elapsed;— So far as the Executive Officer (Lieut. Higginson) can judge, and he is the only officer of the Housatonic whom I have seen it did not exceed five or seven minutes.

Admiral Dahlgren's report to the Secretary of the Navy advising him of the sinking of the U.S.S. "Housatonic."
Report courtesy of the U.S. National Archives.

can be seen of her, and the gale which is now prevailing will do much to make a complete wreck of that once noble ship.

Ensign Hazeltine got into the second boat, and had he remained in it would have been saved; but as the ship careened over he jumped on board. The last ever seen of him he was floating among the fragments of the wreck, a corpse.

At low tide the water is about six feet above the rail of the *Housatonic*. If the weather moderates, her guns, and many valuable articles and the pay masters safe will be recovered. She can not be raised, as her stern is completely blown off, clean to the ward room hatch. She was loaded down with coal and provisions, which will be a total loss. Many of the survivors had quite large sums of money laid away to send home by the next mail. the loss to them is severe."[233]

As the days following the attack on the *Housatonic* turned to weeks, the jubilation once felt over the sinking of an enemy ship soon faded in unhappy Charleston. With the number of exploding shells being dropped into the city increasing each day, it was obvious to all those who remained that it was only a matter of time before the city's garrison would have to abandon Charleston and link up with General Johnston's ragged army trying to halt the enemy's advance in nearby Georgia.

From the book of letters sent from Charleston headquarters for the month of April 1864, we find a note to General Maury of Mobile, informing him as to the fate of Dixon and his brave crew of adventurers. Although nothing was known at the time as to why the *Hunley* had not returned, Captain Grey of the Charleston Torpedo Service informs the general as to what he believes to have been the fate of the missing submarine:

"Charleston, S.C., April 29, 1864. General: In answer to a communication of yours, received through headquarters, relative to Lieutenant Dixon and crew, I beg leave to state that I was not informed as to the service in which Lieutenant Dixon was engaged or under what orders he was acting. I am informed that he requested Commodore Tucker to furnish him some men, which he did. Their names are as follows, Viz: Arnold Becker, C. Simkins, James A. Wicks, F. Collins, and Ridgeway, all of the Navy, and Corporal C.F. Carlson, of Captain Wagner's company of artillery.

The United States sloop of war *Housatonic* was attacked and destroyed on the night of the 17th of February. Since that time no information has been received of either the boat or crew. I am of the opinion that, the torpedoes being placed at the bow of the boat, she went into the hole made in the *Housatonic* by explosion of torpedoes and did not have sufficient power to back out, consequently sunk with her.

I have the honor to be, General, very respectfully, your obedient servant, M. M. Grey, Captain in Charge of Torpedoes."[234]

As the spring of 1864 slowly warmed into summer, the badly battered Confederacy defiantly prepared for what would become her final acts. In far off Virginia, General Lee, outnumbered nearly two to one, faced the most recent of President Lincoln's generals, Ulysses S. Grant in what would become a death struggle for the Confederate Capital at Richmond. To the west, General William T. Sherman would cut a path sixty miles wide across Georgia, lay siege to Atlanta, burn the proud city then march on towards the most hated of all the Confederate states: South Carolina, the birth place of the secessionist movement.

While the federal grip on the worn-out Confederacy continued to tighten, it would appear that Baxter Watson, now planting underwater mines with James McClintock in Mobile Bay, had not yet given up on a dream of his to build yet a fourth submarine boat. In the collection of letters received by Confederate President Jefferson Davis, we find the following late war communication from far off Alabama.

"Mobile, October 10th, 1864, The Honorable President Davis: Sir: Being the inventor of the Submarine boat that destroyed the Yankee vessel *Housatonic* in Charleston harbor in February last, and being unable to build another. I have concluded to lay the matter before you, and ask your assistance and influence in the matter, as I have exhausted all the capital that I had in building and experimenting with that one which was lost in Charleston.

A boat of that description I am satisfied after three years experience can not be used successfully without Electro-Magnetism as power, the air in the boat will not sustain so many men long enough for the time required. (Watson appears to have been unaware of Dixon's 2 1/2 hour submerged duration test.) I have tried to procure an Electro Magnetic engine, but so far have not accomplished it.

I can procure an engine of this description by going to New York or Washington City, but the amount of five thousand dollars in exchange necessary is more that I can raise.

I can fully satisfy you that this is of much value to the Confederacy and would like to have the government take the matter in hand. If you desire it, I will be happy to give you a full description, and all the necessary proofs of the utility of the enterprise. Your humble subscriber Baxter Watson, (Address care of Park & Lyons Mobile Alabama)."[235]

With the war in it's final stages and the Confederate Capital practically surrounded by an enemy army, one can only imagine how much consideration was given to the proposed construction of an electrically powered submarine boat. While the weary armies of Generals Lee and Grant faced one another from the muddy trenches of Petersburg, Union divers outside Charleston were completing a week long survey of several wrecked blockade runners along with the submerged hull of the *Housatonic*. From the following report sent to Dahlgren, we find that by November, 1864, it was known within the fleet that the *Hunley* had not returned, and that the wreck of this Confederate secret weapon might be found near its victim:

"U.S. Schooner *G.W. Blunt*, November 27, 1864. Sir: After a careful examination of the wrecks of the sunken blockade runners and *Housatonic*, I have the honor to make the following report:

I find that the wrecks of the blockade runners are so badly broken up as to be worthless. The *Housatonic* is very much worm-eaten, as I find from pieces which have been brought up. She is in an upright position; has settled in the sand about 5 feet, forming a bank of mud and sand around her bed; the mud has collected in her in small quantities. The cabin is completely demolished, as are also all the bulkheads abaft the mainmast; the coal is scattered about her lower decks in heaps, as well as muskets, small arms, and quantities of rubbish.

I tried to find the magazine, but the weather has been so unfavorable and the swell so great that it was not safe to keep a diver in the wreck. I took advantage of all the good weather that I had, and examined as much as was possible.

The propeller is in an upright position; the shaft appears to be broken. The rudder post and rudder have been partly blown off; the upper parts of both are in their proper places, while the lower parts have been forced aft. The stern frame rests upon the

rudder post and propeller; any part of it can be easily slung with chain slings, and a powerful steamer can detach each part.

I have also caused the bottom to be dragged to an area of 500 yards around the wreck, finding nothing of the torpedo boat. On the 24th the drag ropes caught something heavy. On sending a diver down to examine it, proved to be a quantity of rubbish. The examination being completed, I could accomplish nothing further, unless it is the intention to raise the wreck or propeller, in which case it will be necessary to have more machinery. Very respectfully, your obedient servant, W. L. Churchill, Lieutenant Commanding."[236]

Upon reading the diver's report, Admiral Dahlgren forwarded a copy to the Secretary of the Navy along with the following note: "Flag-Steamer *Philadelphia*, November 28, 1864. Sir: I transmit herewith a report of the squadron diver in relation to the wrecks of the *Housatonic* and some blockade runners which were driven ashore at different times by vessels of the blockade.

It is to be presumed that all the perishable articles are now valueless; the metallic parts will be recovered whenever the services of the divers can be spared from the vessels in service."[237]

With nothing found of the missing *Hunley*, federal ships on blockade duty continued to maintain their strangle hold on defiant Charleston with little fear of attack. With the city's defenses near collapse, and the federal batteries on Morris Island continuing to pound the ruins of Fort Sumter, it would seem that Baxter Watson in far-off Mobile, having not gotten a response to his letter to Jefferson Davis, decided to write to Beauregard shortly after the start of the new year to try and gain support for the construction of his electric powered submarine.

With Beauregard having been transferred to the Army of Northern Virginia some months before, it's doubtful that the following letter ever reached him while commanding ragged troops in the muddy trenches around Petersburg:

"Mobile, Alabama, January 6th, 1865. General Beauregard: Being the inventor of the submarine boat that destroyed the *Housatonic* in Charleston in February last, and losing all I had with her. I have concluded to lay the matter before you, and request your assistance in building another for the same place.

That boat as you know was a complete success as far as the boat was concerned, but was a comparative failure through mismanagement, a fault over which I had no control, as my supervision of her ceased as soon as she was in the water.

I propose to build another provided I can get the necessary assistance to do so. It will require an electromagnetic engine to propel a boat of that description, as a boat of that kind is impracticable with any other kind of power. I firmly believe that I can destroy the blockade in Charleston in a short time if I get the assistance. Your Servant, Baxter Watson."[238]

While the ashes of Atlanta continued to smolder, Sherman's triumphant army marched towards Columbia, determined to unleash their vengeance on the state capital that had been first to succeed. As the Union army moved in from the west, it appeared to many who remained in unhappy Charleston that time had run out regarding dreams of independence.

From the ruins of a shattered city, we again find Smythe penning a letter to his mother: "January 9th, 1865. Dearest Mother: I must write in haste as I must go down to Sullivan's Island presently, and do not know if I shall be back in time to get my letter in the mail. On duty last night, and it was cold. I assure you Sherman keeps quiet.

As for Columbia, I should not attempt to move anything. That place will be defended at all hazards, even Charleston will be given up to hold it. About this place I don't know what to think. I have heard several times that General Lee's army will be sent here, and Richmond left, rather than allow Sherman to devastate this state as he has done to Georgia.

The city here is in a very lawless condition, robberies and assaults every night. It is horrible and dangerous to go out after dark, especially down town where there is no light on the streets. Augustine."

Within a month after Smythe had written this sad letter to his mother, military commanders of Charleston were planning to evacuate the city and join up with General Johnston's ragged army, desperately trying to stop Sherman's advance through South Carolina. On the night of February 17, 1865, exactly one year to the day after the crew of the *Hunley* had fatally ushered in the age of underwater warfare, the garrisons of Fort Sumter and Sullivan's Island furled their colors for the last time and withdrew from the ruins of Charleston.

In a matter of weeks, Wilmington and Mobile would fall to the federal forces, and on April 9, 1865, General Robert E. Lee put an end to the conflict by surrendering the Army of Northern Virginia to Grant at a little Virginia crossroads named Appomattox Court House; four long years of terrible slaughter had come to an end.

As the tattered soldiers of the defeated Confederacy slowly staggered home to a new way of life, they were met by an unsympathetic army of occupation, put in place to insure that new laws, and the Emancipation Proclamation proposed by the late President Lincoln would be followed and obeyed. While the devastated South dealt with an economy that lay in ruins, and many northerners eager to pick her bones flocked to her war ravaged cities with their carpetbags packed with everything they owned except scruples, bold plans were being put into motion designed to breath new life into the poverty stricken south land.

By the late 1860's, plans for removing the various wrecks and obstructions that severely hindered navigation in southern ports were being acted upon from Norfolk, Virginia to Mobile, Alabama. With southern harbors free of obstructions, commerce once more flowed from recently blockaded ports to cities around the world. Her many commerce vessels once again flying the stars and stripes of the United States of America.

During this time of resurrection, a news article appeared in the Charleston Daily Republican, October 8, 1870 (cited briefly in Chapter Three) which alleged that the wreck of the *Hunley* had been found. Quoting from the article titled *The Remarkable Career of a Remarkable Craft* we read the following extract: "We all know the fate of the brave *Housatonic*. Brave Dixon guided the torpedo fairly against her, the explosion tore up the great ship's sides, so that she went down with all her crew within two minutes.

The torpedo vessel also disappeared forever from mortal view. Whether she went down with her enemy or whether she drifted out to sea to bury her gallant dead, was never known, and their fate was left till the great day when the sea shall give up her dead.

But within a few weeks past, divers in submarine armor have visited the wreck of the *Housatonic*, and they have found the little torpedo vessel lying by her huge victim, and within are the bones of the most devoted and daring men that ever went to war."

Although I have chosen to discuss these early

alleged sightings of the *Hunley* in the conclusion, I would like to share the following unfootnoted passage that appeared in a well written book published in Charleston for the Civil War Centennial. "Several years after the war one Angus Smith, who had taken a contract to remove Confederate wrecks and other obstructions from Charleston harbor, reported that he had been on top of the *Hunley* and found out the cause of her sinking, but did not say what it was. He found the submarine alongside the sunken *Housatonic*, and declared that she could be raised at any time and, in his opinion, was as good as the day she sank."²³⁹

As the years passed, many rumors circulated around Charleston claiming that the *Hunley* had either been sucked into the *Housatonic* as she sank, or lay beside her victim partially buried in the sand. However, these reports were not supported by divers who visited the wreck only days after the sinking and found no trace of the submarine. As stated earlier, I will discuss this question further in the conclusion.

With commerce once again flowing freely from the busy port of Charleston, it would appear that the hidden wreck of the once proud *Housatonic* was becoming more and more of a navigational hazard as ship traffic increased in the post-war harbor. With the rotting upper deck of the old warship being less than ten feet beneath the surface, it was decided that the height of the wreck should be lowered so that trading vessels could freely pass over her collapsed and decaying hull.

On April 20, 1870, a report concerning the condition of the wrecks obstructing Charleston Harbor and its approaches was submitted by Captain Ludlow to the United States Corps of Engineers. This informative report included the following description of the *Housatonic*:

"The *Housatonic* was a wooden vessel blown up at anchor by a torpedo boat which sunk with her. The wrecks of the two lie nearly four miles due east of the *Weehawken Light Ship* in 4 1/2 fathoms of water. The wreck has been blasted, the stern blown off and portions of the machinery taken out. Two boilers are still in her weighing 40 and 50 tons each. The wooden sheathing inside and the flanking outside are eaten by worms down to the copper. It is a dangerous wreck lying in deep water in the track of northerly bound vessels, and should be removed. The estimated cost to obtain 20 feet of water is $10,000. All these amounts are as nearly as possible estimated for the actual cost of removal,

and if contracts are made, the contractor is supposed to look for his profit, to the value of the material raised."²⁴⁰

At about the same time that Charleston harbor officials were trying to find a contractor capable of demolishing the wreck of the *Housatonic*, James McClintock was arranging passage to Halifax, Nova Scotia to attend secret meetings with British engineering officers (who wished to construct a submarine boat of their own). From these extensive interviews conducted during the fall of 1872 (briefly touched on in chapter one) come the following extracts taken from a report which is still on file at the British Admiralty in London.

"Halifax, Nova Scotia. October 21, 1872. My dear sir: The enclosed is the report and other papers concerning the submarine boat invented by Mr. McClintock of Mobile, and ordered to be reported on by Captain Nicholson and Mr. Ellis, Chief Engineer of the *Royal Alfred*.

Mr. McClintock appeared to us to be a very intelligent self taught man, whose skills as a mechanic, in all sorts of submarine engineering had been developed during the late civil war in America. He produced two documents to show the extent of torpedo work he had done for the government of the Confederate States. We venture to submit that the vast experience he must have acquired in this work could be of great value to any government intended in perfecting a system of torpedo defense.

Mr. McClintock's position in his own country might be seriously compromised if it were known that he had come here to communicate his invention. He hates his countrymen and hopes some day to be a British subject. I think it would be very advisable to bring Mr. McClintock to England, and afford him all necessary means to construct, or superintend the construction of a boat.

The want of time for official experiment while in a state of war prevented his invention ever receiving the attention which it undoubtedly deserved, and left him entirely to his own resources in developing it. Enclosures 1, 2, 3 and 4 show that as a mater of fact Mr. McClintock's boats have been maneuvered underwater, and that one of them did actually destroy the *Housatonic* a vessel of the U.S. Navy.

Captain Nicholson and Mr. Ellis were strongly impressed with the great intelligence of Mr. McClintock, and with his knowledge of all points, chemical and mechanical, connected with

U.S. Navy diver being suited up in what was once considered "state of the art" gear. Photo courtesy of U.S. Naval Historical Center.

DIVING FOR THE HOUSATONIC.

AN HISTORIC DERELICT AT ENTRANCE OF HARBOR.

Investigations of the Merrit & Chapman Co About Complete and Report to be Submitted—The Wreck May be Destroyed with Dynamite. Capt Stuart's Successor to Arrive To-morrow.

Thorough investigation has been made by the force of divers who were sent here this week by the Merrit & Chapman Wrecking and Dredging Company, of Norfolk, of the wreck of the frigate Housatonic, which was sunk in the harbor by a Confederate torpedo boat in 1863, and a report will shortly be submitted to the Government. The wreck is situated about four hundred yards southeast of the harbor entrance, and has caused much trouble to vessels trying to enter and leave the port. It is thought that the Government will use the diving company's information and they will probably be given the contract to remove the obstruction.

The story of the sinking of the Housatonic by a Confederate torpedo boat is well known here and has often been written in these columns. After the war no efforts were made to have the wreck removed and soon the derelict became the foundation of a sand bar, which built itself up in the path of the commerce of this port, and to mariners it has always been a cause of much anguish. Recently strong efforts were brought forward to have this obstruction cleared away if possible, and the local engineer officer, Capt E. R. Stuart, U. S. A., who is always ready to assist Charleston, arranged to have an investigation made by a diving concern.

One of the largest concerns of its kind in the world, the Merrit & Chapman Company, asked permission to make the investigation, and, the request being granted, they immediately sent down a large diving outfit under the charge of Diving Superintendent Tucker. Mr Tucker, on his arrival in Charleston, commenced work, and in two or three days he completed his investigation and is now busy on his report, which will be very interesting. The submarine trip of the divers revealed the old Housatonic much the worse for the stay under water, and she was, of course, far beyond recognition. She was of wooden construction and most of her timbers have disappeared, having been washed away by storms. Among things seen below were two boilers and much of the armament of the old-time battle ship, and it is thought that a good amount of salvage can be obtained from the old iron that can be easily gotten out of the old fighting machine. Should the Housatonic be removed dynamite will be used in large quantities, and the last death of the old reminder of the War Between the States will be a grand sight.

The report of Superintendent Tucker will be turned over to Capt Stuart, who will, after going over it with care, send his recommendations to the chief of engineers at Washington. The indications are that the report will show that the wreck can be removed and the result will doubtless be the clearing of the channel of a hindrance which has caused trouble for years.

This 1908 news article relates one of the many efforts that were made to locate the "Hunley."

Torpedoes and Submarine vessels."[241]

From the report "and other papers concerning the submarine boat" found in this file at the British Admiralty come letters of recommendation from underwater explosives expert Matthew F. Maury (then a professor at the Virginia Military Institute in Lexington, Virginia), and several ex-Confederate naval officers whom had witnessed a demonstration of the *Hunley's* attack capabilities in the Mobile River (excerpts quoted in chapter one)

Unfortunately a response to this in depth report was not filed with the papers discussed above, and it may remain a mystery as to how impressed officers of the British Admiralty had been with Mr. McClintock's testimony.

At about the same time that James McClintock was trying to persuade British naval officers to build a submarine vessel of his design, in far off South Carolina an underwater adventurer was then considering the feasibility of removing the wreck of the *Housatonic*.

On the afternoon of September 20, 1872, the Corps of Engineers accepted a bid from a Professor Benjamin Maillefert for the removal of the wrecks *Weehawken* and *Housatonic* to a low-tide depth of twenty feet, as well as the missing submarine boat *Hunley*, if the wreckage of the vessel could be located.

Throughout the winter and spring of 1872 and 1873, the wreck sites of the two ships were carefully surveyed by divers so as to find the best locations to place the explosive charges. By the summer of 1873, it would appear that the site survey of the *Housatonic* site had been completed and demolition of the wreck begun; for in a report filed by Major Gillmore dated August 28, 1873, we read:

"The wooden gun-boat *Housatonic* sunk outside the bar in 4 1/2 fathoms of water, was removed to a low water depth of 20 1/2 feet. The torpedo-boat, sunk at the same time and place, could not be found."[242]

For several years following the demolition of the *Housatonic's* rotting super structure, she lay forgotten off Sullivan's Island with little attention having been given her or the missing submarine that had sent her to the bottom in the winter of 1864. After spending several years in obscurity, her decaying hull once more became a nuisance to navigation when new jetties were added and the main channel changed in 1879. Following the completion of the new channel, ship captains unfamiliar with the location of the wrecked sloop of war reported scraping their hulls on the rusting boilers that protruded from the sand bottom.

For several years after, a large buoy could be seen attached to what remained of the once proud warship, warning visiting sea captains of the hidden obstruction. Government charts of the period mark the location as the *Housatonic Wreck*, but make no mention as to the alleged wreck site of the submarine boat that destroyed her.[243]

Throughout the later part of the 19th century, distorted accounts of the *Hunley* could occasionally be seen in the Charleston papers, recounting the exploits and gallantry of her lost crew for the aging Confederate veterans, and new generations of Charlestonians. In far-off Mobile, William Alexander became something of a local celebrity, occasionally speaking to community historical societies about his adventures aboard the Confederate submarine that had been built in their city.

While rumors and theories concerning the fate of the missing Hunley slowly entered the folklore of the reconstructed south, the United States government was beginning a bold project to incorporate, in several volumes, a complete history of the Naval actions of the Civil War. For the first time since that war, the general public would be able to read actual dispatches and reports concerning virtually all aspects of the war at sea. Included in the records were documents and reports concerning the exploits of the *Hunley* and her destruction of the *Housatonic*.

After years of compiling thousands of documents related to naval actions of the Civil War, the government printing office released a multi-volume work titled Official Records of the Union and Confederate Navies in the War of the Rebellion. Shortly after the release of this comprehensive collection of letters, reports, documents and dispatches, an aging William Alexander obtained a copy and read for the first time in almost forty years the official accounts of the sinking of the *Housatonic* and mysterious disappearance of the submarine boat from which he had been transferred less than two weeks before her disappearance.

As part of my research into the history of the *Hunley*, I spent a day searching through the collection of letters received by the Department of Naval Archives relating to the *Hunley* that has been compiled for over a century. Within the collection

NAME	*Housatonic*	PAGE 1

CLASS. *Sloop of War*	TONNAGE. *1240*	RATE.

KEEL LAID.	LAUNCHED. *Nov 20" 1861*	AT *Boston Mass*

HULL.

BUILDER.	MATERIAL.	ACQUISITION.	COST.	TOTAL COST.	CHANGES.
Government			$121,526.71	$231,526.71	

PROPULSION.	RIG.	LENGTH.	BEAM.	DEPTH.	DRAFT.	FINAL DISPOSITION.	PRICE.	HISTORY.
Screw		*207'*	*38'*	*16' 10'*		*Sunk out side of Charleston bar by Confederate torpedo boat Feby 17" 1864*		*Capt C.W. Pickering was in command*

ENGINES.

BUILDER.	DATE.	No.	KIND.	COST.	COAL.	COAL PER HOUR.	H.P.	SPEED. MAX.	SPEED. AVERAGE	BOILERS. No.	BOILERS. KIND.	PRES.	STACKS
Globe Works Boston		*2*	*Horizontal Direct Action*							*2* *1*	*main Auxilliary*	*30 lb*	

BATTERY.

ORIGINAL. DATE.	No.	KIND.	CALIBER.	GUN No.	HISTORY.
1862 Sept 2"	*1 3 1 2 2 1*	*Parrott Rifle " Dahl. S.B. 33 cwt Howitzer " Rifle*	*100 30 XI 32 24 12 12*	*pdr " " pdr " "*	*South Atlantic Squadron No Log Books of this Vessel*

CHANGES. DATE.	No.				
1863 Apr 30		*add 2-33 cwt 32 pdr*			
June 2"/63		*Remove Howitzers*			
Nov 27/63		*Same as Apr 30th*			

Description of the "Housatonic" listing armament and boilers.
Document courtesy of the U.S. Naval Archives, Washington Navy Yard.

of faded letters seeking information about the vessel, I was pleasantly surprised to discover two letters received from William Alexander - One correcting the archives on a recently written article, and the other trying to generate interest in locating the missing submarine. From these two letters I would like to share the following with the reader:

"Mobile, Alabama November 20th, 1902. Acting Superintendent Naval War Department, Washington, D.C. Dear Sir: From the index copy volume 15 Naval War Records, I received, many thanks: The initials *F.L. Hunley* page 692 are incorrect, They should be *H.L. Hunley* for whom the submarine boat was named.

I have seen for the first time, and with great interest, the official reports in regard to the loss of the *Housatonic*, and the efforts made to find the torpedo boat. Commander Churchill says on page 334. 'The *Housatonic* has settled in the mud about five feet, dragged the bottom an area of 500 yards - found only rubbish.' so far. so good: but. The submarine torpedo boat *H.L. Hunley* is there - or thereabouts! This and all the reports confirm this statement.

I consider it of the greatest importance, in the light of experience of the loss of the *Housatonic* that the government make investigation of the known facts and probabilities connected with the fate of the torpedo boat.

The government needs this information today. We are spending millions on coast defense. The *H.L. Hunley* is the only submarine torpedo boat ever built in this, or any other country, that accomplished the purpose for which a submarine boat is designed. That is a boat operated at sea, under water by a crew sinking an enemy war vessel during time of war. Other *Hunleys* can do likewise and not be lost.

I would be most obliged if you could address me if you have any information as to whether the hull of the *Housatonic* was ever fished up. Very respectfully W. A. Alexander. P.S. There are 3 or 4 men still living in Mobile and vicinity who assisted me in building the submarine."[244]

Although I was unable to locate a response to Alexander's letter, there's a good chance that the navy may have been quite interested in what he had to tell them regarding the characteristics of his lost Confederate submarine; for just five years prior to receiving this communication, the U.S. Navy had commissioned the first submarine into their fleet. In the summer of 1897 (over thirty years after the

Hunley had proven to the navies of the world that no vessel was safe from underwater attack), the United States Navy commissioned the *Plunger*, a relatively small submarine developed by John P. Holland into service. Although the craft was slow, and never came up to expectations, it was obvious to the navy that the submarine had come of age, and would soon become an integral part of naval strategy.[245]

As development of underwater vehicles started to take hold around the world, interest regarding the first successful submarine attack and fate of the missing *Hunley* appears to have grown throughout the nostalgic South. From a copy of a speech given by an elderly William Alexander to the Iberville Historical Society on December 15, 1903 (Just three days before Wilber and Orville Wright would fly at Kitty Hawk, North Carolina), we can get some idea of the pride he felt in having built the first successful military submarine some forty years before. From the lengthy speech now on file at the Mobile City Museum, I would like to share the following extract with the reader.

After reading the article he had written for the *New Orleans Picayune* the year before, he continued as follows: "In the article just read I state that 'after the close of the war, the government divers working on the wreck of the *Housatonic*, discovered the torpedo boat with the wreck.' I have since been informed by Capt. Charles W. Stewart, Superintendent of Naval War Records at Washington, that the many statements as to the discovery of the torpedo boat in the wreck are not authentic. This I find to be correct from the following extract from the report of the divers sent to examine the wreck and taken from volume 15, Naval War Records just published.

'U.S. Schooner *G.W. Blunt*, November 27th, 1864. Sir: After a careful examination of the sunken blockade runners and the *Housatonic*, I have the honor to make the following report: I find that the wreck of the blockade runners are so badly broken up as to be worthless. The *Housatonic* is very much worm eaten as I find from the pieces that have been brought up She has settled in the sand about five feet. I have also caused the bottom to be dragged for an area of 500 yards around the wreck, finding nothing of the torpedo boat. W. L. Churchill, Lieut. Commanding.'

I informed Capt. Stewart that this report, while it corrected the error of my statements as to the finding of the torpedo boat by the divers, it confirmed my conjectures as to what happened to the torpedo boat after the explosion, and as the wreck of the *Housatonic* had settled in the sand five feet, she had settled the torpedo boat in the sand five feet beneath her.

It is sad indeed to contemplate the fate of those nine brave men! In regard to their sufferings of course all is conjecture. I can say however, that if the *Hunley* was not hurt by the explosion of the torpedo, or the settling of the *Housatonic* upon her, I know from previous understanding between Dixon and myself, while we were operating the boat together at Charleston, that in the event of our inability from any cause to rise to the surface, the sea cocks were to be opened and the boat flooded. If this were carried out their sufferings were soon ended. And there they rest! rest from their labors! But these were not in vain."[246]

For the remainder of his life, William Alexander probably spent many a sleepless night pondering the mystery as to the disappearance of his lost comrades.

As commerce of every description continued to increase during the early years of the twentieth century, surviving documentation would suggest that the wreck of the *Housatonic* lying outside the busy harbor of Charleston was becoming too much of a nautical hazard for its continued existence to be tolerated, for in the July 12, 1908 edition of the *Charleston News and Courier*, we read the following article concerning the proposed fate of the once proud warship:

"Diving for the *Housatonic*, an historic derelict at entrance of harbor. Thorough investigation has been made by the force of divers who were sent here this week by the Merrit & Chapman Wrecking and Dredging Company, of Norfolk, of the wreck of the frigate *Housatonic*, which was sunk in the harbor by a Confederate torpedo boat in 1864.

The wreck is situated about four hundred yards southeast of the harbor entrance, and has caused much trouble to the vessels trying to enter and leave the port. It is thought that the government will use the diving companies information and they will probably be given the contract to remove the obstruction.

The story of the sinking of the *Housatonic* by a Confederate torpedo boat is well known here and has often been written of in these columns. After the war no efforts were made to have the wreck removed and soon the derelict became the foundation of a sand bar, which built itself up in the path of commerce of this port, and to mariners it has always been a cause of much anguish. Recently strong efforts were brought forward to have this obstruction cleared away if possible, and the local engineer officer, Capt. N. R. Stuart who is always ready to assist Charleston arranged to have an investigation made by a diving concern.

The submarine trip of the divers revealed the old *Housatonic* much the worse for the stay under water, and she was, of course, far beyond recognition. She was of wooden construction and most of her timbers have disappeared, having been washed away by storms. Among things seen below were two boilers and much of the armament of the old time battle ship, and it is thought that a good amount of salvage can be obtained from the old iron that can be easily gotten out of the old fighting machine. Should the *Housatonic* be removed, dynamite will be used in great quantities, and the last death of the old reminder of the War Between the States will be a grand sight."[247]

A little over a year after the above article appeared in the Charleston papers, a contract to remove what was left of the *Housatonic* was awarded to a local diver named William Virden. On February 19, 1909, a survey of the wreckage was begun prior to final demolition and within a couple of weeks following the completion of this task, the boilers of the once mighty sloop-of-war were blasted and buried in the sand. After several days of dynamiting what remained of the once proud *Housatonic*, the wreckage was lowered to an acceptable height; and all that remains of her today lies hidden beneath the shifting sands off Sullivan's Island.[248]

While going through the letters received over the past century concerning the *Hunley* at the Naval Archives, I happened upon a fascinating note requesting information as to whether the wreckage of the *Hunley* had ever been located. From the contents of this letter, it would appear that at some time after the end of the Civil War, the legendary showman P.T. Barnum had offered an extremely large reward for the recovery of this unique diving machine. From all the research I have done on the history of the Confederate submarine, this I feel is one of the more surprising discoveries that has come to light. I have found no other mention regarding Barnum's interest in the *Hunley*, except within this interesting communication which I would like to share with the reader.

"Biloxi Mississippi, April 27th, 1915. Dear Mr.

William Alexander as he appeared in the Spring of 1902. Alexander gave us the best first hand accounts of the "Hunley." Courtesy of the Museum of the City of Mobile.

Secretary: The question: was the torpedo boat *Fish*, that sunk the *U.S.S. Housatonic* off the harbor of Charleston S.C., in the war between the sections, ever recovered? An article in the 'State' of Columbia S.C., by former Lt. C. L. Stanton C.S.N., claims that it was.

Captain Jas Smith, diver of Charleston S.C. (Apparently the son of Angus Smith!), told me that his father and partner, both divers, had searched five acres or more of the sea bottom around the *Housatonic* in vain, P. T. Barnum having offered $100,000 for the *Fish* for 'show' purposes. Will your Department settle the question? (Gen) James Gadsden Holmes, 2nd."[249] Unfortunately the archives failed to keep records regarding communications sent.

As the years passed, and the number of aging Civil War veterans noticeably dwindled from the annual Fourth of July parades around the country, the War Between the States slowly faded from the nation's memory. While the country turned her attentions westward, the defeated veterans of the lost cause affirmed their allegiance to the United States and went about rebuilding their lives and a new South.

In the years following Lee's surrender at Appomattox, Beauregard returned to his home town of New Orleans and became the president of a railroad company. He wrote several articles about his experiences during the war and managed the Louisiana state lottery with another ex-Confederate General, Jubal Early, until his death in 1893.[250]

General Thomas Jordan, the man who according to Beauregard had convinced to allow Dixon to resume diving operations after the death of Horace Hunley, migrated to Cuba after the War and became leader of a revolutionary group there. By 1870, Spain had placed a $100,000 reward (today's equivalent of $2,000,000) on his head, dead or alive. With the crushing of the revolution, Jordan returned to the United States where he became the editor of the Financial and Mining Record of New York. He died in New York City, November 27, 1895.[251]

Emma Holmes, who referred to the *Hunley* in her diary as the *Porpoise*, remained in South Carolina during Reconstruction and accepted a position in a girls academy soon after the war. She died at home just weeks before her seventy-second birthday in 1910.[252]

John K. Scott, the one time skipper of the *Pioneer* who had worked along side Horace Hunley

at the New Orleans customs house, survived his enlistment with a Louisiana infantry regiment and returned to a maritime career following the end of the war.[253] At the age of 43 on March 1, 1874, Scott fell from a Louisiana steam boat and was drowned in the Red River Near Shreveport. The last line of his *New Orleans Picayune* obituary stated "Saint Louis papers please copy." [254]

General Dabney Maury "Old Puss in Boots," the man who had first met with Horace Hunley and his partners after the fall of New Orleans, defended Mobile to the end, giving up the city only after Lee had surrendered. He became the founder of the Southern Historical Society. He spent four years as the United States Minister to Columbia and died while visiting his son in Peoria, Illinois, January 11, 1900.[255]

Charles Pickering, the captain who emptied both chambers of his double barrel shotgun into the forward hatch of the *Hunley* on February 17, 1864, lived a long full life after the war. He died in 1914, almost fifty years to the day after the attack on his vessel.[256]

Chief Engineer James Tomb who towed the *Hunley* to the mouth of the harbor several times, and later wrote of his experiences with the submarine after the war, migrated to St. Louis, Missouri, and became a hotel manager. As late as 1906, he was still running the Benton Hotel on Pine Street, often reminiscing in the parlor with other aging veterans who had taken part in the siege of Charleston.[257]

Jeremiah Donivan, the 18-year-old volunteer who accompanied the McClintock and Whitney crew to Charleston in August of 1863 went on to serve as a sailor in the Spanish-American War, and in later life became a foreman for the Alabama Dry-docks and Shipping Company. He died at home on November 19, 1928, and according to the Mobile papers, had been the last surviving member of any of the various crews of the *Hunley*.[258]

Mr. Henry J. Leovy, the pre-war friend and associate of Horace Hunley who apparently took over his $5000 dollar share of the torpedo boat following captain Hunley's death, continued his duties with the Secret Service until the end of the war. In April of 1865 following the collapse of the Confederate capital, Leovy accompanied President Jefferson Davis's entourage in their escape southward, and remained with them until the group disbanded some weeks later in rural Georgia.[259] Following his parole Leovy returned to practicing

No. 2

I, the undersigned, Prisoner of War, belonging to the Army of the _Trans-Mississippi Dept._ having been surrendered by _Genl E. K. Smith_ C. S. A., Commanding said Department, to Maj. Gen. E. R. S. Canby, U. S. A., Commanding Army and Division of West Mississippi, do hereby give my solemn **Parole of Honor**, that I will not hereafter serve in the Armies of the Confederate States, or in any military capacity whatever, against the United States of America, or render aid to the enemies of the latter, until duly exchanged, or otherwise released from the obligations of this Parole by the authorities of the Government of the United States.

Done at _Lavaca, Texas_
this _8th_ day of _July_ 1865.

E C Singer
Comdg Singers Special
Service Company

W Bailey
Maj. 7th U. S. C. T. & Prov. Mar.

The above named officer will not be disturbed by the United States authorities, as long as he observes his Parole, and the laws in force where he resides.

W Bailey
Maj. 7th U. S. C. T.
Prov. Mar. Lavaca
Texas

E. C. Singer parole papers show that he was on duty near Houston, Texas at the end of the war. National Archives

law in his home town of New Orleans, and wrote several books on the Louisiana judicial system. On October 9, 1902 Leovy collapsed on Canal street from a sudden illness and died the following day.[260] He was laid to rest at the Trinity Church in Pass Christian, Louisiana next to his wife and a son whom the couple had named after his old friend Horace Lawson Hunley.[261]

General R.S. Ripley, the man who insisted that divers Smith and Broadfoot only get half of what the referees in the case had agreed upon until the *Hunley* proved successful, surrendered at the end of the War while fighting with General Johnston's army in North Carolina. He moved to England soon after, where he engaged in a manufacturing venture. He died in New York City March 29, 1887.[262]

David Broadfoot, the diver who twice helped raise the *Hunley*, hung up his deep sea diving gear soon after the war and joined his father's shoe repair and upholstery business.[263] In the years that

followed, he occasionally assisted his old friend and partner Angus Smith in salvaging some of the wrecks that hindered navigation at the mouth of the harbor.[264] He died of chronic heart disease in 1897. He was 79 years old.[265]

Angus Smith, of Smith and Broadfoot, continued in his occupation as wrecker and diver well into his fifties. He participated in clearing several wrecks after the war, and became rather wealthy from selling the scrap iron and brass he had salvaged from the old Civil War wrecks that lay off Charleston.[266]

Lieutenant Charles Hasker, one of only four men who escaped death at the Fort Johnson dock, was captured on Morris Island soon after the *Hunley's* tragic accident. He was returned to Confederate service following a prisoner exchange and continued to serve in the Confederate Navy until the end of the war. He never lost his interest in submarines and corresponded frequently with Simon Lake (called the father of the modern

E.C. Singer, Confederate underwater explosive expert and investor in the "Hunley," built the explosive device that destroyed the "Housatonic." This article about him was published when he was in his mid 90's. Taken from the San Antonio Express, courtesy of the U.S. Library of Congress.

This beautiful building located on East Bay Street at the foot of Broad Street in Charleston survived both the American Revolution and the Civil War. It was originally built as an Exchange Building or Custom's House for the British government, and now houses the "Old Exchange Museum." Although this was a main thoroughfare in a major city, you will note that it was unpaved. Civil War photo from the collections of the U.S. National Archives.

submarine) before his death in 1898.[267]

Conrad Wise Chapman, the young artist-soldier whose paintings, and sketches have appeared several times within these pages, journeyed to Europe soon after the war to continue with his artistic studies. Many of his wartime and post-war paintings are now in the collection of the Valentine Museum in Richmond, Virginia. He continued to produce works of art until his death in 1910.[268]

Augustine Smythe, the young sailor attached to the C.S.S. Palmetto State whose various letters I have quoted, married Charleston native Louisa McCord soon after the war and attended a local law school. In 1880 he was elected to the South Carolina Senate where he served for the next fourteen years. He became a 32nd degree Mason by 1900, and later wrote several articles about the siege of Charleston for the United Daughters of the Confederacy's national magazine.[269] He died of pneumonia, June 24, 1914, at Flat Rock, North Carolina. He was 72 years old.[270]

Captain E.C. Singer, founder of the Mobile group of engineers who financed and built the Hunley, returned to his home in Texas after the war and continued to tinker with mechanical devices of every description. He died at his home in San Antonio in his mid-nineties shortly after the start of World War I.[271]

Lieutenant James Williams, who's letter to wife Lizzie confirmed the good-luck gold coin story, continued to serve in the 21st Alabama, and was promoted to lieutenant colonel by the war's end. From excerpts of his letter of August 7, 1863, we can get some idea as to his fears for his good friend Dixon.[272]

"Dear Lizzie: I have heard that the sub-marine is off for Charleston, I suppose that Dixon went with it. With favorable circumstances it will succeed, and I hope to hear a report of its success before this month is out; still there are so many things which may ruin the enterprise that I am not so sanguine of its triumph as Dixon."

In honor of his old war buddy who he once wrote of as "one of the best fellows that ever lived," he and his wife Lizzie named their first born son George Dixon Williams.

Baxter Watson, Co-designer of the Pioneer and submarine advocate who petitioned both the Confederate War Department, and General Beauregard for funds to build yet a fourth (electrically powered) submarine boat, never received the necessary money he requested for the "Electro Magnetic engine". With no funding received for his proposed vessel, Watson continued to work at the Park and Lyons machine shop with other members of the Singer Submarine Corps until the end of the war. Unfortunately nothing is known of Baxter Watson's postwar activities other than the fact that he died in New Orleans in his late thirties during the turbulent years of reconstruction. [273]

James McClintock, perhaps the man who first envisioned the building of the Pioneer in New Orleans, returned to Mobile, Alabama, after being relieved of the Hunley's command in Charleston, and continued to serve the Confederacy with his partner Baxter Watson by deploying underwater contact mines in Mobile Bay. He took part in the final defense of the city of Mobile with General Maury's army and surrendered with them in 1865.[274]

In 1867 McClintock was captain of the steam diving bell boat Glide.[275] The following year he wrote to underwater explosive expert Matthew Maury, trying to gain support for approaching the Europeans with his submarine idea. Within this extensively quoted letter we have seen that he gave a very interesting, but unfortunately brief, history of the three submarines he helped to construct. In the summer of 1879, while demonstrating an underwater contact mine to the United States government in Boston Harbor, something went amiss causing the explosive device to detonate prematurely. He was killed instantly.[276]

Queenie Bennett, George Dixon's Mobile sweetheart, was devastated by the news of her fiance's death. Shortly after the war she accepted a teaching position at Mobile's Barton Academy For Young Ladies, and continued to live at home with her mother and father until 1871 when she married William Walker (a gentleman she had known from church for several years), and moved to Clark County, Mississippi.[277]

In the years that followed, she had several children, two of which were Ruth and Queenie Walker. In the early years of the twentieth century, these two daughters consented to allowing an Alabama paper to print two letters that their mother Queenie had received from Dixon while in Charleston. Unfortunately, this short article has long since been lost, along with her letters from George that she had kept until her death. Queenie Bennett Walker died, August 3, 1883, following complications due to the birth of twins.[278]

Lieutenant William Alexander, perhaps the man

most responsible for passing on the history of the Confederate submarine to future generations, completed the breach loading cannon for which he had been called back from Charleston to design, just prior to the end of the war. During the evacuation of Mobile in the Spring of 1865, the cannon was put aboard a steamer and accompanied the last ragged remnants of the Confederate Army to the interior of Alabama. With the approach of the Union Army the gun was thrown overboard to escape capture.[279]

At the end of hostilities, Alexander along with most every one else who had fought in the Confederate Army, signed an oath of allegiance to the United States and returned to his occupation as a consulting engineer in Mobile. He married a local girl, Margaret Spence, and in the years that followed had eight children.[280]

Throughout the rest of his life one can only wonder at how often he must have pondered the questions as to the fate of his missing comrades lost somewhere off the coast of South Carolina. How many times in his twilight years while passing through the world of dreams did he once more find himself a young man in the *Hunley*, miles out to sea in the middle of the night, breathlessly listening to the throbbing propeller of an approaching enemy picket boat, only to awake again as an elderly man lying next to his sleeping wife in the darkness.

During the summer of 1898, members of the Charleston Memorial Association (who were then attempting to find out all the names of the various crew members who had died aboard the *Hunley*), contacted Alexander seeking information. From the following excerpt taken from an article written by one of the memorial association members, comes a brief explanation as to why that group desperately sought Alexander's testimony.

"Few feats of naval warfare approach in exalted courage the volunteering of those men who faced almost certain death, and that, not in the excitement of battle, but sealed up in a shell that had so many times become a grave. Absolute secrecy was essential to their success, and hence scant mention of them appears in the official communications and none whatever in the newspapers of the time. So little was known of the movements of the torpedo boat, even by officers then stationed in Charleston, that a private letter written by one of them immediately after the attack of the *Housatonic*, speaks of the fish-boat having escaped all injury and gone to Georgetown."

In response to the memorial associations request, Alexander sent a four page letter to the groups chair person naming all those whom he could remember, as well as a brief history of the submarine. [281]

Of the final crew of the *Hunley* Alexander stated the following. "In regard to the names of the fourth crew I am familiar with Dixon, Ridgeway, Miller, Wicks, Collins, and I think Simpkins but Becker and Carlson (?) I can't place. I have a note from Dixon dated the day he went out for the last time, mentioning Becker's name to me - also saying in another note that he expected to get men from the German Artillery, perhaps these were the men.

At this late date it is hard for me to recall names and dates. It's so long ago - my memory fails to make clear many particulars of special interest. I was a member of this last crew until a few days before she went out for the last time. How often I have regretted not keeping a diary."[282]

As the years passed, Alexander joined the Masons and the local chapter of the United Confederate Veterans.[283] As we have seen during the course of this story, he wrote of his adventures in the *Hunley* at least twice during the early years of the twentieth century; and thanks to his efforts, we now have what will probably prove to be the most complete history of the Confederate submarine ever to come to light written by some one who was actually there.

In his later years, Alexander became the chief electrician for the city of Mobile, and lived with his wife at 13 South Catherine Street, where on May 13, 1914, just over fifty years after he had been called away from his duties aboard the *Hunley*, William Alexander, surrounded by his wife, children, and grandchildren, died in his sleep.[284] The many questions as to the fate of his lost comrades at last being answered.

CHAPTER SIX
Importance & Discovery of the *Hunley*

"The South will then be seen in her true position and receive the justice and admiration due her for the many revolutions she accomplished." – William Alexander (Iberville Historical Society, 1903)

In the autumn of 1914, just over fifty years after Dixon and the crew of the *Hunley* had awkwardly ushered in the birth of underwater warfare, the British Submarine *E-9* torpedoed and sank the German cruiser *Hela* while lying at anchor near Wilhelmshaven in the North Sea, thus becoming the second submarine in history to have destroyed an enemy vessel in time of war. From that day forward, the submarine has played a strategic role in the world's navies.[285]

If the reader has turned to this page, it could be assumed that the contents of the previous chapters have been duly noted and critiqued. When I first started writing this history of the Confederate submarine, I must admit that I couldn't envision the day that I would actually be writing the conclusion to the story. Although I included almost everything I was able to discover regarding the events surrounding history's first successful submarine attack, there are certain facts and observations I purposely left out so as not to confuse or distract the reader. At this point I would like to share a few of my observations regarding the events written of here, as well as discuss information I found to be somewhat confusing.

One of the nagging questions I continually pondered throughout the writing of this narrative was the question as to the hierarchy of command aboard the submarine. At first glance it seems obvious that the helmsman was in command of the vessel with his first officer being the man at the rear ballast tank pump and sea valves. I would never have questioned this seemingly obvious arrangement had it not been for Captain Hunley's August 21st requisition for "Nine gray jackets, three to be trimmed with gold braid."[286] The obvious question to be asked upon reading this requisition would be, why were three uniforms fashioned to distinguish rank, instead of just two? While continuing with my research into the history of this Confederate submarine, it occurred to me one day that Charles Hasker (one of the four men

who had been able to escape the sinking Hunley at the Fort Johnson dock), like John Payne, was an officer in the Confederate Navy. Since Charles Sprague had been assigned to the submarine as her torpedo expert only days before the sinking, and made his escape along with one other through the after hatch, it could be assumed that he may have been the one responsible for manning the rear tank and ballast pumps.

According to Hasker's account of the sinking, he had only been able to escape the doomed vessel because he was sitting nearest the open hatch at the bow. Judging from the fact that both he and Payne were officers and situated next to one another, could it not be assumed that he may have been Payne's advisor and first officer?

Since the crew of the submarine was seated between the skipper and the operator of the aft ballast tank valves, they would have been privy to every judgment being discussed between the two officers. It may have been decided that the advisor, or first officer, would be placed at the skipper's side, turning the propeller shaft with the others, and act in an advisory capacity whenever circumstances dictated. This hierarchy of command seems more realistic when one realizes that the alternative would be to discuss problems and tactics over the heads of their crew.

If it had not been for *Hunley's* uniform requisition, mixed with the fact that both Payne and Hasker were Confederate naval officers, I never would have given the question as to the chain of command any thought. As a last word on this subject, I would like to ask the question as to what agent Dillingham's duties were aboard the *Hunley*? Surely a man who had operated behind enemy lines as a special agent and saboteur would have been delegated more responsibility than helping to turn the vessel's heavy propeller shaft.

Another small mystery that presented itself during the course of my investigation was the question as to who was in charge of the submarine after Hunley's death. From the post-war writings of Beauregard, we are informed that he allowed the *Hunley* to continue operations only after discussing the matter in depth with his chief of staff, Thomas Jordan. We are told in these writings that, only after much debate and petitioning from Dixon and Alexander was permission granted for the two to go aboard the *C.S.S. Indian Chief* and call for volunteers.

In writing of this phase in our story, I quoted both Beauregard's and Alexander's recollections of these events. However, while searching through Beauregard's book of endorsements sent during this period, I happened upon an interesting and somewhat baffling response to the letter received from Dixon requesting command of the submarine after his return from Mobile on November 12, 1863. From the general's following response to this request, it would appear that there was some confusion as to who was in charge of the vessel.

"November 13th, 1863. To: Lieut. Dixon G.E.: The Fish Torpedo Boat having been duly transferred by me to Captain H.L. Hunley before his demise and he having cleaned and obtained it as owner, it is no longer under my control, hence I can not grant the request herein contained, but I will afford proper assistance to whoever has lawful charge of said boat and will give him authority to navigate in this bay with it, and to attack the enemy's vessels blockading this harbor. General Beauregard."

From evidence presented in Chapter Three, it could be assumed that this confusion as to who had control of the *Hunley* was sorted out within 24 hours, for on the 14th of November we have a requisition from Dixon requesting cleaning supplies which he signed the bottom of the document "Lt. G.E. Dixon, Commanding Submarine Boat." Since General Beauregard was unaware as to ownership of the *Hunley* on the 13th of November, and considered the craft to have been under the control of Captain Hunley, the question arises as to whether or not any money had actually been paid to Singer's group of engineers who owned the vessel.

During the course of my investigation, I was contacted by Frank Furman, who was researching Confederate torpedo boats and underwater contact mines. While discussing our mutual interests, he informed me that his great grandfather, Henry Marshall, had been a Louisiana representative in the Confederate Congress and was an acquaintance of Horace Hunley. Furman also told me of a family letter (now in the Marshall Furman papers, Hill Memorial Library, Louisiana State University) that described the accident in Charleston harbor that claimed Hunley's life.

Upon receiving a copy of this letter I was surprised to discover that McClintock may have lingered in Charleston (after being relieved of the *Hunley's* command in late August) significantly longer than I had once assumed. The letter read:

"James Island, S.C. December 9th, 1863. My Friend: In compliance with my promise, I went yesterday to the city and hunted up McClintock the owner I believe of the submarine boat. I interrogated him in reference to the fatal mishap that attended Hunley in his last experimental trip.

I learned from him that the boat has been raised; that when found she was lying flat on the bottom filled with water; with her valve - that of the purpose for introducing the water ballast - wide open. The boat was entirely uninjured, no starting of joints or seams.

McClintock explains the catastrophe by assuming that having opened the valve to gain a greater depth, the crew lost their presence of mind, and so failed to stop the influx of water. There is however nothing that militates against the explanation you gave me in Richmond of the way in which you were sure the accident occurred.

But on the contrary, it is much more reasonable to say that the horizon of the boat was lost by reason of the mobile and unconfined water ballast; thereby precipitating the crew in a huddle to one end, than that men who had so often been down in the same boat should have suddenly become so scared as to forget how to close her valve.

I failed to elicit any information from McClintock in regard to his intentions as to further experiments. The attention of the people here seems to be directed to building small boats on the model of the *David* used by Glassel against the *Ironsides*. Sincerely your friend, Delkemper."

This beautiful memorial to the three crews who lost their lives during diving operations aboard the "Hunley" was an 1889 gift to the city of Charleston from the Daughters of the Confederacy. It is located at White Point Gardens (a.k.a. "the Battery") at the tip of the Charleston peninsula. Photo by M. Ragan.

Since the post-war writings of Alexander fail to mention McClintock as having any involvement with the *Hunley* after late August, I am at a loss to understand why he was apparently still in Charleston by early December.

On another note, as the reader will recall from the last chapter, Alexander stated in his speech to the Iberville Historical Society in 1903 that, in the event that the *Hunley* ever became trapped while beneath the surface, the sea cocks were to be opened and the vessel flooded. By performing this drastic act, it was thought that the sufferings of the crew would come to an end with less misery than a slow death by asphyxiation. It would certainly be a quicker and more noble end to a hopeless situation.

However, as strange as it may seem, flooding the sub would have been their only realistic means of escaping from the trapped vessel. At a depth of just ten feet beneath the surface, the pressure on a hatch is so great that no one would ever be able to open it. Only by flooding the hull, and equalizing the pressure within the craft to the pressure outside the submarine could the hatches be pushed open. Even if the *Hunley* were trapped thirty feet beneath the surface, the water within the craft would not rise above chest level before the pressure would be equalized. If this fact were known to the *Hunley's* crew, they could have waited for the air and water pressure to equalize in their doomed vessel, and made their escape long before being asphyxiated. In my own submarine I have a two inch ball-valve at the rear of the craft that serves no other purpose than to flood the hull in the event that the sub ever becomes entangled. This is actually a standard feature on all modern small submarines. Once the air pressure inside becomes equal to the water pressure outside, the occupants can easily push the hatch open, and swim for the surface. Of course, today we equip our subs with emergency scuba gear to make the ascent safer.

Another interesting piece of information concerning the final fate of the *Hunley* is the alleged sighting of a blue signal light after her attack on the *Housatonic*. As stated in the testimony of Seaman Flemming during the Union Navy's Court of Inquiry: "When the *Canandaigua* got astern, and was lying athwart, of the *Housatonic*, about four ship lengths off, while I was in the fore rigging, I saw a blue light on the water just ahead of the *Canandaigua*, and on the starboard quarter of the *Housatonic*." Since a blue light was the signal the *Hunley* was to use to communicate her wishes to the fort on Sullivan's Island, it appears that Flemming may have actually seen her signaling.

With the *Housatonic* being slightly over 200 feet long, we can assume that the blue light seen by Flemming was roughly 800 feet away, facing towards shore. Since Captain Green of the *Canandaigua* states that his vessel did not reach the *Housatonic* until after 9:30 p.m., we can say with some confidence that the signal light seen by Flemming was observed over 45 minutes after the attack. With only about 800 to 1000 feet being covered during this period of time, it's very possible that the submarine was crippled in some way, and was experiencing great difficulty maneuvering back towards shore.

With enemy picket boats presumably converging on the site of the attack, Dixon and his crew surely would have tried to get out of the area as quickly as possible. With such a short distance being covered in such a long period of time, could it not be assumed that the submarine was seriously damaged? In the concussion that quickly enveloped the vessel after the torpedo was detonated, rivets could have been loosened, shafts bent or crew members injured.

Federal divers, who visited the site only days after the sinking, found no trace of the *Hunley*. Several months later, when the navy dragged chains for 500 yards around the wreck in the hope of snagging the torpedo boat, they somehow missed her and found nothing but a large pile of rubbish.

At this point I would like to address the question as to the alleged sightings of the *Hunley* by hard-hat divers shortly after the end of the war. The first claim that the submarine had been discovered, was made in the Charleston Republican's story of October 8, 1870, titled "The Remarkable Career of a Remarkable Craft." In this article it is written that "Within a few weeks past, divers in submarine armor have visited the wreck of the *Housatonic*, and they have found the little torpedo vessel lying by her huge victim."[287]

Question by the Court.

Did you see this object at any time after you fired at it?

Answer I did not. When the "Canandaigua" got astern, and lying athwart, of the "Housatonic", about four ships'lengths off, while I was in the fore-rigging, I saw a blue light on the water just ahead of the "Canandaigua", and on the starboard quarter of the "Housatonic".

Question by the Court.

Do you know who unshackled the cable? if so, state who.

Answer. I do not know.

Question by the Court.

How long after you first discovered this object did they beat to quarters?

This page is from the official record of the Court of Inquiry held concerning the loss of the U.S.S. "Housatonic." It mentions a "blue light on the water." Could this have been the "Hunley's" signal that was "observed and answered" by Battery Marshall on Sullivan's Island? Reproduced courtesy of the U.S. National Archives.

The author passes his metal detector to a crew member after checking a wreck site found while searching for the "Hunley."
Photo by Stan Fulton.

Another source stated that diver Angus Smith had seen the *Hunley* after the war, and considered her to be in excellent condition. However, as mentioned in the last chapter, the great showman P.T. Barnum apparently offered a reward of $100,000 for the recovery of the *Hunley* sometime after the War. That would be 1995's equivalent of over two million dollars. With such a large reward posted for the recovery of the submarine, you can be sure that she would have been salvaged if she had truly been found by Smith or any of the other divers of that era.

In view of the unclaimed reward and other evidence, I feel that the statements as to the early discovery of the *Hunley's* final resting place are in error, and were either misquoted or purposely hoaxed. This is supported by William Alexander's 1903 speech to the Iberville Historical Society, in which he stated: "I have since been informed by Captain Charles W. Stewart, Superintendent of Naval War Records at Washington, that the many statements as to the discovery of the torpedo boat in the wreck are not authentic."

Numerous poorly researched short stories, "official" reports, books, and news articles written during the past 131 years have resulted in confusion as to the number of sinkings of the *Hunley*. If everything written were true, the *Hunley* sank at least six different times during her short career at a cost of over thirty-five lives. The first alleged sinking took place in the Mobile River before the submarine ever came to Charleston and supposedly killed the entire crew. Two other fatal accidents are said to have taken place while the *Hunley* was under the command of Payne. The fourth deadly sinking is said to have been the October 15th accident that cost the life of Captain Hunley. The fifth sinking was alleged to have taken place on, or about January 18, 1864, while under the command of two naval officers, and the last, or sixth sinking was obviously the loss of the submarine with all hands on the night of February 17, 1864.

As evidence that all but three of these alleged sinkings are bogus, and without substance, I would first like to quote a letter from J.D. Braman, one of the five men who bought shares in the *Hunley*, and a member of the Singer Submarine Corps. In this letter to his wife, dated to within three weeks after the attack on the *Housatonic*, Braman summarizes the history of the vessel; and since he was one of the owners of the craft, who better would have known the status of the submarine?

"March 3, 1864, My Dear Wife: Since we have been on this side of the river we have gotten up a great many projects and have been interested in many new schemes, the particulars of which are too lengthy for an ordinary letter. Among the number, however, was a submarine boat, built at this place, of which Whitney and myself bought one-fifth for $3,000. We took her to Charleston, for the purpose of operating there, and a few days after her arrival there, she sunk through carelessness and her crew of five men drowned.

Another crew of eight men went on from here, raised her, and while experimenting with her in the harbor, sunk her and all eight were drowned. Lieutenant Dixon then went on from here and got another crew in Charleston. A few nights ago he went out, attacked and sunk the steam sloop of war *Housatonic*, but, unfortunately (like his predecessors in this desperate and untried adventure), fear that he and his crew were all lost. I enclose you a slip from our paper, giving an account of the affair, which will be interesting to you, as Singer and myself built the torpedoes with which the ship was destroyed."[288]

In post-war accounts of the *Hunley*, written by General Beauregard and William Alexander, both men agree that the total number of sinkings, including the loss on February 17, was three. Five men drowned in the Fort Johnson sinking on August 29; seven men were asphyxiated with Captain Hunley on October 15; and nine died shortly after the attack on the *Housatonic*. During the course of my research, I found no letters, requisitions, orders, or dispatches even hinting at any other accidents except the ones written of in these pages.

Since many accounts of the *Hunley* have included these unsubstantiated accidents without question, I have chosen to mention them here so that the reader may have a more complete and rounded history of the *Hunley*. A history which includes not only the facts, but the rumors and legends that have grown up around the *Hunley's* mysterious loss.

While researching the construction and history of the *Hunley* in Mobile Alabama, about three weeks before our submarine tests off Sullivan's Island, I happened upon an old newspaper story about the submarine that included a poem glorifying the exploits and bravery of her crew. At first glance I thought this to be rather tacky, and was about to pass over it, until I noticed that the poem was attributed to Captain Klaxon, a World War One British submarine commander who had written the lyrics soon after the war. At this point I would like to share the following lines with the reader regarding the first successful submarine attack, penned by a retired British submarine captain in 1924.[289]

> Too proud to fight? I'm not so sure - our skipper now and then
> Has lectured to us on patrol of foreign ships and men,
> and other nation's submarines, when cruising round the Bight;
> And seems to me - when they begin - the Yankee chaps can fight.
> Why, if I was in the army (which I ain't and no regrets),
> And had my pick of generals, from London's latest pets
> To Hannibal and Wellington, to follow whom I chose,
> I wouldn't think about it long - I'd give the job to those
> Who fought across a continent for three long years and more
> (I bet the neutral papers didn't say in sixty four of Jackson, Sherman, Lee and Grant, 'The Yankees only shout' -
> That lot was somewhere near the front when pluck was handed out).
> But what the skipper said of this: 'there's only been
> but one Successful submarine attack before this war begun,
> And it wasn't on a liner of the easy German plan,

> But on a well-found man-of-war, and Dixon was the man
> Who showed us how to do the trick, a tip for me and you,
> And I'd like to keep the standard up for Dixon and his crew.
> For they hadn't got a submarine that cost a hundred thou'
> But a leaky little biscuit-box, and stuck up on her bow
> A spar torpedo like a mine, and they and Dixon knew
> That if they sank the enemy they'd sink the *Hunley* too.
> She'd drowned a crew or two before - they dredged her up again,
> And manned and pushed her off to sea. My oath, it's pretty plain.
> They had some guts to give away and tried another trip
> In a craft they knew was rather more a coffin than a ship.
> And they carried out a good attack, and did it very well.
> As a model for the future, why it beats the books to Hell.
> A tradition for the U.S.A., and, yes, - for England, too:
> For they were men with English names, and kin to me and you;
> And I'd like to claim an ancestor with Dixon when he died
> at the bottom of the ocean at the *Housatonic's* side."

Judging from the contents of his poem, it would appear that retired submarine commander, Captain Klaxon, was rather proud of the fact that Dixon and his crew were of English descent and "kin to me and you." He also points out that this first successful submarine attack should be viewed with pride by the United States as well ("A tradition for the U.S.A., and yes, - for England, too."), regardless of the fact that the *Hunley* was in reality an invention of the Confederate States.

Although this first submarine to destroy a vessel in time of war was of Confederate design

The author used this rented Cesna to get a bird's eye view of Breach Inlet and the surrounding area before he began his search for the "Hunley." Photo by Greg Cottrell.

The author's K-250 submarine, "Alex," pictured on Sullivan's Island, was used in the search, and allowed unique insight into the problems faced by the "Hunley's" crew. Photo by M. Ragan.

and manufacture, it should not be forgotten that every man aboard her on the night of February 17, 1864, was an American. A friend of mine from South Carolina made the statement that "The name of Lt. George Dixon would be known by every school boy if in fact the *Hunley* had been a Union submarine that sank a Confederate ship."

When one looks at the number of men (22) who died aboard the *Hunley* during her harbor trials and final attack compared with the number of men (5) who perished on the *Housatonic*, the words of Beauregard's telegram to Dixon while he was in Mobile ring very true: "I can have nothing more to do with that submarine boat, it's more dangerous to those who use it than the enemy."

Even though the *Hunley* proved fatal to just about every man who entered her dark and shadowy hull, I think that the reader will agree that the dedication to duty and bravery shown by those Confederate citizens and sailors has not been seen except on rare occasions in our history.

While researching the history of the *Hunley*, I journeyed to Charleston and Sullivan's Island at least a dozen times from my home near Annapolis, Maryland. During World War II, my grandfather was an officer stationed at Fort Moultrie on Sullivan's Island, and my father spent several of his boyhood years there. My father's stories of his adventures on Sullivan's Island during the war years sound as though they could have been taken from a Mark Twain novel, and they undoubtedly played a role in my own fascination with Sullivan's Island and the story of the *Hunley*.

While sitting on the beach near Breach Inlet on a moonlit night, it's quite easy to imagine the little *Hunley* moving past on her way out to do battle with the blockading fleet. The sound of the surf and the grass-covered sand dunes that dominate the landscape quickly erase the long span of time that separates us from Dixon and his daring crew. Several times while gazing over the moonlit horizon, I couldn't help but wonder as to where they now rested.

During the early summer of 1993, I was able to finance and organize a modest search for the *Hunley* with several friends and enthusiasts. The object of our quest was to relocate what was left of the sloop-of-war *Housatonic*, then work our way back along the *Hunley's* obvious course towards Sullivan's Island, while magnetically searching the bottom with a ship towed magnetometer. With the aid of a loran navigational system, and a topographical profiler, we would be able to pin point each anomaly located by the magnetometer as well as discern whether or not the object detected protruded from the sand.

Since the submarine's bow and stern were shaped like a wedge, I theorized that within a matter of weeks after her loss, she had already vanished into the soft mud sand sediments that make up the sea floor off Sullivan's Island. Evidence of this quick settling seemed to be supported by the swift disappearance of a group of ships, known as the Stone Fleet, purposely sunk by the federal navy during the first months of the Civil War. The vessels of the Stone Fleet were old New England whaling ships that had been loaded with stones and towed to Charleston to be sunk as obstructions to the blockade runner traffic. The scuttled vessels soon disappeared into the soft sand bottom.

During the summers of 1980 and 1981, Clive Cussler, author of numerous best selling adventure novels with an underwater twist, funded two expeditions in search of the lost Confederate submarine. Utilizing some of the most up-to-date underwater electronic equipment of the day, Cussler and NUMA (a non-profit organization) located the wreck site of the *Housatonic*, as well as several other wrecks and numerous objects buried beneath the sea floor. The wrecks and buried objects had shown up during a wide ranging magnetometer search which measured anomalies in the earth's natural magnetic field. Several of the unidentified anomalies indicated large amounts of buried iron, but none seemed the right size for the *Hunley*.

While researching the history of the *Hunley*, I was in communication with Cussler on several occasions, after explaining my proposed plans to search for the wrecked sub, he graciously supplied me with a chart showing the coordinates to the wreck site of the *Housatonic* which he had plotted during his 1981 survey.

The author in the hatch of his two man submarine. Photo by Beth Simmons.

The author's two man submarine alongside of the "Hunley," which carried a crew of nine. Photo by M. Ragan.

In 1989 Hugo, the most powerful hurricane ever to hit South Carolina, cut a path directly over the area in question. Our team hoped that the ferocity of this storm might have completely exposed the *Hunley* or, at least removed enough sand and silt from around the submarine's iron hull, to allow us to detect it with our magnetometer, pinpoint it with our sonar, and visually confirm it with our divers.

By early June, 1993, our group was ready to search for the final resting place of the *Hunley* and her long lost crew of Confederate adventurers. On the morning of June 10 we set out from Charleston harbor in search of the wreck site of the *Housatonic*, lying beneath the sands about 3 1/2 miles off Sullivan's Island. The sea was rough that day and several of our group, including myself, soon became nauseous from the constant rolling of the vessel and the diesel fumes that filled the air. The slow speed we had to maintain during our towing of the magnetometer and surveying of the bottom only added to the monotonous motion of the ship in the never-ending swells.

By early afternoon we had crisscrossed over the coordinates supplied us by Cussler with our magnetometer and found the wreckage of the *Housatonic* to be scattered over a large area, which we interpreted to have been in the shape of a huge oval. We soon anchored our vessel over the wreck site and suited up for a near zero visibility dive with our underwater metal detector. Divers Greg Cottrell, Stan Fulton, and myself were soon on the dark bottom, groping around in the soft sediments for any sign of the once powerful ship that lay buried beneath us. Although I was able to hit upon several metallic objects buried beneath the bottom with the metal detector, we found no trace of the vessel protruding above the sands. With the visibility being only about eight inches, we had great difficulty staying together and soon lost one another in the black murky sediments we had kicked up. (Since much of the ship still exists beneath the mud sand bottom, perhaps one day an excavation can be conducted to remove artifacts from this first ship to fall victim to a submarine.) Upon returning to our vessel later that afternoon, we were all exhausted and wished for nothing more than a hot shower and a cold drink.

On the following morning, we returned to the docks to begin our search for the main target of our expedition - the final resting place of the lost Confederate submarine *H.L. Hunley*. By mid-morning we had left the harbor far behind, and were slowly approaching Breach Inlet, constantly monitoring the depth sounder so as not to run aground on one of the many hidden sand bars. Upon reaching the mouth of the narrow inlet we anchored the ship, and readied our magnetometer, and underwater electronic gear for the search. Our plan was to take a loran generated course heading on the wreck site of the *Housatonic* that lay on the horizon, deploy the magnetometer, and steer for the wreck, while monitoring the sea floor with the bottom profiler.

Within forty-five minutes after deploying the magnetometer, we got our first strike. We circled the area of the anomaly and found that metallic debris seemed to litter the ocean floor in all directions. After recording the location of the mysterious site with the loran, we came to the unsubstantiated conclusion that the wreckage we had found could very well have been that of the iron hull of a blockade runner that had run aground and been broken up and scattered by storms and hurricanes ever since. The conclusion that the wreckage we had found was that of a blockade runner was not that far fetched, for within the general area of our search we knew of at least one other blockade runner wreck site. Although the wreckage we discovered was not shown on any chart, it was obvious that we had found the remains of some long lost vessel that had never made it to port.

After the exhilaration of finding the supposed wreck site of a lost blockade runner had passed, we re-calibrated the magnetometer and continued on our course heading towards the wreck of the *Housatonic*, still over a mile and a half in front of our bow. Over the course of the next couple of hours, we discovered two more uncharted anomalies that caused the magnetometer's control panel to sound off sharply. The bottom profiler indicated that the large metallic objects beneath us were buried and did not protrude from the sand,

This proton magnetometer and a towable metal detector (not pictured) were used to search for the "Hunley." The diagram illustrates how the instruments were used. Photo courtesy of J.W. Fishers Mfg. Inc.

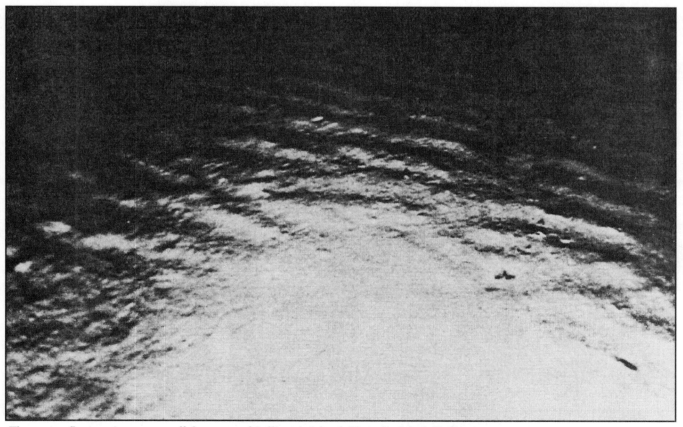

The ocean floor as it appears off the coast of Sullivan's Island. Photo by Mark K. Ragan.

Greg Cottrell monitors the controls of a J.W. Fishers "Pulse Three" towable metal detector used during the author's 1993 "Hunley" expedition. Photo by M. Ragan.

J.W. Fishers "Pulse Three" towable metal detector, used in the author's search for the "Hunley" is brought aboard. Photo by Stan Fulton.

228

while the depth sounder indicated that our finds lay beneath 22 feet and 26 feet of water.

Within weeks after our moderately financed expedition was concluded, I had the paper on which we had recorded our loran coordinates notarized, so as to add some validity to our alleged discoveries. For the record, our two greatest strikes were found at loran coordinates 45500.4/60489.9 and 45500.3/60489.4 between 10 and 11 a.m., June 11, 1993. Although the signals given off by both of these two buried anomalies were very powerful, we had no way of determining whether either was the final resting place of Lt. Dixon and the crew of the *Hunley*.

During the following summer of 1994, Clive Cussler, his NUMA dive team, and archaeologists from SCIAA, returned to Charleston to renew their search. Although the official expedition ended without the announcement of any new discoveries, several NUMA divers from the Charleston area, at Cussler's direction, continued a concentrated magnetometer search for several months. This on again/off again expedition was well known to me, and I was in communication with Cussler regarding the progress on several occasions during the fall and winter of 1994. As grid after grid of ocean floor was meticulously searched off the coast of Sullivan's island, my optimism at a successful discovery eroded as the cold winter months wore on into the early spring of the following year.

At about 7:00 on the morning of May 11, 1995 all my hopes were realized when I received an excited phone call from Queenie Bennett's great-granddaughter. We had not spoken in at least a couple of months, so I was quite surprised to hear from her at such an early hour. Within a matter of seconds after answering the telephone, she informed me that the *Hunley* had been found by NUMA, and that the announcement was being broadcast on the various morning news programs. To say the least, I was shocked by this revelation and, on later reflection, I was truly delighted that fate had chosen the great-granddaughter of Lt. Dixon's fiancee to be the bearer of news that I, quite honestly, never expected to hear. Later that afternoon I received a telephone call from Clive Cussler who was the successful expedition's financier, and leader. During the course of our conversation, Cussler unselfishly shared many details of the expedition, the discovery, and the vessel's condition, including some that had not been revealed to the media.

Since the *Hunley* is currently claimed as the property of the United States government, Cussler stated that his continued involvement with the recovery of the little submarine would be greatly minimized, and that the anticipated cost of recovering the wreck could be as much as $200,000. (A figure near the total amount put up by Cussler during NUMA's 15 year quest to find the elusive vessel.) Newspaper accounts have since reported that the total costs of salvage, preservation, and display could run as high as $20,000,000.

The wreck of the Confederate diving machine had been uncovered by divers Ralph Wilbanks, Wes Hall and Harry Pecorelli exactly one week before news of the thrilling find was released to the world. A buoy had been attached to the partially buried vessel for two days, while Cussler's team photographed and video taped the forward conning tower and exposed hull that had been temporarily freed from the surrounding silt.

Cussler revealed that the forward hatch remained bolted shut from the inside, and that the left observation viewport was either missing, or had been broken out at some time in the past. (Perhaps shot out by one of the many *Housatonic* crew members who fired their muskets during the attack?) Wilbanks had reached through the glassless port and found the partially buried vessel to be completely filled with silt. The presence of the silt greatly increases the odds that the crew's remains, and whatever else was aboard the little vessel on that cold winter night, might be found well preserved.

In a subsequent conversation, NUMA's chief diver, Ralph Wilbanks, said he had partially uncovered the *Hunley's* port diving plane, and that the wreckage appeared to be lying at an angle on her side. The snorkel assembly was in the up position, but the four foot long breathing tubes had been broken off at the elbows. (This interesting tidbit may be useful when trying to piece together

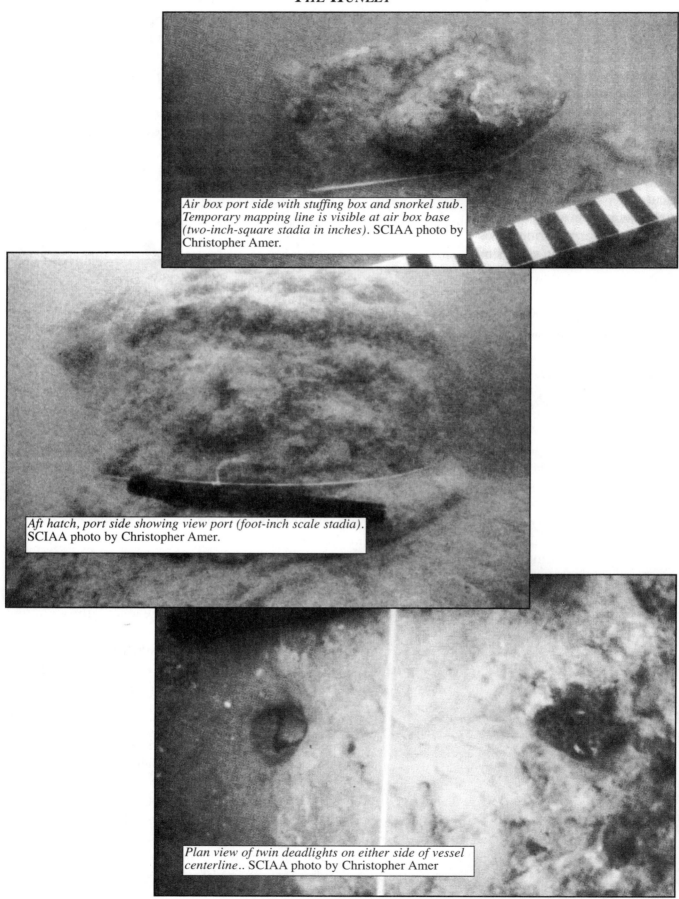

Air box port side with stuffing box and snorkel stub. Temporary mapping line is visible at air box base (two-inch-square stadia in inches). SCIAA photo by Christopher Amer.

Aft hatch, port side showing view port (foot-inch scale stadia). SCIAA photo by Christopher Amer.

Plan view of twin deadlights on either side of vessel centerline.. SCIAA photo by Christopher Amer

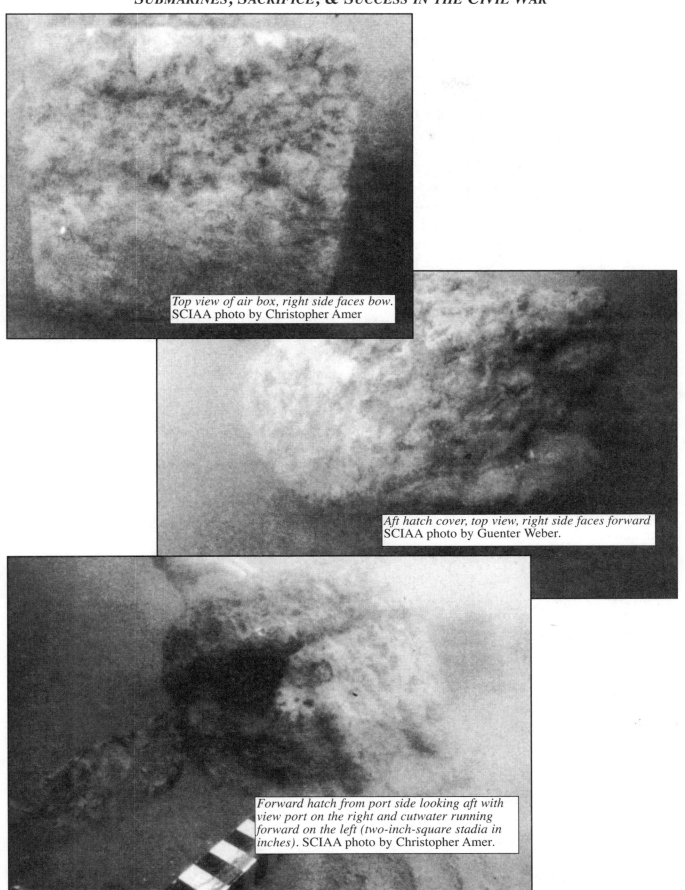

Top view of air box, right side faces bow.
SCIAA photo by Christopher Amer

Aft hatch cover, top view, right side faces forward
SCIAA photo by Guenter Weber.

Forward hatch from port side looking aft with view port on the right and cutwater running forward on the left (two-inch-square stadia in inches). SCIAA photo by Christopher Amer.

the post attack situation aboard Lt. Dixon's battered, and perhaps crippled, submarine.) Wilbanks said that the vessel was in remarkably good condition, despite having been lost over 130 years.

Now that there is no question that the *Hunley* has been found, I can only hope that I may be allowed in some small way, to help with the difficult, yet fascinating, work of research, recovery, and preservation that will unquestionably take place in the months and years to come. However, before her hull can be raised, conserved and displayed, the actual ownership and thus the final fate of the *Hunley* must be carefully decided by state and federal judges, politicians, and other government officials.

At this point I would like to end my narrative with several paragraphs taken from William Alexander's 1903 speech before the Iberville Historical Society. What better way to end this book, than with words spoken by the last surviving member of Dixon's daring crew of Confederate submariners?

"When the historian shall in the future write the impartial history of the War Between the States, the South will then be seen in her true position and receive the justice and admiration due her for the many revolutions she accomplished during that trying period.

It should always be remembered that when the war began it found the South, as she had been for many generations, an agricultural people, dependent almost entirely on the north to raise her food for both man and beast, to make all her shoes, hats and clothing, farming implements, and in fact, all and every kind of manufacturing article she needed - this because her lands and attention were all required to raise the staple to cloth the world.

This was the situation when the federal government committed the first overt act and inaugurated war upon the South by attempting with the Star of the West to reinforce Fort Sumter and thus dominate South Carolina. Then almost before the South had time to look around her, she was hemmed in on land by northern armies, and her sea ports blockaded by war vessels. But the necessity arose, and in a day she became a manufacturing people, supplying her needs not only with food and clothing - but also equipped her army and navy with guns, war vessels and munitions of war manufactured by herself. Nor was this all, the South revolutionized the construction of the war vessels of the world.

From the article I have just read of the operations of the *Hunley*, it will be remembered that she rested on the bottom of Charleston harbor - the entire crew of eight men actively engaged for two hours and thirty-five minutes before coming to the surface.

They were the first. so far as history records, in all the world to demonstrate the possibility of successfully operating a submarine torpedo boat, years before much attention had been given to the subject. The *Hunley* accomplished the purpose for which a submarine torpedo boat was designed, vis., to operate under water at sea, exploding a torpedo under and sinking the war vessel of an enemy in time of war. By this event the subject of successfully operating submarine torpedo boats received an impetus, moving the governments of every nation to make them important auxiliaries to their fleets. The plans of all the modern productions of submarine torpedo boats, when compared with the *Hunley*, are copied from the *Hunley*. Submarine navigation arrived with the *Hunley* forty years ago, and the *Hunley* was the product of Mobile, Alabama - a city in the South."

Needless to say, I am in complete agreement with the excellent points Alexander made about the importance of the *Hunley*.

With the *Hunley's* final resting place at last having been unquestionably found, perhaps one day the rusty little submarine's long sealed hatches will again swing open; and upon re-entering the resurrected vessel a badly mangled gold coin bearing the mark of a Yankee bullet may be found amidst the fragile bones of her once daring crew - mute testimony to long ago lovers tragically separated by war, and the sacrifice and success of the *Hunley's* brave crew.

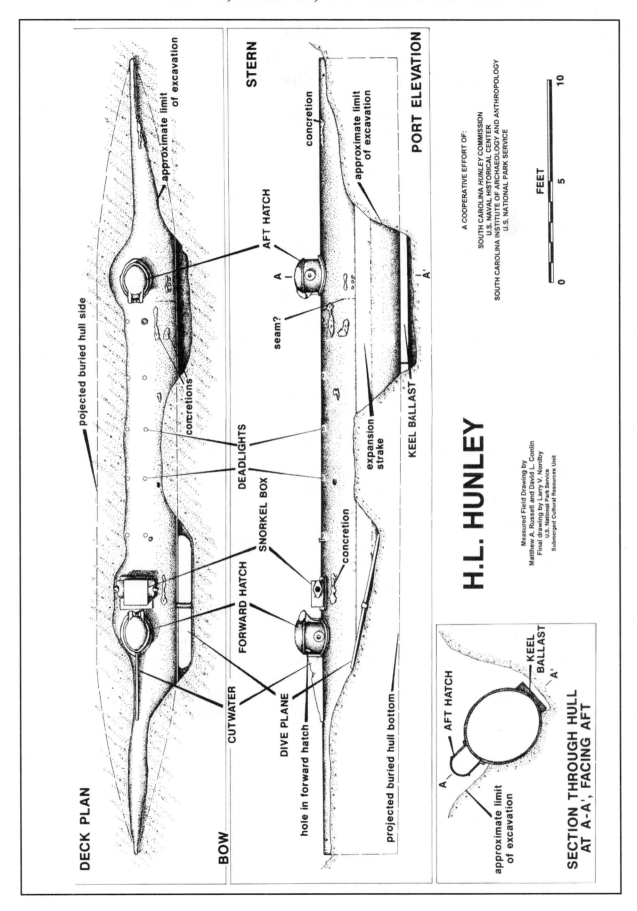

DECK PLAN

BOW

STERN

approximate limit
of excavation

pojected buried hull side

concretions

concretion

DEADLIGHTS

SNORKEL BOX

FORWARD HATCH

CUTWATER

DIVE PLANE

hole in forward hatch

AFT HATCH

A

seam?

A

concretion

approximate limit
of excavation

PORT ELEVATION

expansion
strake

KEEL BALLAST

A'

projected buried hull bottom

H.L. HUNLEY

A COOPERATIVE EFFORT OF:
SOUTH CAROLINA *Hunley* COMMISSION
U.S. NAVAL HISTORICAL CENTER
SOUTH CAROLINA INSTITUTE OF ARCHAEOLOGY AND ANTHROPOLOGY
U.S. NATIONAL PARK SERVICE

0   5   10
FEET

Measured Field Drawing by
Matthew A. Russell and David L. Conlin
Final drawing by Larry V. Nordby
U.S. National Park Service
Submerged Cultural Resources Unit

A   AFT HATCH

KEEL
BALLAST

A   A'

approximate limit
of excavation

SECTION THROUGH HULL
AT A-A'; FACING AFT

1996 Archaeological site diagram shows the extent of the excavation. The vessel was re-buried soon after.

233

APPENDIX
Acknowledgment of Lee Spence's Claim
Regarding Discovery of the *Hunley* in 1970

Edward Lee Spence has publicly claimed and demanded credit as the first discoverer of the wreck of the *Hunley*. This author does not personally believe that Spence ever found the wreck as he has claimed, therefore this author absolutely does not believe Spence deserves such credit. However, this author does acknowledge that he has not examined all of Spence's evidence and acknowledges that the *Hunley* is within the specific limited geographical area Spence first filed with various State and Federal agencies in the 1970s, filed with the Federal District Court in 1980, and published in one of his books in 1995. Although Spence's mapping and description of the *Hunley's* location as an area rather than as at a specific point followed a practice used by salvors that has previously been acceptable to the courts, such mapping and description does not necessarily constitute proof of discovery.

Theoretically, Spence could have based his area on his interpretation of the historical record rather than on actual field work. In his defense, Spence points out that his area substantially matches an area historical records show was unsuccessfully searched by the United States Navy in 1865 and by various salvage groups who worked in the area during the remainder of the time period government archaeologists now agree the wreck would have been exposed, and says it isn't reasonable to think he would have gone against such easily available historical records to select such an area and then use it to make a false claim to the court. Spence also points out that he has sworn affidavits from various individuals who were with him at the time of his alleged discovery and/or went back to the site with him over the years, but this author reminds the reader that such affidavits, even if honestly given, are still just the affiants' beliefs or opinions and do not technically constitute proof. Spence also tries to bolster his claims stating that his area is smaller than that frequently used in salvage claims and he claims that an adequately trained, three man team using a small boat, equipped with basic scuba, a metal probe, a simple water jet for digging, a GPS unit for positioning, and a decent magnetometer, working at a search rate equivalent to that reported by the NUMA search team, should be able, in the space of just one morning, to start and complete a thorough magnetometer search of the entire area and, that afternoon, should be able to adequately examine any and all magnetic anomalies of a magnitude that might be expected for the *Hunley*, and thereby positively identify the wreck of the *Hunley*.

Regardless of whether such search and identification is theoretically possible, which this author acknowledges it is, it still doesn't constitute proof. Both Spence and two of his associates have sworn that they dove on the wreck in 1970, but this author disputes and rejects those claims on the basis of scientific and archaeological evidence, which this author believes proves that the *Hunley* was completely buried in the ocean's floor within thirty years after its sinking in 1864, and that the wreck was not uncovered until after it was located by the NUMA search team in 1995.

1. Official Records of the Union and Confederate Navies in the War of the Rebellion, Series 1, Volume 15, p. 335

2. The Blockade (Alexandria, VA, Time-Life Books, 1983), p. 12

3. William Morrison Robinson, Jr. The Confederate Privateers, (New Haven, CT, Yale University Press, 1928), p. 17

4. Statement of Isaac Ball, July 26, 1919, as to Civil War activities of Rev. Franklin G. Smith. Copy in authors collection

5. F.G. Smith, "Submarine Warfare," *Mobile Advisor and Register*, June 26, 1861

6. Miscellaneous papers in Eustace Williams Collection, Special Collections Division, Mobile City Library, Mobile, Ala

7. McClintock File, Confederate Papers Relating to Civilian or Business Firms, RG 109, Entry M-346, National Archives, Washington, DC

8. James R. McClintock's letter to Matthew Maury, Volume 46 of the Matthew Maury Papers, Items 9087-9094, Manuscript Division, Library of Congress, Washington, DC. See also footnote 252.

9. R.H. Duncan, The Captain and Submarine *CSS H.L. Hunley*, (S.C. Toof and Co., Memphis, TN, 1965), p. 58

10. McClintock's letter to Matthew F. Maury

11. Letter from file titled "Submarine Warfare" on file at the British Admiralty FILE "ADM 1/6236/99455"

12. Robinson, The Confederate Privateers, p. 167

13. G.W. Baird, "Submarine Torpedo Boats," *Journal of American Societies of Naval Engineers*, 14, 3 (1902), pp. 845-855

14. January, 1864 letter from Engineer Shock in "Letters Received by the Secretary of the Navy from Officers Below the Rank of Commander" Record Group 45, National Archive, Washington, D.C.

15. John K. Scott, Compiled Service Records of Confederate Soldiers Who Served in Organizations From the State of Louisiana, RG 109, Entry M-320, National Archives, Washington, DC

16. Miscellaneous notes, Eustace Williams Collection, Special Collections Division, Mobile Public Library, Mobile, Ala

17. William A. Alexander, Speech given before the Iberville Historical Society, December 15, 1903, Alexander File, Mobile City Museum, Mobile, Ala

18. B. Rasco, "Two Cranes in Use Here Probably Lifted *Hunley*," *The Mobile Press Register*, February 15, 1959

19. Official Records of the Union and Confederate Navies, Series 1, Vol. 15, pp. 229

20. Annual Report of the Commissioner of Patents (Parrish & Williams Confederate Imprints 1733), January 1863. Page 8. Found in the Brockenbrough Library, Museum of the Confederacy. Richmond, Va.

21. Franklin Buchanan Letterbook, Southern Historical Collection, U. of North Carolina at Chapel Hill. Chapel Hill, NC

22. "Treasury of Early Submarines (1775-1903)," *U.S. Naval Institute Proceedings*, May, 1967, p 102

23. Buchanan Letterbook

24. Ibid.

25. Official Records of the Union and Confederate Navies, Series 1, Vol. 19, pp.628

26. Alexander "The True Stories of the Confederate Submarine Boats," *Picayune*, New Orleans, LA, June 29, 1902

27. S.H. Schell, "Submarine Weapons Tested at Mobile During the Civil War." *The Alabama Review*. July 1992

28. Buchanan Letterbook

29. Duncan, The Captain and Submarine, p. 61

30. Ibid., pp. 62-63

31. H.N. Hill, "Texan Gave World First Successful Submarine Torpedo," *San Antonio Express*, July 30, 1916, San Antonio, Tx.

32. Ibid.

33. Ibid.

34. Alexander, "The True Stories of the Confederate Submarine Boats"

35. Francis Pearce, Letters received by the Confederate Secretary of War, 1861-1865, RG 109, Entry M-437, National Archives

36. Duncan, The Captain and Submarine, p. 62

37. Eustace Williams Collection, Special Collections Division, Mobile Public Library, Mobile, Ala

38. Buchanan Letterbook

39. Slaughter letter from file ADM 1/6236/39455 "Submarine Warfare" on file at the British Admiralty

40. Murphey letter Ibid.

41. Buchanan Letterbook

42. General J.E. Slaughter File, Compiled Service Records of Confederate General and Staff Officers, and Non-regimental Enlisted men. Record Group 109. National Archives

43. Buchanan Letterbook.

44. Beauregard, Letters and Telegrams Sent, 1st. Military District, Department of South Carolina, Georgia, and Florida, 1863-1864, RG 109, National Archives

45. Official Records of the Union and Confederate Navies, Series 1, Vol. 15, p. 229

46. Ellen Shackelford Gift Papers. Letter dated August 8, 1863 Southern Historical Collection, University of North Carolina at Chapel Hill, Chapel Hill, N.C.

47. B.A. Whitney, Un-filed Papers and Slips Belonging in Confederate Compiled Service Records, RG 109, Entry M-347, National Archives

48. Beauregard to Maury, Telegrams Sent, Dept. SC, GA, FL, 1863-1864, RG 109

49. James L. Nichols, Confederate Engineers, (Confederate Publishing Co., Tuscaloosa, 1957) p. 68

50. Ibid., p. 69

51. Letters Sent, Dept. of SC, GA & FL, 1863-1864, RG 109

52. Hill, "Texan Gave World First Successful Submarine Torpedo"

53. B.A. Whitney, Un-filed Papers, RG 109, Entry M-347

54. Hill, "Texan Gave World First Successful Submarine Torpedo"

55. Horace L. Hunley's letter to McClintock, Eustace

Williams Collection, Special Collections Division, Mobile Public Library, Mobile, Ala

56. Jordan to McClintock, Letters Sent, Dept. of SC, GA & FL, 1863-1864, RG 109

57. Letters Sent, Dept. of SC, GA & FL, 1863-1864, RG 109

58. H. Johnson, "Jeremiah Donivan, Survivor of *Hunley*, Died in His Bed," *The Mobile Register*, Mobile, Ala, November 19, 1948

59. Dunn orders of August 10, 1863, Confederate Navy Subject File. Record Group 109. Entry BM (Charleston papers relating to torpedoes), National Archives

60. The War of the Rebellion: A Compilation of the Official Records of the Union and Confederate Armies, (Washington, DC, 1901), Series 1, Vol. 28, Pt. 2, p. 670

61. Theodore Honour, letter to wife Beckie, Honour File, South Carolina Library, Columbia, SC

62. Area File of Naval Records Collection. Record Group 45, Entry M-625, Area 8, Confederate States Navy, Reel 414, National Archives

63. Emma Holmes, The Diary of Miss Emma Holmes 1861-1866, (Louisiana State University Press, Baton Rouge, LA, 1979)

64. S.G. Haynes, Letters Received by the Secretary of the Navy: Miscellaneous Letters, August-September, 1863, RG 45, Entry M-124, National Archives

65. *Hunley*, Un-filed Papers, RG 109, Entry M-347

66. Milton F. Perry, Infernal Machines: The Story of Confederate Submarine and Mine Warfare, Louisiana State University Press, Baton Rouge, LA, 1965, p. 138

67. James E. Kloeppel, Danger Beneath the Waves, (Sandlapper Publishing, Inc., Orangeburg, SC, 1987). p 35

68. Honour, letter to wife Beckie

69. The War of the Rebellion: A Compilation of the Official Records of the Union and Confederate Armies, Series 1, Vol. 28, Pt 2, p. 670

70. The War of the Rebellion: A Compilation of the Official Records of the Union and Confederate Armies, Series 1, Vol. 28, Pt. 2, p. 670

71. Smith and Broadfoot File, Confederate Papers Relating to Citizens or Business Firms, RG 109, Entry M-346, National Archives

72. Hill, "Texan Gave World First Successful Submarine Torpedo"

73. Letters Sent, Dept. of SC, GA & FL, 1863-1864, RG 109

74. Duncan, The Captain and Submarine, p. 70

75. D. Wilkinson, "The Peripatetic Coffin," Oceans, #4, 1978

76. Letters Sent by Engineering Department. Record Group 109, Entry 4157, Page 467, National Archives

77. C.L. Stanton, "Submarines and Torpedo Boats," *Confederate Veteran*, Volume XXII, #4, Nashville, TN, April, 1914, pp. 398-399

78. Ibid. pp. 398-399

79. McClintock's letter to Matthew F. Maury

80. William H. Metzger, "Brother Charles Hazelwood Hasker and the Fish" manuscript in the collection of DR. Charles Perry

81. Honour, letter to wife Beckie

82. The War of the Rebellion: A Compilation of the

Official Records of the Union and Confederate Armies, Series 1, Volume 28, part 2, p. 551

83. Augustine Smythe, Communication from 1890's Augustine Smythe file, South Carolina Historical Society, Charleston, S.C.

84. Telegrams Sent, Department of South Carolina, Georgia and Florida 1863-1864, Record Group 109, National Archives

85. Smith and Broadfoot File, RG 109, Entry M-346

86 "Rebel Submarine Machine Sunk" September 30, 1863, New York Herald.

87. Francis T. Miller, The Photographic History of the Civil War, (New York: Thomas Yoseloff Inc., 1957), p. 24

88. Maury to Charleston, Telegrams Sent, Dept. SC, GA, FL, 1863-1864, RG 109

89. Ripley to Beauregard, Letters Received, Dept. of SC, GA & FL, 1862-1864, RG 109

90. Nichols, Confederate Engineers, p 70

91. Horace L. Hunley, Confederate Papers Relating to Citizens or Business Firms, RG 109, Entry M-346

92. Beauregard to Trezevant, September 22, 1863, Letters Sent, Dept. of SC, GA & FL, 1863-1864, RG 109, National Archives

93. Letter to R.S. Ripley, Letters Sent, Dept. of SC, GA & FL, 1863-1864, RG 109

94. Area File of Naval Records Collection, Record Group 45, Entry M-625, Area 8, Confederate States Navy, Reel 414, National Archives

95. P.G.T. Beauregard, "Torpedo Service in the Harbor and Water Defenses of Charleston," *Southern Historical Society Papers*, 5, 4 (1878)

96. *Hunley*, Un-filed Papers, RG 109, Entry M-347

97. E. Lee Spence, *Treasures of the Confederate Coast: The "Real Rhett Butler" & Other Revelations*, p. 82

98. "Dixon Builder of the Submarine *Hunley*, Went to death in the Deep" *The Mobile Daily Herald*, Mobile Alabama, November 15, 1904

99. Ibid

100. *Hunley* File, caption on photograph of tombstone, South Carolina Historical Society, Charleston, SC

101. "Melancholy Occurrence," *Charleston Mercury*, Charleston, SC, October 16, 1863

102. A.A. Hoehling, Damn the Torpedoes (John F. Blair, Publisher, 1989) pp. 77-87

103. *Hunley*, Un-filed papers, RG 109, Entry M-347

104. Official Records of the Union and Confederate Navies, Series 1, Vol. 15, p. 692

105. P.G.T. Beauregard, "Torpedo Service in the Harbor and Water Defenses of Charleston"

106. A. Smith, Confederate Papers Relating to Citizens or Business Firms, RG 109, Entry M-346

107. Letters Sent, Dept. of SC, GA & FL, 1863-1864, RG 109

108. Henry Dillingham, Letters received by the Confederate Secretary of War, 1861-1865. RG 109, Entry M-437, National Archives; Letter dated April 25, 1865 listing names of known rebel saboteurs, (Index for "Dillingham, Henry"); The War of the Rebellion, A Compilation of the Official Records of the Union and Confederate Armies, Series 1, Vol. 28, Pt 2, pp. 194, 195

109. R.W. Dunn file, Letter of April 9, 1864 in Confederate Papers Relating to Citizens or Business Firms, Record Group 109, Entry M-346, National Archives

110. Letters Sent, Dept. of SC, GA & FL, 1863-1864, RG 109

111. Official Records of the Union and Confederate Navies in the War of the Rebellion, Series 1, Volume 15, p. 693

112. Letters Received, Department of South Carolina, Georgia and Florida. 1862-1864, Record Group 109, National Archives

113. Letters Sent, Department of South Carolina, Georgia and Florida, 1862-1864, Record Group 109, National Archives

114. Smith and Broadfoot, RG 109, Entry M-346

115. Alexander, "The True Stories of the Confederate Submarine Boats"

116. Letters Sent, Department of South Carolina, Georgia and Florida, 1862-1864, Record Group 109, National Archives

117. Augusta Constitutionalist, Augusta, Georgia

118. "My friends on Morris Island," Collection #19, Georgia Historical Society

119. Gardner Smith, letter to Mrs. V.W. Barrow, *Hunley* File, Mobile City Museum, Mobile, Ala

120. Beauregard, "Torpedo Service in the Harbor and Water Defense of Charleston," *Southern Historical Society Papers*, p. 153

121. Letters Sent, Dept. of SC, GA & FL, 1863-1864, RG 109

122. "Last Honors to a Devoted Patriot," *Charleston Mercury*, Charleston, SC, November 9, 1863

123. "Dixon, Builder of the Submarine *Hunley*, Went to Death in the Deep," *The Mobile Daily Herald*, Mobile, Ala, November 15, 1904

124. Telegrams sent, and orders, Dept. of SC, GA & FL, 1863-1864, RG 109, (Chapter 2, Volume 45)

125. J.I. Hartwell, "An Alabama Hero," *Montgomery Advisor*, Montgomery, Ala, March 11, 1900

126. Smith and Broadfoot File, RG 109, Entry M-346

127. Ripley, Endorsements, Telegrams Sent, Dept. SC, GA, FL, 1863-1864, RG 109

128. Register of Letters Received, Department of South Carolina, Georgia, and Florida, October 1862 - November 1864, (Dixon Letter)

129. Beauregard, "Torpedo Service in the Harbor and Water Defenses of Charleston," *Southern Historical Society Papers*, pp. 145-161

130. Jordan to Garner, Telegrams Sent, Dept. SC, GA, FL, 1863-1864, RG 109

131. Dixon to Jordan, Letters Received, Department of SC, GA & FL, 1862-1864, RG 109

132. Letters Sent, Dept. of SC, Ga & Fl, 1863-1864, RG 109

133. George E. Dixon, Compiled Service Records of Confederate Soldiers who Served in Organizations From the State of Alabama, RG 109, Entry M-311, National Archives

134. "Contents of Yankee Mail Bag," *Mercury*, Charleston, SC, September, 2, 1863

135. Official Records of the Union and Confederate Navies, Series 1, Vol. 15, p 337

136. Information compiled by Naval Archivist Becky Livingston for South Carolina state representatives who wished to know from which states the *Hunley* crew members enlisted. Records cited were Rg 109, Entry T-829, Charleston Station Payrolls and Shipping Articles, Roll 166 & 173

137. Augustine Smythe, Communications from 1890's, Smythe file, South Carolina Historical Society, Charleston, SC

138. "Lieutenant Dixon's Last Letter" *Hunley* File, Mobile Museum, Mobile, Al.

139. Painting of *Hunley* on wharf, by Conrad Chapman, which was based on photograph believed taken by Cook on December 6, 1863

140. The Blockade, (Time-Life Books Inc., Alexandria, VA, 1983), p. 98

141. Ibid. p. 96

142. The Blockade, (Time-Life Books Inc., Alexandria, VA, 1983), p. 94

143. Smythe Letters, South Carolina Historical Society, Charleston, SC, February 21, 1864

144. General Orders, Dept. of SC, GA & FL, July 1862-January 1864, RG 109

145. Augustine Smythe, Communication from 1890's, Smythe file, South Carolina Historical Society, Charleston, SC

146. David Broadfoot, Confederate Papers Relating to Citizens or Business Firms, RG 109, Entry M-346

147. Dixon, Compiled Service Records, RG 109, Entry M-311

148. Official Records of the Union and Confederate Navies, Series 1, Vol. 15, p. 335

149. Robert S. Solomon, The *C.S.S. David*: The Story of the First Successful Torpedo Boat, p. 22

150. Naval File of Naval Records Collection, Record Group 45, Entry M-625, Area 8.

151. Perry, Infernal Machines, Baton Rouge: Louisiana State University Press, 1965, p. 85

152. Ibid.

153. Official Records of the Union and Confederate Navies, Series 1, Vol. 15, pp 20-21

154. Charleston to Garner, Telegrams Sent, Dept. SC, GA, FL, 1863-1864, RG 109

155. Official Records of the Union and Confederate Navies, Series 1, Vol. 15, p. 334

156. Area File of Naval Records Collection, RG 45, Entry M-625, Area 8, National Archives

157. Alexander, "The True Stories of the Confederate Submarine Boats"

158. Letters Sent, Dept. of SC, GA & FL, 1863-1864, RG 109

159. Alexander, "The True Stories of the Confederate Submarine Boats"

160. Letters Sent, Dept. of SC, GA & FL, 1863-1864, RG 109

161. Letters received by the Secretary of the Navy From Commanding Officers of Squadrons, January-March, 1864, RG 45, Entry M-89

162. Requisition dated October 10, 1863, *Hunley*, Un-filed Papers, RG 109, Entry M-347

163. Letters Sent by Engineering Department, Record Group 109, entry 4158, page 261, National Archives

164. Ibid September 15, 1863

165. Smythe Letters, SC Historical Society, November 20, 1863

166. Alexander, "The True Stories of the Confederate Submarine Boats"

167. Orders and Circular, Dept. of SC, GA & FL, September 1863-March 1864, RG 109

168. W.B. Fort "The First Submarine in the Confederate Navy" *Confederate Veteran*. Vol. XXVI, #10, October 1918.

169. Letters Received by the Secretary of the Navy From Commanding Officers of Squadrons, January-February 1864, RG 45, Entry M-89

170. Dahlgren to Welles, Letters Received by the Secretary of the Navy From Commanding Officers of Squadrons, January-February 1864, RG 45, Entry M-89, National Archives

171. Letter of Hope Barker of Riverdale, GA, to John Hunley of New Orleans, LA, February 9, 1989 (Note: Mrs. Barker's husband was the great-grandson of James A. Wicks' oldest daughter, Eliza, who married Henry Ross Barker on September 26, 1874. Eliza's place and date of birth were given as New York, New York, May 17, 1853. Her younger sisters were Josephine, Lori, and, and, and Laura. Wicks was married to Catherine Kelly, who had been born in England.)

172. Alexander, "The True Stories of the Confederate Submarine Boats"

173. Ibid.

174. Dahlgren to Green, Area File of Naval Records Collection, RG 45, Entry M-625, Area 8, National Archives

175. Endorsements on Letters Received, Dept. of SC, GA & FL, November 1862-February 1864, (Feb. 10, 1864), RG 109

176. Alexander, "The True Stories of the Confederate Submarine Boats"

177. "Lt. Dixon's Last Letter," clipping in Mobile City Museum

178. Reports, Dept. of SC, GA & FL, 1863-1864, RG 109

179. Alexander, "The Heroes of the *Hunley*," *Munsey Magazine*, August, 1903

180. Hartwell, "An Alabama Hero," Montgomery Advisor, March, 11, 1900

181. "Lt. Dixon's Last letter," clipping in Mobile City Museum

182. Jordan to Garner, Telegrams Sent, Dept. SC, GA, FL, 1863-1864, RG 109

183. Alexander, "The True Stories of the Confederate Submarine Boats"

184. Alexander, "The Heroes of the *Hunley*," *Munsey Magazine*

185. R.S. Ripley (General, CSA), October 16, 1863, Letters Sent, Dept. of SC, GA & FL, 1863-1864, RG 109

186. Compiled Service Records of Confederate Soldiers Who Served in Organizations from the State of SC, RG 109

187. Letters Sent, Dept. of SC, GA & FL, 1863-1864, RG 109

188. Endorsements on Letters Received, Dept. of SC, GA & FL, November 1862-February 1864, RG 109, Chapter 2, February 10, 1864

189. Proceedings of the Naval Court of Inquiry, February, 26, 1864, Case #4345, RG 45, National Archives

190. Official Records of the Union and Confederate Navies, Series 2, Vol. 1, p 104

191. J.N. Cordozo, Reminiscences Charleston, (Joseph Walker, Charleston, SC, 1866), pp.124-125

192. Proceedings of the Court of Inquiry, Case #4345, RG 45

193. *Daily Courier*, Charleston, SC, February 17, 1864

194. *New York Times*, February 27, 1864

195. Alexander, "The True Stories of the Confederate Submarine Boats"

196. "South Carolina Confederate Twins," *Confederate Veteran*, Volume XXXIII, #9, Nashville, TN, September, 1925, p. 328

197. Letters Sent by the Engineering department, Record Group 109, Entry 628, box 4, page 523, National Archives

198. General Gillmore's Personal Papers 1861-1865, National Archives

199. Proceedings of the Court of Inquiry, case #4345

200. Cardozo, J.N., Reminiscences Charleston, Joseph Walker, Charleston, SC, 1866, p. 124

201. Proceedings of the Naval Court of Inquiry, Case #4345

202. Official Records of the Union and Confederate Navies in the War of the Rebellion, (Washington, DC, 1901), Series 2, Vol. 1, p 104

203. Proceedings of the Naval Court of Inquiry, Case #4345

204. Ibid.

205. Alexander, "The True Stories of the Confederate Submarine Boats"

206. Official Records of the Union and Confederate Navies, Series 1, Vol. 15, p. 332

207. Ibid., p 335

208. "South Carolina Confederate Twins," *Confederate Veteran*, Volume XXXIII, #9, Nashville, TN, September, 1925, p. 328

209. Official Records of the Union and Confederate Navies, Series 1, Vol. 15, p. 335

210. Ibid., p. 327

211. Ibid., p. 328

212. Dixon, Compiled Service Records, RG 109, Entry M-311

213. Reports, Dept. of SC, GA & FL, 1863- 1864, RG 109, # 74

214. Letters Received, Dept. of SC, GA & FL, 1862-64, RG 109

215. Official Records of the Union and Confederate Navies, Series 1, Vol. 15, p. 331

216. Official Records of the Union and Confederate Navies, Series 1, Vol. 15, p. 330

217. Beauregard to Cooper, Telegrams Sent, Dept. SC, GA, FL, 1863-1864, RG 109

218. Area File of Naval Records Collection, RG 45, Entry M-625, Area 8

219. Alexander, "The True Stories of the Confederate Submarine Boats"

220. Smythe Letters, South Carolina Historical Society, February 28, 1864

221. Beauregard to Inspector General, Telegrams Sent, Dept. SC, GA, FL, 1863-1864, RG 109

222. Letter of February 28, 1864, Smythe Letters, South Carolina Historical Society

223. *Charleston Daily Courier*, February 29, 1864

224. British Consul to Charleston, letter of, Eustace Williams Collection, Special Collections Division, Mobile Public Library, Mobile, Ala

225. Proceedings of the Naval Court of Inquiry, Case #4345

226. Official Records of the Union and Confederate Navies, Series 1, Vol. 15, p. 332

227. *Charleston Mercury*, (Charleston, SC), March 3, 1864

228. Dixon, Compiled Service Records, RG 109, Entry M-311

229. H.L. Hunley Will on file at St. Tammany Parish Court House, St. Tammany Parish, La.

230. Official Records of the Union and Confederate Navies, Series 1, Vol. 15, p. 337

231. Deserter's testimony, March 16, 1864, Area File of Naval Records Collection, RG 45, Entry M-625, Area 8

232. Ibid.

233. *Charleston Mercury*, (Charleston, SC), March 14, 1864

234. Gray to Maury, April 29, 1864, Letters Sent, Dept. of SC, GA & FL, 1863-1864, RG 109

235. Baxter Watson letter of October 10, 1864, Letters received by the Confederate Secretary of War, 1861-1865. RG 109, Entry M-409, National Archives

236. Official Records of the Union and Confederate Navies, Series 1, Vol. 15, p. 334

237. Ibid., p. 334

238. Baxter Watson letter in *Hunley* File, Mobile Historic Preservation Society, Mobile, Ala

239. Maxwell C. Orvin, In South Carolina Waters 1861-1865, (Southern Publishing Co., Charleston, SC, 1961)

240. Miscellaneous Wrecks, 1871-1888, RG 77, File #1125, National Archives, Southeast Region

241. British Admiralty file "Submarine Warfare" ADM 1/6236/39455

242. Miscellaneous Wrecks, 1871-1888, Rg 77, File #1125, National Archives, Southeast Region

243. Late 19th century map of Charleston Harbor, on file in Charleston City Museum, Charleston, SC

244. William A. Alexander, November 20, 1902, Letters received by the Naval Archives, *Hunley* file, Washington Navy Yard, Washington, DC

245. Bill Gunston, Submarines, (Blandford Press Ltd., Dorset, England, 1976), p. 48

246. Alexander, 1903 Speech, Iberville Historical Society

247. "Diving for the *Housatonic*," *Charleston News & Courier*, Charleston, SC, July 12, 1908

248. E. Milby Burton, The Siege of Charleston, USC Press, Columbia, SC, 1970, p. 239 (footnoted as: Annual Report of Chief of Engineers, US Army, 1909, Part II, p. 1316)

249. Holmes, April 27, 1915, Letters received by the Naval Archives, *Hunley* file, Washington Navy Yard, Washington, DC

250. Ezra J. Warner, Generals in Gray, Louisiana State University Press, Baton Rouge, LA, 1959, p. 23

251. Warner, Generals in Gray, p. 168

252. Holmes, The Diary of Miss Emma Holmes (in conclusion); "Charleston County Death Records, 1821-1926," Volume 150, Reg. #19

253. John K. Scott Obituary, *New Orleans Picayune*, March 10, 1874

254. Abid.

255. Warner, Generals in Gray, pp. 215-216

256. Miscellaneous note in Eustace Williams Collection, Special Collections Division, Mobile City Library, Mobile, Ala

257. Perry, Infernal Machines, p. 193

258. Enclosures in letter of John Hunley, New Orleans, LA, to Mary F. Donivan of Mobile, Ala, February 20, 1989, (transcripted notes of conversation between John T. Hunley and Mary F. Donivan, February 17, 1989, taken at Radisson Admiral Semmes Hotel, Mobile, Ala; clipping "Jeremiah Donivan, Survivor of *Hunley*, Died in His Bed," *The Mobile Register*, Mobile, Ala, November 19, 1948, clipping "Veteran of 3 Wars Answers Last Call," "Man Who Served in Three Wars Dies in Mobile")

259. Louis Genella collection, Manuscript Division, Tulane University, Louisiana

260. Henry J. Leovy Obituary, *New Orleans Picayune*, October 2, 1902

261. Louis Genella collection, Manuscript Division, Tulane University, Louisiana

262. Warner, Generals in Gray, p. 257

263. Charleston City Directory, Charleston, SC, 1881, p. 151

264. 1870 U.S. Census for Charleston County, SC

265. "Charleston County Death Records, 1821-1926," Volume 98, #1362

266. 1870 U.S. Census for Charleston County, SC

267. Stanton, "Submarines and Torpedo Boats," *Confederate Veteran*, Volume XXII, #4, pp. 398-399

268. Chapman File, Conrad Wise Chapman Collection, Valentine Museum, Richmond, Virginia

269. Compiler's annotation in Smythe Letters, South Carolina Historical Society

270. "Charleston County Death Records, 1821-1926," Volume 165, Reg. # O.T. 30

271. Hill, "Texan Gave World First Successful Submarine Torpedo"

272. John Kent Folmar, "From That Terrible Field," University of Alabama, *University of Alabama Press*, 1981, pp. 117, 118

273. Louis Genella Collection, Tulane University

274. Description of McClintock from McClintock's grandson, Eustace Williams Collection, Special Collections Division, Mobile City Library, Mobile, Ala

275. Way's Packet Directory 1848-1983, compiled by Frederick Way, Jr. (Ohio University, Athens, OH, 1983, p. 189, #2352)

276. Description of McClintock, Eustace Williams Collection

277. Conversation of November 12, 1994, between Mark Ragan and Queenie Bennet's great-granddaughter (she does not wish to have her name disclosed at this time)

278. Ibid.

279. Alexander, 1903 Speech, Iberville Historical Society

280. "Builder of First Sub Dead," *Mobile Register*, Mobile, Ala, May 14, 1914

281. Augustine Smythe Communications from 1890's. South Carolina Historical Society, Charleston, SC

282. Ibid.

283. "Builder of First Sub Dead," *Mobile Register*,

Mobile, Al, May 14, 1914

  284. Ibid.

  285. Bill Gunston, Submarines, (Blandford Press Ltd., Dorset, England, 1976), p. 56

  286. *Hunley*, Un-filed Papers, RG 109, Entry M-347

  287. "Remarkable Career of a Remarkable Craft," *Daily Republican*, Charleston, SC, October 8, 1870

  288. Official Records of the Union and Confederate Navies in the War of the Rebellion, (Washington, DC, 1901), Series 1, Vol. 26, p. 188

  289. Edwin Craighead, *"The Hunley," The Mobile Register*, Mobile, Ala, September 14, 1924

Salvaged Submarine Remanned

BIBLIOGRAPHY
Manuscripts

Atlanta Federal Archives and Records Center, East Point, Georgia
    Record Group 77:
    Miscellaneous Wrecks, 1871-1888
Author's Collection
    Letter written by Isaac Ball regarding Civil War activities of Rev. Franklin G. Smith (July 26, 1919)
British Admiralty Archives
    "Submarine warfare" ADM 1/6236/99455
Hill Memorial Library, Louisiana State University
    Marshall Furman Papers
Library of Congress, Washington, District of Columbia
    Matthew F. Maury Papers
    E. Willis scrapbook Torpedoes and Torpedo Boats
Mobile Public Library, Mobile, Alabama
    Eustace Williams Collection
Museum of the Confederacy, Eleanor S. Brockenbrough Library, Richmond, Virginia
    Annual Reports of the Confederate Commissioner of Patents, 1861-1865
National Archives, Washington, District of Columbia
    Record Group 393:
        Gillmore Papers (Department of the South).
    Record Group 45:
        Letters Received by the Secretary of the Navy from Officers Below the Rank of Commander
        Letters Sent by the Secretary of the Navy to Officers, 1798-1868
        Miscellaneous Letters sent by the Secretary of the Navy, 1798-1886
        Proceedings of the Naval Court of Inquiry, Case #4345, February 26, 1864
    Record Group 109:
        Charleston Station Payrolls and Shipping Articles, Entry T-829.
        Compiled Service Records of Confederate Generals and Staff Officers, and Non-regimental Enlisted Men
        Compiled Service Records of Confederate Soldiers Who Served in Organizations From the State of Alabama
        Compiled Service Records of Confederate Soldiers who served in Organizations From the State of South Carolina
        Confederate Papers Relating to Citizens or Business Firms
        Endorsements on Letters Received, Department of Alabama, Mississippi, and Louisiana, November 1863-May 1865
        Endorsements on Letters Received, Department of South Carolina, Georgia, and Florida, November 1862-Feb. 1864
        General Orders, Department of South Carolina, Georgia, and Florida, July 1862-January 1864
        General and Special Orders of Sub-commands, Department of South, Carolina, Georgia, and Florida, 1863-1864
        Index to the Letters Received by the Confederate Adjutant and Inspector General and by the Confederate
            Quartermaster General, 1861 -1865
        Index to the Letters Received by the Confederate Secretary of War, 1861-1865
        Inspection Reports, Department of South Carolina, Georgia, and Florida, 1863-1864
        Letters Received by the Confederate Adjutant and Inspector General, 1861-1865
        Letters Received by the Confederate Secretary of War, 1861-1865
        Letters Received, Department of South Carolina, Georgia, and Florida, 1862 -1864
        Letters Received by the Secretary of the Navy From Commanding Officers of Squadrons, 1841-1886
        Letters Received by the Secretary of the Navy: Miscellaneous Letters, 1801-1884
        Letters received by the Secretary of the Navy from Officers Below the Rank of Commander, 1802-1884
        Letters Sent by the Chief of Artillery, Department of Alabama, Mississippi, and Louisiana, 1864-1865
        Letters Sent by Confederate Engineering Department.
        Letters Sent, Department of Alabama, Mississippi, and Louisiana, 1864-1865
        Letters Sent, Department of South Carolina, Georgia, and Florida, July 1862 - April 1864
        Letters Sent, Department of South Carolina, Georgia, and Florida, 1863 -1864
        Letters sent, Engineer Office, District of the Gulf, 1863-1865
        Letters, Telegrams, and Orders, Department of South Carolina, Georgia, and Florida, March, 1864
        Letters and Telegrams Received, Department of Alabama, Mississippi, and East Louisiana, 1862-1865
        Letters and Telegrams Sent and Endorsements on Letters Received by the Engineer Office, Department of South
            Carolina, Georgia, and Florida, 1863-1864
        Miscellaneous Papers, Department of South Carolina, Georgia, and Florida, 1861-1862; 1864
        Orders, District of the Gulf, 1862-1865
        Orders and Circular, Department of Alabama, Mississippi, and Louisiana, 1862-1865
        Orders and Circular, Department of South Carolina, Georgia, and Florida, September 1863 - March 1864

Orders and Circular, 1st. Military District, Department of South Carolina, Georgia, and Florida, 1862-1863
Papers Pertaining to Vessels of or Involved With the Confederate States of America, "Vessel Papers"
Receipts for General Orders, Department of South Carolina, Georgia, and Florida
Records of Civilian Employment, Department of South Carolina, Georgia, and Florida, 1863
Records Relating to Confederate Naval and Marine Personnel
Register of Letters and Telegrams Received, Department of Alabama, Mississippi, and Louisiana, 1862-1865
Registers of Letters Received, Department of South Carolina, Georgia, and Florida, October 1862 - November 1864
Reports, Department of South Carolina, Georgia, and Florida, 1863-1864
Special Orders and Circular, Department of South Carolina, Georgia, and Florida, September 1862 - December 1863
Telegrams Sent, Department of Alabama, Mississippi, and Louisiana, January 1864 - April 1865
Telegrams Sent, and Orders, Department of South Carolina, Georgia, and Florida, 1863-1864
Unfilled Papers and Slips Belonging in Confederate Compiled Service Records
Naval Archives, Washington Navy Yard, Washington, District of Columbia
Letters Received (Hunley File)
Collection of Dr. Charles Perry, Charleston, South Carolina
"Brother Charles Hazelwood Hasker and the Fish" H. Metzger
South Carolina Historical Society, Charleston, South Carolina
Smythe Papers
Augustine Smythe, Communication from 1890's
South Caroliniana Library, Columbia, South Carolina
Papers of Theodore A. Honour
St. Tammany Parish Court House Records, St. Tammany Parish, Louisiana.
Will of H.L. Hunley
Manuscript Division, Tulane University, Louisiana.
Louis Gennella Collection
Valentine Museum, Richmond, Virginia
Conrad Wise Chapman Collection
Southern Historical Collection, University of North Carolina at Chapel Hill, Chapel Hill, North Carolina
Letterbook of Franklin Buchanan
Ellen Shackelford Gift Papers

Books

Bergeron, Arthur W. Confederate Mobile. University Press of Mississippi, 1991, Jackson, MS
The Blockade. Time-Life Books Inc., Alexandria, VA, 1983
Brewer, *Willis. Alabama: Her History, Resources, War Record, and Public Men.* Barrett & Brown, Montgomery, AL, 1872
Burton, E. Milby. *The Siege of Charleston.* Columbia: University of South Carolina Press, 1970.
Cardozo, J.N. *Reminiscences Charleston.* Charleston: Joseph Walker, 1866.
Civil War Naval Chronology, 1861-1865. Washington: Government Printing Office, 1971.
Coker, PC III. *Charleston's Maritime Heritage 1670-1865.* CokerCraft Press, Charleston, SC, 1987.
Craighead, Edwin. "The Hunley." From *Mobile's Past.* Mobile: The Powers Printing Co., 1925.
Davis, B. *The Civil War: Strange and Fascinating Facts.* New York: Fairfax Press, 1982.
Delaney, Caldwell. *Confederate Mobile: A Pictorial History.* Mobile: Haunted Book Shop, 1971.
Dorset, Phyllis Flanders. "C.S.S. Pioneer." *Historic Ships Afloat.* New York: Macmillan Co., 1967.
Duncan, Ruth Henley. *The Captain and Submarine, C.S.S. H.L. Hunley.* Memphis: S.C. Toof and Co., 1965.
Durkin, J.T. Stephen R. *Mallory: Confederate Navy Chief.* Chapel Hill: University of North Carolina Press, 1954.
Folmar, John Kent. From *That Terrible Field: Civil War Letters of James M. Williams,* Twenty-First Alabama *Infantry Volunteers.* University of Alabama: University of Alabama Press, 1981.
Fyfe, Herbert C. *Submarine Warfare: Past and Present.* New York: E.P. Dutton, 1907.
Gunston, Bill. *Submarines.* Dorset: Blandford Press Ltd., 1976.
Hoehling, A.A. *Damn The Torpedoes! Naval Incidents of the Civil War.* Winston-Salem: John F. Blair Publisher, 1989.
Holmes, Emma. *The Diary of Miss Emma Holmes 1861-1866.* Baton Rouge: Louisiana State University Press, 1979.
Horton, E. *The Illustrated History of the Submarine.* London: Sidgwick & Jackson., 1974.
Hoyt, Edwin Palmer. *From the Turtle to the Nautilus: The Story of Submarines.* Boston: Little, Brown & Co., 1963.
Johnson, John. *The Defense of Charleston Harbor.* Charleston: Walker, Evans and Cogswell, 1890.
Kloeppel, James E. *Danger Beneath the Waves: A History of the Confederate Submarine H.L. Hunley.* Orangeburg: Sandlapper Publishing, Inc., 1987.
Lake, Simon. *The Submarine in War and Peace: Its Development and its Possibilities.* Philadelphia: J.B. Lippincott, 1918.
Lipscomb, Frank Woodgate. *Historic Submarines.* London: Hugh Evelyn Limited, 1970.
Manigault, Edward. *Siege Train: The Journal of a Confederate Artilleryman in the Defense of Charleston.* Columbia: University of South Carolina Press, 1986.

Melton, Maurice. *The Confederate Ironclads*. South Brunswick: Thomas Yoseloff, 1968.

Middleton, D. *Submarine: The Ultimate Naval Weapon - Its Past, Present & Future*. Chicago: Play Boy Press, 1976.

Miller, Francis Trevel. *The Photographic History of the Civil War*. New York: Thomas Yoseloff Inc., 1957.

Moebs, Thomas Truxton. *Confederate States Navy Research Guide*. Williamsburg: Moebs Pub. Co., 1991.

Nichols, James Lynn. *Confederate Engineers*. Tuscaloosa: Confederate Publishing Co., 1957.

Norlin, F.E. *A Short History of Undersea Craft*. Newport: Naval Torpedo Station, 1960.

The Official Records of the Union and Confederate Navies in the War of the Rebellion. Washington: Government Printing Office, Series 1, Volumes 15, Series 2, Volume 1

Ortzen, Len. *Stories of Famous Submarines*. London: Redwood Press Limited, 1973.

Orvin, Maxwell Clayton. *In South Carolina Waters 1861-1865*. Charleston: Southern Publishing Co., 1961.

Parker, William Hawar. *The Confederate States Navy*. Atlanta, 1899.

Perry, Milton F. *Infernal Machines: The Story of Confederate Submarine and Mine Warfare*. Baton Rouge: Louisiana State University Press, 1965.

Robinson, William Morrison, Jr. *The Confederate Privateers*. New Haven: Yale University Press, 1928.

Roland, A. *Underwater Warfare in the Age of the Sail*. Indiana University: Indiana University Press, 1978.

Roman, Alfred. *The Military Operations of General Beauregard in the War Between the States, 1861-1865*. New York: Harper & Brothers, 1884.

Roscoe, Theodore. *Picture History of the U.S. Navy from Old Navy to New, 1776-1897*. New York: Charles Scribner's and Sons Ltd., 1956.

Scharf, J. Thomas. *History of the Confederate States Navy*. Albany: Joseph McDonough, 1894.

Solomon, Robert S., M.D. *The C.S.S. David: The Story of the First Successful Torpedo Boat*. Columbia: R.L. Bryan Co., 1970.

Spence, E. Lee. *Shipwrecks of South Carolina & Georgia, 1861-1865*. Sullivan's Island: Sea Research Society, 1984.

Spence, E. Lee. *Treasures of the Confederate Coast: The "Real Rhett Butler" & Other Revelations*. Charleston: Narwhal Press, 1995.

Stern, Philip Van Doren. *The Confederate Navy: A Pictorial History*. Garden City: Doubleday, 1962.

Still, William N. *Confederate Shipbuilding*. Columbia: University of South Carolina, 1987.

Way, Frederick Jr. (compiler). *Way's Packet Directory 1848-1983*. Athens: Ohio University, 1983.

The War of the Rebellion: A Compilation of the Official Records of the Union and Confederate Armies. Washington: Government Printing Office, 1901, Series 1, Volume 28, Part 2

Warner, Ezra J. *Generals in Gray*. Baton Rouge: Louisiana State University Press, 1959.

Wells, Thomas Henerson. *The Confederate Navy: A Study in Organization*. U. of Ala.: University of Alabama Press, 1971.

Articles in Magazines

Alexander, William A. "The Confederate Submarine Torpedo Boat Hunley." *Gulf States Historical Magazine*. (September, 1902).

Alexander, William A. "Thrilling Chapter in the History of the Confederate States Navy." *Southern Historical Society Papers*. (1902).

Alexander, William A. "The Heroes of the Hunley." *Munsey Magazine*. (August, 1903).

Arthur, S.C. "Pioneer: The First Submarine Boat Now on Exhibition in Jackson Square, New Orleans." *Alabama Historical Quarterly*. (Fall, 1947).

Augusta Constitutionalist, Augusta, Georgia (October 19, 1863).

Baird, G.W. "Submarine Torpedo Boats." *Journal of American Societies of Naval Engineers*. volume 14, #2, (1902).

Beard, W.E. "The Log of the C.S. Submarine." *U.S. Naval Institute Proceedings*. (1916).

Beauregard, P.G.T. "Torpedo Service in the Harbor and Water Defense of Charleston." *Southern Historical Society Papers*. (April 1878).

Blair, C.H. "Submarines of the Confederate Navy." *U.S. Naval Institute Proceedings*. (October, 1952).

Bowman, B. "The Hunley: Ill-fated Confederate Submarine." *Civil War History*. (September, 1959).

"Builder of First Submarine Dead." *The Mobile Register*. (May 14, 1914).

Doran, C. "First Submarine in Actual Warfare." *Confederate Veteran*. (1908).

"Fighting Hunley. Made in Mobile." *Port of Mobile*, (December, 1973).

Ford, A.P. "The First Submarine Boat." *Confederate Veteran*. Volume XVI, #11, (November, 1908), 563-564.

Fort, W.B. "The First Submarine in the Confederate Navy." *Confederate Veteran*. Volume XXVI, #10, (October, 1918), 459.

Hagerman, G. "Confederate Submarines." *U.S. Naval Institute Proceedings*. (September, 1977).

Hanks, C.C. "They Called Her a Coffin." *Our Navy*. (March 1944).

Kelln, A.L. "Confederate Submarines." *Virginia Magazine of History and Biography*. (July, 1953).

Kelln, A.L. "Confederate Submarines and PT Boats." *All Hands*. (April, 1956).

Von Kolnitz, H. "The Confederate Submarine." *U.S. Naval Institute Proceedings*. (October, 1937).

Levy, Gordon S. "Torpedo Boat at Louisiana Soldiers' Home." *Confederate Veteran*. Volume XVII, #9, (Sept., 1909), 459.

"Loss of the *Housatonic*." Correspondence Section, *Army and Navy Journal*. (March 5, 1864).

Mazet, Horace S. "Tragedy and the Confederate Submarines." *U.S. Naval Institute Proceedings*. (May, 1942).

Morris, D.R. "The Rebels and the Pig Boat." *Argosy*. (October, 1954).

Olmstead, Charles H. "Reminiscences of Service in Charleston Harbor in 1863." *Southern Historical Society Papers*. (1883).

Powles, J.M. "Hunley Sinks the *Housatonic*!!" *Navy Magazine*. (January, 1965).

Schell, S.H. "Submarine Weapons Tested at Mobile During the Civil War." *The Alabama Review*. (July 1992).

Shugg, W. "Profit of the Deep: The H.L. Hunley." *Civil War Times Illustrated*. (1973).

Sims, L. "The Submarine That Wouldn't Come Up." *American Heritage*. (1958).

"South Carolina Confederate Twins." *Confederate Veteran*. Volume XXXIII, #9, (September, 1925), 328.

Stanton, C.L. "Submarines and Torpedo Boats." *Confederate Veteran*. Volume XXII, #4, (April, 1914), 398-399.

Still, William N. "Confederate Naval Strategy." *Journal of Southern History*. (August, 1961).

"Submarine Engines." *Army and Navy Journal*. (March 19, 1864).

Thomson, D.W. "Three Confederate Submarines." *U.S. Naval Institute Proceedings*. (January, 1941).

Tomb, J.H. "Submarines and Torpedo Boats, C.S.N." *Confederate Veteran*. Volume XXII, #4, (April, 1914), 168-169.

"Treasury of Early Submarines (1775-1903)." *U.S. Naval Institute Proceedings*. (May, 1967).

Villard, O.S. "The Submarine and the Torpedo in the Blockade of the Confederacy." *Harpers Monthly Magazine*. (June, 1916).

Wilkinson, D. "Peripatetic Coffin." *Oceans*. #4, (1978).

Articles in Newspapers

Alexander, William A. "The True Stories of the Confederate Submarine Boats." *Picayune*. (June 29, 1902).

Arthur, S.C. "Early New Orleans Submarine Sired Davids." *Times Picayune*. June 14, 1942.

"Captain McElroy Gives History of U-Boat Used in Confederate Navy." *The Mobile Register*. (November 5, 1924).

Charleston Mercury. (February 29, 1864).

Charleston News and Courier. (October 16, 1863; November 9, 1863; February 29, 1864; May, 10, 1899).

"Confederates Built First Successful Submarine Boat." *Montgomery Advertiser*. (May 26, 1907).

"Confederate Sub Search Called Off." *The Mobile Register*. (June 27, 1981).

Craighead, Edwin. "The Hunley." *The Mobile Register*. (September 14, 1924).

"Did You Know the First Submarine was Built Right Here in Mobile?" *Mobile Press Register*. (April 11, 1948).

"Dixon, Builder of the Submarine Hunley, Went to death in the Deep." *The Mobile Daily Herald*. (November 15, 1904).

Dunigan, T. "Descendants Of Builder Unveil Plaque." *The Mobile Press Register*. (July 7, 1957).

"First American Ship Ever Sunk by a Submarine." *St. Louis Post Dispatch*. (February 18, 1917).

"First Submarine Was Made in Alabama." *Montgomery Advisor Journal*. (February 19, 1961).

"First Torpedo Boat." *New Orleans Picayune*. (April 2, 1909).

"First War Submarine Built Here." *The Mobile Register*. (November 24, 1948).

Foster, J. "Is the Submarine in the Arcade of the Presbyter Really the Pioneer?" *Times Picayune*. (May 14, 1961).

Hartwell, J.I. "An Alabama Hero." *Montgomery Advisor*. (March 11, 1900).

Hearin, E.S. "Hunley Focal Point of Civil War Gathering." *Mobile Register*. (February 2, 1989).

Hill, H.N. "Texan Gave World First Successful Submarine Torpedo." *San Antonio Express*. (July 30, 1916).

"Hunley - Pioneer Puzzles." *New Orleans Times Picayune*. (December 4, 1967).

Johnson, H. "Jeremiah Donivan, Survivor of Hunley, Died in His Bed." *The Mobile Register*. (November 19, 1948).

Little, R.H. "The First Submarine to Sink a Hostile Warship." *Chicago Tribune*. (November 29, 1936).

"Loss of the *Housatonic*." *New York Times*, (February 27, 1864).

"Mobile Honors Crew of 1864 Submarine." *New York Times*. (April 26, 1948).

"Nautilus Gets Papers on Confederate Hunley." *Charleston News & Courier*. (January 25, 1958).

"Navy Still Plans Hunt for Hunley," *Charleston News & Courier*. (August 28, 1957).

New Orleans Picayune. (February 15, 1868).

Obituary, Henry J. Leovy. *New Orleans Picayune*, (October 2, 1902).

Obituary, John K. Scott. *New Orleans Picayune*, (March 10, 1874).

Rasco, B. "Two Cranes in Use Here Probably Lifted Hunley." *The Mobile Press Register*. (February 15, 1959).

"Rebel Submarine Machine Sunk." *New York Herald*. (September 30, 1863).

"Remarkable Career of a Remarkable Craft." *Charleston Daily Republican*. (October 8, 1870).

"Salvage of Submarine Hunley Has Chance for Success." *Charleston News and Courier*. (June 18, 1957).

"Veteran of Three Wars Answers Last Call." *The Mobile Register*. (November 19, 1928).

Wainwright, T. "First Submarine to Send Man of War to Davy Jones' Locker Was Built in Mobile." *The Mobile Register*. (August 30, 1931).

"Yankee Gun Boat Found." *The Mobile Register*. (July 19, 1981).

---

m7087-C
21 TX